"I have had the honor of speaking in Sia[...]
Christ's church where Dr. Tan serves as p[...]
a place of joyful worship, loving fellowsh[...]
congregation thrives in large measure due [...] many years of pastoral care
of Pastor Siang-Yang Tan. In *Shepherding God's People*, Dr. Tan shares with
us the wisdom of his years of academic and pastoral insight. This book is
packed with exhaustive research and lived experience. I recommend it highly."

—**Richard J. Foster,** author of Celebration of Discipline
and Streams of Living Water

"Siang-Yang Tan is an astute, experienced, and wise guide for those called to
shepherd Christ's church. In *Shepherding God's People*, readers will discover
a wealth of knowledge and counsel for carrying out their pastoral vocations
powerfully, sanely, and safely. Highly recommended."

—**Chris Hall,** president, Renovaré

"Dr. Tan loves the Lord and has a heart for ministry that jumps off every page
in *Shepherding God's People*. I have been honored to watch my friend and
colleague have a deep and lasting impact as he trains leaders around the world
to point others toward Christ. A must-have for everyone who has influence in
the life of another—that means *you*."

—**Tim Clinton,** president, American Association of Christian Counselors;
executive director, James Dobson Family Institute

"Rarely does a person in ministry discover a book that combines comprehensive scholarly research, deep spiritual wisdom, and practical resources for
the nitty-gritty work of nurturing a community of faith. Dr. Tan has written
such a book. *Shepherding God's People* will serve as an invaluable primer for
men and women entering ministry and as a source of deep enrichment and
encouragement for veteran pastors."

—**Laura R. Harbert,** former Dean of Chapel and Spiritual Formation,
Fuller Theological Seminary; adjunct affiliate professor,
Fuller Graduate School of Psychology

"In an exceptionally well-researched book, supported by years of experience
as pastor, psychologist, and friend, it is hard to imagine an area of interest to
pastors that has not been insightfully covered in Dr. Tan's book. *Shepherding
God's People* deserves wide and careful reading."

—**Larry Crabb,** founder and director of New Way Ministries

"I'm keeping this book close at hand because of its holistic, God-drenched,
imminently practical view of pastoring. Incredibly, Siang-Yang Tan actually
lives this out as pastor in his own church."

—**Jan Johnson,** author of *Meeting God in Scripture*;
board chair of Dallas Willard Ministries

"Siang-Yang Tan is a pastor's pastor. And this book is full of wisdom accrued the honest way—through more than two decades of pastoral experience. In a culture that idolizes cults of personality, and where many pastoral leadership models all too closely resemble the corporate world, *Shepherding God's People* is a welcome and needed reminder that humility, godliness, love, and a life of prayer are the keys to a fruitful and God-honoring ministry. This book is both practical and learned, as one would expect from a pastor theologian like Tan. Whether you are just starting out as a pastor or have been in pastoral ministry for many years, there is much wisdom to be gleaned here."

—**Rev. Gerald Hiestand**, senior pastor, Calvary Memorial Church;
director, Center for Pastor Theologians

"Full disclosure: I am completely biased. Siang-Yang Tan is one of my best friends. He is also my pastor—even though I've heard him preach only once. He is my pastor because for over three decades he has sought me out and prayed with me and for me as we have navigated both the highs and lows of life. If tomorrow brings unexpected joy or tragedy, Siang-Yang Tan is the person I would want to tell. It is not surprising that he has written this comprehensive, transparent, practical, formational, and Spirit-filled book for the present and next generation of soul shepherds."

—**Gary W. Moon**, founding executive director of the Martin Institute and
Dallas Willard Center, Westmont College; author of *Apprenticeship
with Jesus* and *Becoming Dallas Willard: The Formation
of a Philosopher, Teacher, and Christ-Follower*

"Siang-Yang Tan's *Shepherding God's People* provides a comprehensive overview of pastoral ministry. Tan draws wisdom from contemporary thinking as well as from his own personal ministry experiences. This book is as valuable for its summaries of key ideas in the relevant literature related to its many topics as it is for Tan's own constructive advice growing out of his congregational ministry. *Shepherding God's People* offers a biblically based, Christ-centered, evangelically faithful, and personally practical survey of the multifaceted aspects of a pastor's life and work. Both seminary and undergraduate students, as well as those practicing pastoral ministry, will find Tan's book helpful in clarifying their role and calling."

—**R. Robert Creech**, professor of pastoral leadership
and director of pastoral ministries, George W. Truett
Theological Seminary, Baylor University

SHEPHERDING GOD'S PEOPLE

SHEPHERDING GOD'S PEOPLE

A Guide to Faithful and Fruitful
Pastoral Ministry

Siang-Yang Tan

Foreword by John Ortberg

Baker Academic
a division of Baker Publishing Group
Grand Rapids, Michigan

Published by Baker Academic
a division of Baker Publishing Group
PO Box 6287, Grand Rapids, MI 49516-6287
www.bakeracademic.com

Printed in the United States of America

Library of Congress Cataloging-in-Publication Data
Names: Tan, Siang-Yang, 1954– author.
Title: Shepherding God's people : a guide to faithful and fruitful pastoral ministry / Siang-Yang Tan.
Description: Grand Rapids, MI : Baker Academic, a division of Baker Publishing Group, 2019. | Includes bibliographical references and index.
Identifiers: LCCN 2018053558 | ISBN 9780801097706 (pbk.)
Subjects: LCSH: Pastoral theology.
Classification: LCC BV4011.3 .T36 2019 | DDC 253—dc23
LC record available at https://lccn.loc.gov/2018053558

ISBN: 978-1-5409-6213-3 (casebound)

19 20 21 22 23 24 25   7 6 5 4 3 2 1

In keeping with biblical principles of creation stewardship, Baker Publishing Group advocates the responsible use of our natural resources. As a member of the Green Press Initiative, our company uses recycled paper when possible. The text paper of this book is composed in part of post-consumer waste.

To the memory of my late mother,

Madam Chiow Yang Quek (1927–2017),

who went home to be with the Lord on January 28, 2017, Chinese New Year's Day, now experiencing perfect peace and eternal joy in the love of the Triune God— Father, Son, and Holy Spirit. Her life was an exemplary model of servanthood, humility, caring, and sacrificial love, which are what pastoral ministry and the church are all about, following Jesus Christ as "the Chief Shepherd" (1 Pet. 5:4) and "the good shepherd" who "lays down his life for the sheep" (John 10:11).

Contents

Foreword

JOHN ORTBERG

What a joy it is to have the honor of introducing this book. If you have not yet met Dr. Siang-Yang Tan, allow me to tell you about him. He has thirty-five years of pastoral experience. He has served close to thirty-five years as a professor of psychology at Fuller Theological Seminary. He has been a senior pastor with heavy preaching responsibilities for over twenty years. If you are good at math, you will realize that this makes him at least ninety years old, not counting all that time he was going to school to prepare.

People say that one dog year equals seven human years. I am not sure what the correct exchange rate is for pastoral years, but I know they are exponentially filled with life and demands and challenges and intensity. And while Dr. Tan has not lived as many chronological years as you might guess from his biography, he has energy levels that are high enough to reach the equivalent.

I should know. I have been involved in writing and ministry for many years and also have my roots in the School of Psychology at Fuller. But Dr. Tan is the teacher and then colleague who first opened doors for me to the ministry of writing. We cowrote two books on depression together. And I can remember as though it were yesterday countless hours sitting in his living room—drinking two cups of strong coffee ahead of time to get my energy level up to commensurate levels—enjoying the blast of learning around research and prayer and clinical work and communication. And I can promise you—he is as much fun and as much of a blessing to write with as he is to read.

Once upon a time, in what was known as Christendom (mostly in the West), being a pastor was often thought of in terms of providing religious services for certain life milestones such as birth, illness, marriage, and death (otherwise known as hatch, patch, match, and dispatch). For better or for worse, pastoring has changed.

Because pastoral work is central to the life of the church, because it is complex and demanding and rewarding and has been going on now for millennia, we have badly needed a basic text that can guide both new and experienced pastors into more fruitful shepherding. *Shepherding God's People* is such a book.

It is Spirit-full. Dr. Tan has tremendous awareness of the role and the power of the Holy Spirit for any significant ministry. He himself relies heavily on the Holy Spirit for his learning and research, his pastoral and clinical work, and also his writing. Not only will this book lead you to a more Spirit-empowered ministry but reading it will also be a Spirit-soaked experience.

It is comprehensive. Dr. Tan, as you will see, is a voluminous reader of just about everything. As our culture and organizational forms grow more complex, effective pastoring encompasses more and more disciplines. This can be dismaying or exhilarating, depending on your appetite for learning. You might think of this book as a kind of career syllabus for pastors. It would be difficult to think of a book that significantly contributes to pastoral fruitfulness that Dr. Tan does not reference here. His viewpoint is international, multicultural, theologically both grounded and gracious, multidisciplinary, and developmental.

It is personal. Pastoring, perhaps uniquely among vocations, involves offering something that we must first possess before we can give it away. Outward results may be engineered by human method and technique, at least for a while. But the spiritual shepherding of human beings is a kingdom assignment, and the kingdom (the "range of God's effective will," as Dallas Willard used to say) is not a human project. We can minister it only to the extent that we are living in it. Dr. Tan guides us through the personal, emotional, and spiritual life of the pastor with wisdom and reality.

Enough of the preliminaries. If you are serious about pastoring, you will be wanting to get on with learning.

Read slowly. Go deep. Reflect. Be changed. Let God use Dr. Tan to shepherd you so that you may return the favor to others. I pray that countless pastors will be inspired and informed and that countless people will be blessed because of the wisdom in this book.

Preface

It has been in my heart for some years now to write this book on shepherding God's people as a major description of faithful and fruitful pastoral and church ministry. A number of helpful books have appeared in recent years in this area of pastoral ministry as well as on the church that will be reviewed in this book. I therefore paused several times to prayerfully decide whether I should proceed with this project. Baker Academic was very gracious to give me a contract and to extend the original deadlines so that I could complete the writing of it. I finally decided to finish writing this book because I deeply sensed that the Lord wanted me to do so, for his glory and the blessing of pastors, church leaders, and churches. In granting me many years of experience as a pastor myself, and also as a seminary professor of psychology and a licensed psychologist, the Lord has enabled me to provide biblical, pastoral, psychological, cross-cultural, and international perspectives on pastoral ministry in this book. I trust and pray that it will in some way help pastors and church leaders to shepherd God's people everywhere in a Christ-centered, biblically based, and Spirit-filled way. It can also be used as a text in seminary courses on pastoral ministry, pastoral theology, and practical theology.

The book presents a biblical perspective on pastoral and church ministry that emphasizes faithfulness and fruitfulness in Christ (John 15:5), through the presence and power of the Holy Spirit (Acts 1:8; Eph. 5:18; 6:10–18), made perfect in weakness, brokenness, and humility (2 Cor. 12:9–10) rather than in success or excellence of the wrong kind. I trust and pray that you will be deeply encouraged as you read this book. Each chapter includes a substantial review of the literature available on the topic as well as my own biblical, theological, psychological, cultural, and personal reflections.

I wish you the Lord's best and richest blessings as you serve him in shepherding God's people in faithful and fruitful pastoral ministry that is founded on abiding in Christ (John 15:5) and union and communion with him in the power of the Holy Spirit.

Acknowledgments

I would first like to thank Jim Kinney, associate publisher and editorial director of Baker Academic and Brazos Press, for his support and encouragement for me and for the writing of this book. I am very grateful for the opportunity to write this book for pastors as well as lay church leaders involved in shepherding God's people. I would also like to thank Jim, Julie Zahm, and the rest of the staff at Baker Academic for their helpful editorial feedback and revisions.

I deeply appreciate John Ortberg for so kindly writing the foreword.

I am grateful and indebted to many intercessors and prayer partners for their prayer covering and support for me during the writing of this book. They include the Wednesday night prayer-meeting group and the pastoral staff and lay leaders at my church; prayer partners of Renovaré and the Renovaré board and ministry team; members of the small group that meets at our home; my prayer partner and faculty colleague for many years at Fuller, Jeffrey Bjorck, professor of psychology; and last but not least, my dear brother in Christ and recent prayer partner John Abisheganaden, associate professor and head and senior consultant of the Department of Respiratory and Critical Care Medicine at Tan Tock Seng Hospital in Singapore, who has spent many hours interceding and praying for me.

Special thanks to Fuller Theological Seminary and my church, First Evangelical Church Glendale, for graciously granting me a sabbatical in the fall of 2017, during which I wrote most of this book. I gratefully acknowledge the excellent administrative and word-processing help of Tammi Anderson at Fuller and Liberty (Otie) Javier at my church.

My daughter, Carolyn, who is a practicing attorney in Pasadena, California, provided significant editorial feedback, which has made the book a better one. I am very grateful for her support and help. I am also deeply thankful for the love, patience, support, and prayers of Angela, my wife, and for the interest and support of my son, Andrew, who was recently married to Jenn, a wonderful daughter-in-law. I have dedicated this book to the memory of my late mother, Madam Chiow Yang Quek, who went home to be with the Lord at ninety years of age. She was an exemplary model of servanthood, humility, caring, and sacrificial love.

Above all, I want to thank God for calling me through his loving grace and mercy to be a pastor and servant of Jesus Christ, my Lord and Savior and Best Friend, and for his wisdom, guidance, and strength in the writing of this book. To God—Father, Son, and Holy Spirit—be the glory!

PART 1

BIBLICAL AND THEOLOGICAL FOUNDATIONS OF PASTORAL MINISTRY

1

A Biblical Perspective
on Pastoral and Church Ministry

Serving as a pastor (or church leader) in a local church is a special and wonderful calling from God to shepherd his people or flock. It is a sacred privilege that has both joys and sorrows, peaks and valleys, triumphs and trials, and blessings and burdens, as does life itself. Some have described the pastoral calling as the highest and noblest calling, while others have called it impossible and most stressful. Albert Mohler wrote:

> The Christian pastor holds the greatest office of human responsibility in all creation. He is called to preach the Word, to teach the truth to God's people, to lead God's people in worship, to tend the flock as a caring shepherd, and to mobilize the church for Christian witness and service. The pastor's role also includes an entire complex of administrative and leadership tasks. Souls are entrusted to his care, the truth is entrusted to his stewardship, and eternal realities hang in the balance. Who can fulfill this job description?
>
> Of course, the answer is that no man can fulfill this calling. The Christian pastor must continually acknowledge his absolute dependence upon the grace and mercy of God. As the apostle Paul instructs us, we are but earthen vessels employed for God's glory. On his own, no man is up to this task.[1]

These words actually apply to both men and women called by God to be pastors or church leaders. Although the stresses and burdens of pastoral ministry have been highlighted for some time, recent research and surveys

3

have revealed that the majority of pastors are significantly happy, satisfied, or fulfilled in their ministries. However, a smaller study of over 1,000 pastors attending conferences in Southern California reported that about 90 percent experienced frequent fatigue and had thoughts of quitting ministry.[2] It has also been pointed out that there are around 350,000 churches in North America and that 3,500 of them (1 percent) die every year. Furthermore, about 1,500 ministers or pastors leave their ministries each month for reasons including loss of their jobs or retirement, but a significant number quit because of burnout and other health and family issues. It is estimated that 3,000 new churches are being planted every year, but more churches are closing down than being planted in North America.[3]

These statistics, of course, do not apply to some parts of the world where churches are actually growing and multiplying as the Holy Spirit works in wonderful and sometimes miraculous ways—for example, in parts of Asia, Africa, and Latin America.[4] Nevertheless, pastors everywhere face unique challenges, including spiritual warfare, and the stresses of ministry are real. A biblical perspective on pastoral and church ministry is needed for pastors to be able to serve their churches and shepherd God's people in a Christ-centered, biblically based, and Spirit-filled way. Pastors are called to faithful and fruitful servanthood in Christ, which will be more fully described and explicated under two major headings: (1) a biblical perspective on the church and (2) a biblical perspective on pastoral ministry, focusing on shepherding God's people as God's servant.

A Biblical Perspective on the Church (Ecclesiology)

Ecclesiology, or the doctrine of the church, has often been approached from a pragmatic or functional perspective, focusing more on what churches actually do and the polity or practices of a local church.[5] However, a more theological and biblical perspective of the church, or biblical ecclesiology, has been the focus of some recent authors.

We first need to clarify the meaning of the Greek word *ecclesia* (or *ekklesia*), often translated in the New Testament as "church" in English. Ed Silvoso has pointed out that *ekklesia* is the word translated as "assembly" in Acts 19:32, 39, 41 but as "church" 112 times in other parts of the New Testament.[6] He emphasized that the first description of *ekklesia*, or assembly of the disciples or Christ followers after Pentecost, was in the context of having a meal or eating together: "they were seen *continually* devoting themselves to the apostles' teaching and to fellowship, to the breaking of bread [eating] and to prayer."[7]

Ekklesia was therefore flowing into everyday life such as at mealtimes. Jesus transformed tables into pulpits and ordinary homes into assembly places where strangers were warmly welcomed and the gospel shared with them. He therefore did not limit the assembly or gathering of his disciples to buildings or scheduled, centralized meetings; rather, his *ekklesia*, or church (assembly), was wherever and whenever his disciples gathered together, with him and his presence among them.[8]

The church, then, is the assembly or gathering of God's people as disciples of Christ and others who may be strangers or friends, anywhere and anytime, including out there in the marketplace and in homes where real life happens and not necessarily within the confines or walls of a church building. Silvoso then provided five key paradigms for understanding church, or *ekklesia*, biblically so that both pulpit and marketplace ministers serve together as equal partners:

1. The Great Commission is about discipling nations and not just individuals (Matt. 28:19).
2. The atonement secured redemption not only for individuals but also for the marketplace, which is the heart of the nation (Luke 19:10; see also Eph. 1:7–10; Col. 1:19–20).
3. Labor is worship, and since all believers are ministers, they are to turn their jobs into places of worship to God and ministry to others (Col. 3:23; see also Gal. 6:9–10; Eph. 2:10).
4. Jesus is the One who builds this church, not us. Our assignment is to use the keys of the kingdom to lock and unlock the gates of hades in order for him to build his church where those gates stand (Matt. 16:18–19).
5. The elimination of systemic poverty in its four dimensions—spiritual, relational, motivational, and material—is the premier *social* indicator of transformation (Luke 4:18; see also Acts 4:32–34; Gal. 2:10; Rev. 21:24–27).[9]

The church has also been described as "the living reality of the living God"[10] and as "the family of God."[11] Although defining the church based on the New Testament is not easy, because there are different and various views of the church, Gregg Allison has emphasized that the church refers to the people of God, or "the communion of saints," made up of particular or peculiar people called "sojourners and strangers" (1 Pet. 2:11).[12] Gerald Bray recently pointed out that the apostles did not have a clear and systematic view of what the church should be, but they knew deep inside what it was and expressed it when appropriate. Their thinking about church can be best summarized by the words of the apostle Peter: "You yourselves like living stones are being built up as a spiritual house, to be a holy priesthood, to offer spiritual sacrifices acceptable to God through Jesus Christ. . . . You are a chosen race, a royal priesthood, a holy nation, a people for his own possession, that you may proclaim the excellencies of him who called you out of darkness into his marvelous light. Once you were not a people, but now you are God's people" (1 Pet. 2:5, 9–10 ESV). [13]

John MacArthur has asserted that the most honorable and serious responsibility as well as the highest privilege one can have with the greatest eternal significance is to serve in church ministry. Such service requires a correct understanding of the church and its ministries, with ten fundamental truths:

1. The church is the only institution that our Lord promised to build and to bless (Matt. 16:18).
2. The church is the gathering place of true worshipers (Phil. 3:3).
3. The church is the most precious assembly on earth since Christ purchased it with his own blood (Acts 20:28; 1 Cor. 6:19; Eph. 5:25; Col. 1:20; 1 Pet. 1:18; Rev. 1:5).
4. The church is the earthly expression of the heavenly reality (Matt. 6:10; 18:18).
5. The church will ultimately triumph both universally and locally (Matt. 16:18; Phil. 1:6).
6. The church is the realm of spiritual fellowship (Heb. 10:22–25; 1 John 1:3, 6–7).
7. The church is the proclaimer and protector of divine truth (1 Tim. 3:15; Titus 2:1, 15).
8. The church is the chief place for spiritual edification and growth (Acts 20:32; Eph. 4:11–16; 2 Tim. 3:16–17; 1 Pet. 2:1–2; 2 Pet. 3:18).
9. The church is the launching pad for world evangelization (Mark 16:15; Titus 2:11).
10. The church is the environment where strong spiritual leadership develops and matures (2 Tim. 2:2). [14]

The New Testament, as Ed Hayes has pointed out, contains various images or descriptions of the church, such as the church militant (on earth) and triumphant (in heaven) (1 Thess. 4:15–5:10); a fellowship or community (Acts 2:42, 43–47); the body of Christ (1 Cor. 12; Eph. 1:22–23; 4:15–16); God's household or family (Gal. 6:10; Eph. 2:19; 1 Tim. 3:14, 15; 2 Tim. 2:20–21); the building of God (1 Cor. 3:9; Eph. 2:20–22; 1 Pet. 2:4–6); the bride of Christ (2 Cor. 11:2; Eph. 5:32; Rev. 19:7); and the flock of God (John 10:11, 14; 21:15–19; Acts 20:28–29; 1 Pet. 5:2). Other images or metaphors for the church include the temple of the Holy Spirit, a royal priesthood, a holy nation, a mystery, a vineyard, the heavenly Jerusalem or the city of God, and the pillar and ground of truth.[15]

A Biblical Perspective on Pastoral Ministry: Shepherding God's People as God's Servant

Having a correct biblical perspective on what it means to serve as a pastor (or church leader) is just as crucial as having the multifaceted but biblical perspective on the church that we just reviewed. Pastoral theology is as important as ecclesiology. There are various models of ministry in the New Testament, and therefore there are multiple New Testament patterns for pastoral leadership and ministry in the church, depending on the needs of a particular church, as Derek Tidball has pointed out.[16]

Yet it is still important to emphasize that a pastor or church leader is primarily a shepherd (or undershepherd) of God's people, or the church. The pastor is a faithful and fruitful *servant* of Jesus Christ and his church, before any leadership models or roles are assumed. Biblical servanthood is central and foundational in the Christian life and ministry, including church ministry and pastoring.[17] Leadership does not come first, not even so-called servant leadership. Servanthood, pure and simple, has to do with being a devoted disciple of Jesus Christ: one who serves him and others, including the church, in loving, humble, obedient ways, in union and communion with him or by abiding in him (John 15:15), that result in much fruit that lasts for eternity. Such biblical servanthood means serving our Best Friend, Jesus, the Lord and Head of the church and the universe. Pastoral ministry then involves faithful and fruitful servanthood in Christ by the power of the Holy Spirit, focusing on shepherding God's people and not on secular, corporate models of leadership that are more CEO and managerial in emphasis and orientation. This does not mean that leadership is not important or valid. It is. However, leadership cannot be primary because servanthood is primary according to Scripture—servanthood that is founded on our essential identity in Christ and that takes place in union and communion with him as his beloved (John 15:5; Col. 3:12).

So what is a biblical perspective on pastoral ministry, or pastoring? Let's begin by briefly discussing the calling from the Lord to pastoral ministry.[18]

There is a general calling to all Christians to serve the Lord in the different and manifold ministries of Christ and his church, locally and/or globally. There is also a more specific calling that he gives to some Christians to enter into paid vocational work as a pastor, usually full time. This specific calling can include a strong inner conviction of a calling from the Lord to pastoral ministry, sometimes based on Scripture and prayer, or a prophetic word from the Holy Spirit directly spoken into one's heart or indirectly through a sermon, a reading, a mentor or other person, an experience or circumstance, or some other means God uses. A specific call will also usually include or require some external validation and confirmation from other church leaders—such as pastors and elders or other spiritual mentors and significant others in one's life—and eventually licensing and ordination in churches where pastors are ordained.

Some helpful questions to ask in discerning whether a person may be specifically called to pastoral ministry include the following from Dave Harvey:

Are you godly?
How is your home?
Can you preach?
Can you shepherd?
Do you love the lost?
Who agrees?[19]

Similarly, Gordon Smith has suggested these questions for discerning one's vocation more generally:

What on earth is God doing?
Who are you?
What is your life stage?
What are your life circumstances?
What is the cross you will have to bear?
What are you afraid of?[20]

In terms of what pastoral ministry and leadership in the church should look like, there has been much emphasis on strong and visionary leadership that is based on corporate CEO models that tend to view the church as an organization to be managed and run like any other corporation rather than as a living organism in Christ. This approach is potentially dangerous if the biblical, foot-washing servanthood exemplified by Christ (John 13:1–17) and the shepherd model of pastoring (John 10:11, 14; 21:15–19; Acts 20:28–29; 1 Pet. 5:2) are not given their places of primacy as taught in Scripture. However, more recently there has also been an encouraging development in the publication of books written from a biblical perspective that warn us against simply following business or CEO models for pastoral leadership and ministry in the church. More biblical models of pastors called to be spiritual shepherds of God's people have been rightly advocated and emphasized.[21] Scriptural criteria for spiritual maturity in New Testament texts—such as 1 Timothy 3:1–12 and Titus 1:5–9—for selecting church leaders and pastors are therefore crucial and essential. The biblical emphasis is for pastors and church leaders to be faithful and fruitful servants in Christ who are willing to be countercultural—to be "unnecessary" pastors, as Marva Dawn and Eugene Peterson have asserted (unnecessary according to the world's secular criteria for effective leadership that focus on false expectations of charisma and success, growing numbers and wielding power).[22]

The word "pastor," transliterated from the Latin word *pastor*, actually means "shepherd," with the connotation of feeding a flock of sheep. The Greek word in the New Testament for pastor is *poimen*, again usually translated as "shepherd."[23] Jesus is described in John 10:11, 14 as the "good shepherd" (*poimen*) who lays down his life for the sheep. He is also called the "great shepherd" of the sheep (Heb. 13:20) who keeps on caring for us, and the "Chief Shepherd" (1 Pet. 5:4) who will return in his second coming with eternal rewards for his servants that will never fade away. Pastors therefore follow Jesus as the Chief Shepherd and Head of the church, to serve as his shepherds or undershepherds of his people, or flock of sheep.

The New Testament also emphasizes pastoral and church ministry as shepherding God's people. For example, in Acts 20:28–29 Paul gave the following charge to the pastoral leaders of the church at Ephesus: "Keep watch over yourselves and all the flock of which the Holy Spirit has made you overseers. Be shepherds of the church of God, which he bought with his own blood. I know that after I leave, savage wolves will come in among you and will not spare the flock."

In John 21:15–19, Jesus himself restored Peter to the pastoral or shepherding ministry after he had denied Christ three times by instructing Peter to feed his sheep or lambs and take care of them, out of Peter's love for him, which was affirmed three times:

> When they had finished eating, Jesus said to Simon Peter, "Simon son of John, do you love me more than these?"

"Yes, Lord," he said, "you know that I love you."

Jesus said, "Feed my lambs."

Again Jesus said, "Simon son of John, do you love me?"

He answered, "Yes, Lord, you know that I love you."

Jesus said, "Take care of my sheep."

The third time he said to him, "Simon son of John, do you love me?"

Peter was hurt because Jesus asked him the third time, "Do you love me?"

He said, "Lord, you know all things; you know that I love you."

Jesus said, "Feed my sheep. Very truly I tell you, when you were younger you dressed yourself and went where you wanted; but when you are old you will stretch out your hands, and someone else will dress you and lead you where you do not want to go." Jesus said this to indicate the kind of death by which Peter would glorify God. Then he said to him, "Follow me!"

One more example from the New Testament that points to pastoral ministry as shepherding God's people is 1 Peter 5:1–5:

To the elders among you, I appeal as a fellow elder and a witness of Christ's sufferings who also will share in the glory to be revealed. Be shepherds of God's flock that is under your care, watching over them—not because you must, but because you are willing, as God wants you to be; not pursuing dishonest gain, but eager to serve; not lording it over those entrusted to you, but being examples to the flock. And when the Chief Shepherd appears, you will receive the crown of glory that will never fade away. In the same way, you who are younger, submit yourselves to your elders. All of you, clothe yourselves with humility toward one another, because, "God opposes the proud but shows favor to the humble."

Simon Chan, in *Spiritual Theology*, concluded from Scripture as well as from church history that the distinguishing mark of pastoral ministry or vocation should be as follows:

In the modern church, the role of the pastor is no longer clear cut. The pastor is expected to do a lot of things but is not sure which is "the one thing needful" (Luke 10:42), the essential duty. The recovery of spiritual direction in recent years has once again drawn the attention to the main focus of pastoral care, namely, to help Christians develop their prayer life and discover the will of God. For much of the history of the church, the work of the pastor was quite unambiguous: the "cure of souls." The shepherd is to help the sheep assimilate and live out the spiritual life. In short, the pastor is essentially a spiritual theologian and a guide to godliness. It is this work and nothing else that gives the pastoral vocation its distinguishing mark.[24]

The pastor, as primarily the shepherd of God's people, is called to spiritual leadership in the church that is not easy or glamorous. John MacArthur has pointed out that Paul in 2 Timothy 2 describes the demands of such leadership using seven metaphors. The pastor is "a teacher (v. 2), a soldier (v. 3), an athlete (v. 5), a farmer (v. 6), a workman (v. 15), a vessel (vv. 20–21), and a slave (v. 24). All such images evoke ideas of sacrifice, labor, service, and hardship. They speak eloquently of the complex and varied responsibilities of spiritual leadership. Not one of them makes leadership out to be glamorous. Its requirements are blameless character, spiritual maturity, and above all, a willingness to serve humbly."[25] He went on to emphasize that the favorite metaphor Jesus used to describe spiritual leadership, including pastoral leadership and ministry, "was that of a shepherd—a person who tends God's flock. Every church leader is a shepherd. The word *pastor* itself means 'shepherd.' It is appropriate imagery. A shepherd leads, feeds, nurtures, comforts, corrects, and protects."[26] In Jeremiah 3:15, the Lord promised his people, "I will give you shepherds after my own heart, who will lead you with knowledge and understanding." He also condemned the false and selfish shepherds of Israel who cared only about themselves and their selfish gain and did not truly care for the sheep of Israel (see Isa. 56:10–11; Ezek. 34:1–16). The Lord himself will be like a shepherd who will feed his flock and take good and gentle care of them (Isa. 40:11; Ezek. 34:15).

A shepherd ultimately serves with love, the agape love of Jesus (John 13:34–35). Wes Roberts and Glenn Marshall, writing about God's original intent or purpose for the church, put it this way: "True shepherds are willing to bear the scars, the disappointments, and the hardships of the task because they care deeply for their sheep. One thing is true, if we're going to shepherd our flocks like Jesus: it's about love."[27]

It is clear, therefore, that a pastor is to serve with love as a shepherd, a spiritual theologian, and a guide to godliness, as Simon Chan and others have emphasized from a biblical and church history perspective. However, there may be congregations or churches out there that are looking for a very different kind of pastor, one who functions more as a CEO prepared to manage a religious corporation called the church. Pastors need to resist the ever-present temptation to please such congregations or churches and remain steadfast, with God's grace, to serve as shepherds, spiritual theologians, and guides to godliness or deeper Christlikeness for God's people. In this context, Peterson has strong but good spiritual medicine for us:

> And we are unnecessary to what *congregations* insist that we must do and be: as the experts who help them stay ahead of the competition. . . . They want

pastors who lead. . . . Congregations get their idea of what makes a pastor from the culture, not from the Scriptures: they want a winner; they want their needs met; they want to be part of something zesty and glamorous. . . . With hardly an exception they don't want pastors at all—they want managers of their religious company. They want a pastor they can follow so they won't have to bother with following Jesus anymore.[28]

John Piper has also biblically and strongly critiqued the professionalism or professionalization of pastoral ministry that focuses on expertise, knowledge, skills, and our own competence and abilities to succeed as pastors: "We pastors are being killed by the professionalizing of the pastoral ministry. The mentality of the professional is not the mentality of the prophet. It is not the mentality of the slave of Christ. Professionalism has nothing to do with the essence and heart of the Christian ministry. The more professional we long to be, the more spiritual death we will leave in our wake. For there is no professional childlikeness (Matt. 18:3); there is no professional tenderheartedness (Eph. 4:32); there is no professional panting after God (Ps. 42:1)."[29]

The following prayer from Piper is a fitting conclusion to this first chapter covering a biblical perspective on pastoral and church ministry: "Banish professionalism from our midst, O God, and in its place put passionate prayer, poverty of spirit, hunger for God, rigorous study of holy things, white-hot devotion to Jesus Christ, utter indifference to all material gain, and unremitting labor to rescue the perishing, perfect the saints, and glorify our sovereign Lord. In Jesus' great and powerful name. Amen."[30]

RECOMMENDED READINGS

Allison, Gregg R. *Sojourners and Strangers: The Doctrine of the Church*. Wheaton: Crossway, 2012.

Bisagno, John. *Pastor's Handbook*. Nashville: B&H, 2011.

Bray, Gerald. *The Church: A Theological and Historical Account*. Grand Rapids: Baker Academic, 2016.

Bryant, James, and Mac Brunson. *The New Guidebook for Pastors*. Nashville: B&H, 2007.

Chan, Simon. *Spiritual Theology: A Systematic Study of the Christian Life*. Downers Grove, IL: InterVarsity, 1998.

Croft, Brian. *The Pastor's Ministry: Biblical Priorities for Faithful Shepherds*. Grand Rapids: Zondervan, 2015.

Dawn, Marva, and Eugene Peterson. *The Unnecessary Pastor: Rediscovering the Call.* Grand Rapids: Eerdmans, 2000.

Eswine, Zach. *The Imperfect Pastor: Discovering Joy in Our Limitations through a Daily Apprenticeship with Jesus.* Wheaton: Crossway, 2015.

Hughes, R. Kent, and Douglas Sean O'Donnell. *The Pastor's Book: A Comprehensive and Practical Guide to Pastoral Ministry.* Wheaton: Crossway, 2015.

Laniak, Timothy S. *Shepherds after My Own Heart: Pastoral Traditions and Leadership in the Bible.* Downers Grove, IL: IVP Academic, 2006.

Lee, Cameron, and Kurt Fredrickson. *That Their Work Will Be a Joy: Understanding and Coping with the Challenges of Pastoral Ministry.* Eugene, OR: Cascade Books, 2012.

MacArthur, John, Jr., ed. *Rediscovering Pastoral Ministry: Shaping Contemporary Ministry with Biblical Mandates.* Dallas: Word, 1995.

McIntosh, Gary, and Charles Arn. *What Every Pastor Should Know: 101 Indispensable Rules of Thumb for Leading Your Church.* Grand Rapids: Baker Books, 2013.

Peterson, Eugene. *The Pastor: A Memoir.* New York: HarperOne, 2011.

Piper, John. *Brothers, We Are Not Professionals: A Plea to Pastors for Radical Ministry.* Rev. ed. Nashville: B&H, 2013.

Prime, Derek J., and Alistair Begg. *On Being a Pastor: Understanding Our Calling and Work.* Chicago: Moody, 2004.

Silvoso, Ed. *Ekklesia: Rediscovering God's Instrument for Global Transformation.* Grand Rapids: Chosen, 2017.

Smith, Mandy. *The Vulnerable Pastor: How Human Limitations Empower Our Ministry.* Downers Grove, IL: InterVarsity, 2015.

Stowell, Joseph M. *Shepherding the Church: Effective Spiritual Leadership in a Changing Culture.* Chicago: Moody, 2007.

Willimon, William H. *Pastor: The Theology and Practice of Ordained Ministry.* Rev. ed. Nashville: Abingdon, 2016.

2

The Person and Work of the Holy Spirit as Crucial and Essential for Pastoral Ministry

The person and work of the Holy Spirit, the Third Person of our Triune God (Father, Son, and Holy Spirit), are crucial and essential in the Christian life in general and in all Christian ministries and work and therefore for all Christians, not just pastors and church leaders. Although we may have different theological or denominational views concerning the doctrine of the Holy Spirit (pneumatology),[1] and conflicting perspectives unfortunately still exist that can be divisive,[2] we can all agree that the presence and the power of the Holy Spirit are also crucial and essential in faithful and fruitful pastoral and church ministry. Christian ministry, including pastoral ministry, can be described as "participating in what God is already doing in Christ in the power of the Spirit," or dancing in the dark with the Triune God, in the light of Christ, into the darkness or dark places of this fallen world, as Graham Buxton has put it.[3]

Basic Biblical Truths about the Holy Spirit

R. T. Kendall has succinctly summarized twenty-one things every Christian should know about the Holy Spirit according to the Bible:

  1. The Holy Spirit is God (Acts 5:4; 2 Cor. 3:17).
  2. The Holy is a person (John 14:16; 16:8).

3. The Holy Spirit is eternal (Gen. 1:1; Heb. 9:14).

4. The Holy Spirit is the Spirit of truth (John 14:17; 16:13).

5. The Holy Spirit was involved in creation (Gen. 1:2).

6. The Holy Spirit, using people, wrote the Bible (2 Tim. 3:16; 2 Pet. 1:21).

7. The Holy Spirit is our teacher (John 14:26; 1 John 2:27).

8. The Holy Spirit can be grieved (Eph. 4:30).

9. The Holy Spirit can be quenched (1 Thess. 5:19).

10. The Holy Spirit will be the One who convicts (John 16:8).

11. The Holy Spirit is our guide (John 16:13).

12. The Holy Spirit speaks only what the Father gives him to say (John 16:13).

13. The Holy Spirit will predict the future (John 16:13).

14. The Holy Spirit will glorify Jesus Christ (John 16:14).

15. The Holy Spirit can be blasphemed (Matt. 12:31).

16. The Holy Spirit is our reminder (John 14:26).

17. The Holy Spirit gives power (Acts 1:8).

18. The Holy Spirit manifests through various spiritual gifts (1 Cor. 12:7–10).

19. The Holy Spirit directs people to Jesus and makes him real (John 6:63, 65; 15:26).

20. The Holy Spirit manifests through various fruit (Gal. 5:22–23).

21. The Holy Spirit gives renewed power (Acts 4:31).[4]

In Ephesians 5:18 we are commanded to "be [continually] filled with the Spirit," and Kendall therefore concludes, "We need to be filled—again and again."[5]

How to Be Filled with the Holy Spirit

Douglas Gregg and I wrote a book, *Disciplines of the Holy Spirit*,[6] on how to connect to the Spirit's power and presence using the traditional spiritual disciplines as power connectors (e.g., solitude and silence, listening and guidance, prayer and intercession, study and meditation, repentance and confession, yielding and submission, fasting, worship, fellowship, simplicity, service, and witness). Of course, the Holy Spirit can work in many ways besides through the traditional spiritual disciplines, such as through authentic disciplines, or circumstantial spiritual disciplines (e.g., selflessness, waiting, suffering, persecution, social mercy, forgiveness, mourning, contentment, sacrifice, hope, and fear).[7] The Holy Spirit, as God, is sovereign and can work in his own mysterious and spontaneous ways to anoint us and fall afresh on us (although he is already in us, if we are Christians) at any time without us doing anything or taking any steps. The Holy Spirit is also everywhere and has worked in all kinds of people, circumstances, and situations, including the whole realm of creation, throughout history.[8]

The following are some of the blessings of the Spirit-filled life: "greater love and intimacy with God; exaltation of Jesus as Son of God and Savior; power and boldness to witness and preach; greater wisdom and faith; deep joy (singing and worship); release of spiritual gifts for ministry; victory over sin and temptation; effectiveness and power through prayer; quiet confidence during opposition; deeper trust in Scripture as the Word of God; renewed zeal for evangelism; and fresh love of Christ and others."[9] However, the Holy Spirit can at times also lead us, as he led Jesus, into the wilderness to face temptations and spiritual warfare and sometimes dark nights of the soul (see Matt. 4:1; Luke 4:1–2). The book of Acts shows that the filling of the Spirit can lead to dramatic external manifestations, such as speaking in tongues (see 2:1–4; 10:44–47; 19:1–7), or less dramatic and more quiet experiences, such as boldness in preaching or witnessing, deeper faith and wisdom, and greater joy (see 4:8, 31; 6:3, 5; 11:24; 13:52).

The Holy Spirit's presence and power are essential in our lives as well as in pastoral and church ministries. It is "'not by might nor by power, but by my Spirit,' says the LORD Almighty" (Zech. 4:6), that his work is done. Jesus himself tells us that "apart from me you can do nothing" (John 15:5). We therefore need to yield to the Holy Spirit and ask to be filled with him. We are then empowered by the Spirit not to grieve him (Eph. 4:30) with the sins of the flesh or the sinful nature (e.g., bitterness, rage and anger, brawling, slander, and malice) and not to quench him or put out the Spirit's fire (1 Thess. 5:19) with unbelief and evil.

How then can we as pastors and servants of Jesus Christ, whose own life and ministry on earth were filled with the power of the Holy Spirit (Luke 4:1, 14–15; Acts 10:38) to the glory of the Father, also be filled with the Spirit? Without trying to be simplistic or formulaic, Gregg and I suggested five approaches to being filled with the Spirit:

1. We confess our sins and receive God's forgiveness and cleansing through the precious blood of Jesus Christ (1 John 1:9). The Holy Spirit fills cleansed vessels.

2. We yield or surrender every area of our lives to the control of the Holy Spirit under Christ's lordship (Rom. 12:1–2). Of course, we never do

this perfectly or completely but as best and as sincerely as we can from our hearts.

3. We ask by faith to be filled with the Holy Spirit in obedience to Ephesians 5:18, which makes this command. This is something we should seek continually—every day and moment by moment. Jesus reassures us that it is our heavenly Father's will to "give the Holy Spirit to those who ask him" (Luke 11:13).

4. We give thanks to God by faith for answering our prayer or request to be filled with the Spirit, because it is according to his will and command in Ephesians 5:18 and he answers prayers that are in alignment with his will (1 John 5:14–15).

5. We trust and expect God to do great things, because he is a great God who is almighty, who does extraordinary things in ordinary people such as you and me.[10]

Again, the great things God does through the presence and the power of the Holy Spirit in our lives are great in his sight—they need not be dramatic or spectacular or successful or relevant from a secular, worldly perspective. They are often simple, childlike, ordinary things made great and extraordinary because of the touch of the Almighty God himself, especially manifesting the greatest thing of all, agape love, the fruit of the Spirit (1 Cor. 13; Gal. 5:22–23). God can, of course, also do great things such as signs and wonders involving miracles, healings, deliverances from evil spirits, and explosive church growth with hundreds or thousands coming to Christ, as he did in the book of Acts and in the charismatic and Pentecostal movements of the twentieth century and today.

I have shared elsewhere in my book on servanthood that we should not so much try to do *great things* for God but simply and humbly do things for a *great God*.[11] The emphasis of true servanthood in Christ is on the great God to whom be all the glory and not on the great things per se that often draw glory to us. The great God may ask us to do nothing for a season but to rest in him, to be with him in the wilderness of solitude and silence and sabbaths. He may ask us to do little or small things with great love (which is in essence the greatest thing!), such as bringing chicken soup to a sick neighbor or driving an elderly person across town for a doctor's appointment or tutoring an inner-city kid as a volunteer. And then the great God may at times ask us to do a great or big thing but only for his glory, such as growing a church from fifty to five hundred and even five thousand in five years. But it is all up to God, not us. We need to die to our own selfish ambitions,[12] surrender to his will, and let his kingdom come and his will be done on earth as it is in heaven, as Jesus taught us to pray (Matt. 6:10), and not build or advance our own kingdoms.

Here is a brief prayer that may be helpful for those of us who want to ask for the filling of the Holy Spirit, that we may be anointed with fire from above and be empowered to become more like Jesus in our character and to do more of the works of Jesus in our ministries:

> Dear Father, I come to you and ask in the Name of Jesus for you to cleanse me and fill me with the Holy Spirit and his power and presence, so that I can become more like Jesus in my life and ministries. Thank you so much. In Jesus' Name, Amen!

While these five steps and the suggested prayer for being filled with the Spirit can be helpful, they are not necessary. As mentioned earlier, the Holy Spirit, as God, is sovereign, and he can work in his own sovereign and spontaneous ways to fill us and anoint us afresh with his presence and his power, all by God's sheer grace and goodness and generosity, without us doing anything (e.g., practicing spiritual disciplines) or taking any steps. As Anthony Thiselton has emphasized, the "ascending" ministry of the Spirit, related to initiating and inspiring prayer, worship, and thanksgiving, is as important and parallel to his "descending" ministry of inspiration and empowerment.[13] We need the Holy Spirit's ministry and help even in the practice of spiritual disciplines, such as prayer and worship. Therefore, it is not by self-effort or dependence on our own skills, giftings, methods, or competence that we serve the Lord. It is in dependence on the Lord, and by the power of the Holy Spirit, that we become like Jesus and do the works of Jesus in our pastoral and church ministries. Ultimately, the Holy Spirit is the Spirit of love[14] who moves us to love God and others, even our enemies, and to live out that love in our lives and ministries for others, even unto death if need be. We read in Romans 5:5, "And hope does not put us to shame, because God's love has been poured out into our hearts through the Holy Spirit, who has been given to us."

In John 7:38–39 Jesus says, "'Whoever believes in me, as Scripture has said, rivers of living water will flow from within them.' By this he meant the Spirit, whom those who believed in him were later to receive." He therefore reassured his disciples, anticipating his death and resurrection and ascension and the sending of the Holy Spirit as their Advocate, that these things would all be good for them: "But very truly I tell you, it is for your good that I am going away. Unless I go away, the Advocate will not come to you; but if I go, I will send him to you" (John 16:7). Having the Holy Spirit inside us at the moment of our conversion to Christ when the Spirit baptizes us into the body of Christ is a special blessing (1 Cor. 12:13), but we need to continually be filled with the Spirit afterward (Eph. 5:18). With the presence and the power of the Spirit in us, we are enabled by him to do the works of Jesus and even "greater things" (in seeing even more people come to Christ and be saved and discipled), as Jesus himself promised us: "Very truly I tell you, whoever believes in me will do the works I have been doing, and they will do even greater things than these, because I am going to the Father" (John 14:12). The work of the Holy Spirit is therefore essential for faithful and fruitful pastoral and church ministries.

The Work of the Holy Spirit

The work of the Holy Spirit can be described in various ways, but it includes three major aspects from a biblical perspective: the Spirit's power and gifts, the Spirit's truth, and the Spirit's fruit.[15]

The Spirit's Power and Gifts

As already mentioned, the power of the Holy Spirit is essential in our Christian lives and ministries, including evangelism and witnessing (Acts 1:8). Therefore, we need to be continually filled with the Spirit (Eph. 5:18), to walk in or by the Spirit (Gal. 5:16) so we do not gratify the desires of the flesh or the sinful nature, and to keep in step with the Spirit since we live by the Spirit (Gal. 5:25). As we prayerfully surrender our lives to the Holy Spirit's control and ask to be filled with the Spirit, he empowers and helps us in our Christian lives and ministries. He often does this by supernaturally and sovereignly manifesting himself in us through spiritual gifts, which Paul defined in 1 Corinthians 12:7 as a "manifestation" (*phanerosis* in Greek) of the Holy Spirit. Sam Storms has helpfully pointed out, "*The gifts are God himself working in and through us.* They are concrete, often tangible, visible and vocal disclosures of divine power showcased through human activity. A *charisma* or gift of the Spirit is the Holy Spirit himself coming to clear and sometimes dramatic expression in the lives of God's people as they minister one to another."[16] Storms encouraged all of us, whatever our denominational background and whether we are charismatic or not, to welcome the gifts of the Holy Spirit, including the more dramatic gifts of healing, prophecy, and deliverance; to worship in the Spirit, providing practical steps as to how to do so; and to keep in step with the Spirit.

Peter Wagner described twenty-eight spiritual gifts based on Scripture (e.g., see Rom. 12; 1 Cor. 12; Eph. 4; 1 Pet. 4) using a spiritual gifts inventory that may be helpful for discovering and then using one's spiritual gifts for the blessing of others and the building up of the church. They are prophecy, service, teaching, exhortation, giving, leadership, mercy, wisdom, knowledge, faith, healing, miracles, discerning of spirits, tongues, interpretation of tongues, apostle, helps, administration, evangelist, pastor, celibacy, voluntary poverty, martyrdom, hospitality, missionary, intercession, deliverance, and leading worship.[17] Neil Cole has particularly emphasized the five spiritual gifts of Jesus for reigniting the church with "primal fire," based on Ephesians 4:11–13: focusing on the apostolic gift (apostle) with contagious empowerment, the prophetic gift (prophet) with contagious insight, the evangelistic gift (evangelist) with contagious compassion, the shepherding gift (pastor) with contagious unity, and the teaching gift (teacher) with contagious learning.[18] Other authors have interpreted spiritual gifts not as special *abilities* given to us by the Holy Spirit (the conventional view) but rather as different *ministries* that the Holy Spirit calls us to be involved in to strengthen and build up the church, or the body of Christ.[19]

Spiritual gifts that may be particularly helpful for an effective people-helping or counseling ministry, including pastoral care and counseling in the church, are the gifts of exhortation or encouragement (Rom. 12:8), healing (1 Cor. 12:9, 28), wisdom or a word of wisdom (1 Cor. 12:8), knowledge or a word of knowledge (1 Cor. 12:8), discerning of spirits (1 Cor. 12:10), and mercy (Rom. 12:8). From a more charismatic or Pentecostal perspective, the following spiritual gifts may also be important and relevant for a counseling ministry: prophecy, teaching, faith, miracles, tongues, and intercession.

The Spirit's Truth

The Holy Spirit is called the Spirit of truth in John 14:16–17 and 16:13. He will teach us and guide us into all truth, including psycho-theological truth in the counseling context. He will remind us of all that Jesus taught or said and reveal to us what is to come. The Spirit also inspired the writing of Scripture as God's Word. He will anoint and empower us as pastors and church leaders to teach and preach God's Word and truth in a way that will transform lives and set people free (John 8:32). He will also guide us to use Scripture in our counseling ministries in sensitive, empathic, and deeply helpful ways with our clients or parishioners. The Holy Spirit will never contradict the truth of Scripture, properly interpreted and illuminated by him. His work in all our pastoral responsibilities as we shepherd God's people, including pastoral care, counseling, preaching, and teaching, will always be consistent with the truths of Scripture, including its moral and ethical teachings.

The Spirit's Fruit

The fruit of the Spirit mentioned in Galatians 5:22–23 refers mainly to Christlike love, or *agapē* in Greek, which is characteristic of mature Christ-likeness (Rom. 8:29), the goal and will of God for all his people and the church. It is the Holy Spirit who produces the fruit of the Spirit: love, joy, peace, forbearance (patience), kindness, goodness, faithfulness, gentleness, and self-control (Gal. 5:22–23). We cannot manufacture or fake such Christ-like fruit, which comes forth by the work of the Holy Spirit within us as we abide in Christ (John 15:5). Such agape love from the Spirit of love is not only powerfully therapeutic or healing in counseling ministries but also essential in all our pastoral and church ministries, for without love we are nothing and have accomplished nothing (1 Cor. 13).

All three major aspects of the Holy Spirit's work (power, truth, and love) are crucial in our Christian lives and ministries, and they need to exist in biblical balance. As I have concluded, "Power without love often results in abuse. Power without truth can become heresy. However, power based on truth and used with Christlike love can produce renewal and revival as well as the deep and substantial healing of broken lives."[20]

The Work of the Holy Spirit in Counseling

This chapter ends by exploring how the Holy Spirit can work in the specific context of counseling or helping people, whether in lay counseling, pastoral care and counseling, or professional therapy, serving as one concrete example of how essential the Spirit is in pastoral ministries. He can work implicitly (quietly or covertly) or explicitly (obviously or overtly) as we minister to people in counseling contexts. There are at least five ways the Spirit can help us during a counseling session.

First, the Holy Spirit can provide specific words of knowledge or wisdom (1 Cor. 12:8) to directly help the Christian counselor or pastor more quickly and accurately get to the root problems of the client or parishioner who is being seen for counseling. Charles Swindoll, writing from a more conservative perspective, has described similar experiences of receiving words of knowledge or wisdom as "inner promptings" or nudges from the Spirit.[21] We can be more mindfully aware of and open to the Spirit during a counseling session by using flash prayers from time to time—for example, praying, "Spirit of God, please guide me," "Holy Spirit, please touch the client with your comfort and grace," and "Holy Spirit, grant us wisdom and clarity."

Second, the Holy Spirit can reveal God's will more clearly to both the counselor and the client (or the pastor and the parishioner) and thus give them spiritual direction as they engage in explicit integration practices during a counseling session—for example, praying together, exploring spiritual issues, and/or reading and sharing Scripture together. The Spirit can provide such spiritual direction more implicitly or quietly when such practices are not appropriate, such as when a pastor is counseling a non-Christian client who is not interested in or open to engaging in spiritual disciplines or practices.

Third, the Holy Spirit can directly touch a client in a spontaneous way with his loving grace and healing power according to his sovereign will and timing. This can happen anytime! However, using prayer and especially inner healing prayer, or the healing of memories, can be particularly helpful in facilitating the healing work of the Spirit in such special transcendent moments during a counseling session.

Fourth, the Holy Spirit can help the counselor or pastor with the discerning of spirits (1 Cor. 12:10) or simply spiritual discernment to determine more clearly whether there may be demonization or demonic oppression in the client's life and to differentiate between demonization and mental illness. Sometimes both may be present in a particular client. The Holy Spirit can also empower the counselor or pastor to conduct effective prayers for deliverance and protection from the demonic, if this is necessary, but with informed consent from and collaboration with the client. At times, referring a client to a prayer ministry team experienced in deliverance may be more appropriate.

Fifth, and finally, the Holy Spirit can work a deep and substantial spiritual transformation in the client as well as in the counselor or pastor as they practice the traditional spiritual disciplines (e.g., prayer, silence, Scripture reading and meditation, confession and repentance, forgiveness, inner healing prayer, etc.) in the power of the Spirit during the counseling session or between sessions as homework assignments for the client (and the counselor or pastor too). The Holy Spirit can sovereignly and supernaturally bring both the client and the counselor to deeper levels of spiritual growth or transformation into greater Christlikeness. It is therefore not true that a counselor or pastor can lead a client only as far as the counselor or pastor has gone spiritually and psychologically. The Holy Spirit can bring both the counselor or pastor and the client beyond their present levels. This is God's sovereign work of grace, and therefore to God be the glory![22]

The work of the Holy Spirit in Christian counseling, including pastoral care and counseling, is therefore crucial. Counseling skills and training are still needed and helpful, but they should always be used in dependence on the Holy Spirit. In fact, the Spirit's work is essential in every aspect of pastoral ministry, not just in pastoral care and counseling—for example, in preaching and teaching; corporate worship; intentional disciplemaking and spiritual formation; evangelism, missions, and social concern; leadership; mentoring of church staff and lay volunteer coworkers; church boards, budgets, and buildings; weddings and funerals; small groups and fellowships; integrity and ethics; and leaving and retiring, all of which will be covered in part 2 of this book.

RECOMMENDED READINGS

Fee, Gordon D. *God's Empowering Presence: The Holy Spirit in the Letters of Paul.* Grand Rapids: Baker Academic, 2009.

Horton, Michael. *Rediscovering the Holy Spirit: God's Perfecting Presence in Creation, Redemption, and Everyday Life.* Grand Rapids: Zondervan, 2017.

Kendall, R. T. *Holy Fire: A Balanced, Biblical Look at the Holy Spirit's Work in Our Lives.* Lake Mary, FL: Charisma House, 2014.

Levinson, John R. *Filled with the Spirit.* Grand Rapids: Eerdmans, 2009.

Packer, J. I. *Keep in Step with the Spirit: Finding Fullness in Our Walk with God.* Rev. ed. Grand Rapids: Baker Books, 2005.

Purves, Andrew. *The Crucifixion of Ministry: Surrendering Our Ambitions to the Service of Christ.* Downers Grove, IL: InterVarsity, 2007.

———. *The Resurrection of Ministry: Serving in the Hope of the Risen Lord.* Downers Grove, IL: InterVarsity, 2010.

Sanders, J. Oswald. *The Holy Spirit and His Gifts.* Grand Rapids: Zondervan, 1970.

Storms, Sam. *Practicing the Power: Welcoming the Gifts of the Holy Spirit in Your Life.* Grand Rapids: Zondervan, 2017.

Tan, Siang-Yang, and Douglas H. Gregg. *Disciplines of the Holy Spirit: How to Connect to the Spirit's Power and Presence.* Grand Rapids: Zondervan, 1997.

Thiselton, Anthony C. *The Holy Spirit—In Biblical Teaching, through the Centuries, and Today.* Grand Rapids: Eerdmans, 2013.

Thomas, Gary L. *Authentic Faith: The Power of a Fire-Tested Life.* Grand Rapids: Zondervan, 2002.

Wagner, C. Peter. *Your Spiritual Gifts Can Help Your Church Grow.* Rev. ed. Ventura, CA: Regal, 2005.

Yong, Amos. *Spirit of Love: A Trinitarian Theology of Grace.* Waco: Baylor University Press, 2012.

3

The Spiritual Life of the Pastor

Although splitting up the life of the pastor is a bit artificial, this chapter covers the spiritual life of the pastor, and the next chapter deals with the personal and family life of the pastor. Since the Holy Spirit's work is so crucial and necessary in pastoral ministry, the spiritual life of the pastor is also of paramount importance in pastoral ministry. The character of the pastor is therefore more important and foundational to faithful and fruitful pastoral ministry than other factors that can be overemphasized. They include competence (or excellence) in skills, abilities, giftings, techniques, methods, performance, and chemistry in getting along well with people and working as a good team player with charisma and a winsome personality. This does not mean a pastor has to be spiritually perfect and flawless in character. We are all fallen, imperfect, sinful human beings. A pastor needs to personally acknowledge this fact and live in holy and healthy brokenness and humility, yielding to the Holy Spirit, so that Christ's strength can be made perfect in his or her human weakness (2 Cor. 12:9–10; see also 2 Cor. 3:5; 4:7).

There has been an emphasis on the spiritual life of the pastor recently, and several helpful and biblically based books will be reviewed in this chapter. These books encourage and edify, inspire and instruct, comfort, convict, and challenge us as pastors and church leaders to make our spiritual lives our first priority—to follow Jesus as our first love in devoted discipleship, to walk in the way of weakness and humble brokenness, by the power of the Holy Spirit, and to love God and others. The ultimate goal of the pastor's spiritual life is to become more like Jesus (Rom. 8:29), just as the ultimate goal of the church and the people of God is also to become more like Jesus. Dallas Willard has emphasized that the primary goal of a local church or congregation should be spiritual formation in Christlikeness.[1] Therefore, there is a great need to guard against the many simple distractions in a local church that can so easily derail the pastor and God's people from focusing on this one main goal.

The Secret of Transforming Power in the Life and Ministry of Jesus

Jesus is the only perfect human being who ever lived. As the sinless Son of God, fully divine and fully human, he was tempted like us but never sinned (Heb. 4:14–15). What was the secret of transforming power in the life and ministry of Jesus, our Lord and Savior and the perfect model of a Shepherd-Pastor whom we should follow? In the midst of a busy ministry that touched many people with many different needs, Jesus took time off on a regular basis to pray and be in solitude and communion with the Father by the power of the Holy Spirit (see Matt. 14:23; 26:36; Mark 1:35; 6:46; 14:32; Luke 5:16; 6:12, 22:41; John 17:1; Heb. 5:7). He also lived, ministered, and taught in the power of the Spirit (e.g., see Luke 4:1, 14–15; Acts 1:1–3; 10:36–38). If Jesus needed to spend regular time in prayer and solitude with the Father to be renewed and filled with the transforming power required to touch and change lives, we need to do likewise as pastors and church leaders. Our first priority is to abide or dwell in Christ (John 15:5), in union and communion with him, so that we can be fruitful, become more like him, and do his works, not our own. He calls us to friendship with him, even as his servants or his "beloved dust"[2]: "I no longer call you servants, because a servant does not know his master's business. Instead, I have called you friends, for everything that I learned from my Father I have made known to you. You did not choose me, but I chose you and appointed you so that you might go and bear fruit—fruit that will last—and so that whatever you ask in my name the Father will give you. This is my command: Love each other" (John 15:15–17).

Modeling the Master

We serve Jesus as his friends, with him as our Best Friend.[3] He is our beloved, and we are his beloved. Following him, we need to set aside time daily to be with God in prayer. This includes solitude and silence and unrushed moments of loving union and communion with him who first loved us and continues to woo us to his loving presence (1 John 4:19). This daily time in fellowship with him has often been called quiet time or personal devotion time. When

I first became a Christian around the age of fourteen in Singapore, where I grew up, I was taught how to have a daily quiet time, whether it was for fifteen minutes or half an hour or even a full hour. The formula was simple: pray, read the Bible, and pray. I was taught that to pray is to talk to God and to read the Bible is when God talks to us. However, I focused, like many young (and old!) Christians, on "doing" my quiet time each day. I was often asked, "Have you done your quiet time?" Over the years, the Lord has graciously helped me learn that quiet time is not about *doing* an activity; it is about *being* with him. It is also not a rushed time to do an activity to score spiritual points, to check off on a spiritual to-do list or, worse, on a spiritual scoreboard. I also learned that there needs to be much quiet or silence in my quiet time. After all, it is supposed to be a *quiet* time with the Lord.

So I now share a revised version of the quiet time: be quiet, pray, be quiet, be quiet in prayer, read the Bible, be quiet in Scripture meditation, be quiet, pray, be quiet! There should be a great deal of quiet or silence in our quiet times. This is one of the most significant discoveries in evangelical spirituality and spiritual formation regarding the practice of the spiritual disciplines. We have discovered or, more accurately, rediscovered silence (and solitude). This time alone with God in prayer and in his Word should involve much unrushed, leisurely periods of quiet or silence as we simply wait on the Lord, being still and deeply knowing and experiencing that he is God (Ps. 46:10).

For the past several years, my daily quiet time in the morning has involved such quiet or silence; prayer of different types (e.g., ACTS: adoration, confession, thanksgiving, and supplication, including petition for self and intercession for others using a prayer list); reading and meditating on Scripture using *Daily Light on the Daily Path*, a collection of biblical texts with morning and evening selections originally compiled by Jonathan Bagster many years ago; and reading devotional books such as *God Calling*, edited by A. J. Russell.[4] I have found these devotional readings very helpful and inspirational, enabling me to more clearly hear God's voice. I also systematically read a few chapters of the Bible at night with some prayer before I go to bed, aiming to go through the entire Bible from Genesis to Revelation in a year or two. In my daily morning prayer time of intercession, I use a prayer list containing hundreds of names (including those of many church members). I mention and lift up each person to the Lord for only a couple of seconds, knowing he already knows each one by name and his or her needs. I may pray longer for some if prompted by the Holy Spirit.

I also spend up to ten hours each week studying a biblical text in depth, in sermon preparation, when I have to preach that particular Sunday. I have been preaching about thirty-three times a year in my church as the senior pastor for over twenty years. This discipline of Bible study and meditation and sermon preparation on a regular basis has deepened my knowledge of God's Word. This discipline, together with my devotional reading of Scripture, has also enabled me to be spiritually transformed to become more like Jesus by the power of Scripture, or "the fire of his Word,"[5] read as a love letter from God.

I also use flash prayers during the day to practice the presence of God and to stay dependent on him, thereby to "pray continually" (1 Thess. 5:17) and to "pray in the Spirit on all occasions with all kinds of prayers and requests" (Eph. 6:18). Examples of these quick, short prayers throughout the day include, "Thank you, Lord," "Please help me, Lord," "I am sorry, Lord," "Fill me with the Spirit," "Bring healing to my dear friend," "Guide me, Lord," "Protect us, Lord," "Provide for us, Lord," "Please bring peace to these troubled places," and "Good night, Lord." The Jesus prayer, from the Eastern Orthodox tradition, based on Luke 18:13, has in recent years become a daily flash prayer for me: "Lord Jesus Christ, Son of God, have mercy on me, a sinner." It is truly a powerful and Spirit-inspired prayer for praying continually (1 Thess. 5:17).

In addition to these daily spiritual practices of prayer and reading of and meditating on Scripture, taking periodic retreats of twenty-four or forty-eight hours or longer, at least once a year, can be crucial in our spiritual formation into deeper Christlikeness as pastors and church leaders. We all tend to be far too busy.[6] We need to slow down and pause and rest in and with the Lord.[7] This includes taking more prolonged personal retreats, or "wilderness time," as Emilie Griffin has put it in her wonderful guide to personal spiritual retreat.[8] We may at first experience hunger, restlessness, and sleepiness when we go on a personal spiritual retreat to be in silence and solitude with the Lord. We may even nod off.[9] However, we need not feel guilty or anxious about such very common and human responses to slowing down and resting in the Lord. We can simply eat something if we are hungry, walk around and enjoy the usually beautiful surroundings of a retreat place, and sleep if need be. We will have enough time during a one- or two-day retreat to fast and pray and stay awake to enjoy the Lord and his presence, with love, peace, and joy in the Spirit.

The spiritual life of the pastor or church leader (or any Christian) can be deepened with prayer and Scripture as well as several other traditional spiritual disciplines, which will now be reviewed in more detail.

Prayer

Much has been written on prayer, including several recent and helpful books and Richard Foster's must-read classic *Prayer: Finding the Heart's True*

Home,[10] which contains descriptions of twenty-one types of prayer that go beyond the basic ACTS components and help us grow deeper spiritually in Christ. They include simple prayer, prayer of the forsaken, the prayer of examen, the prayer of tears, the prayer of relinquishment, formation prayer, and covenant prayer (for moving inward in seeking the transformation we need); the prayer of adoration, the prayer of rest, sacramental prayer, unceasing prayer, the prayer of the heart, meditative prayer, and contemplative prayer (for moving upward in seeking the intimacy we need); praying the ordinary, petitionary prayer, intercessory prayer, healing prayer, the prayer of suffering, authoritative prayer, and radical prayer (for moving outward in seeking the ministry we need).[11] Prayer is therefore not just talking to God but also listening to God and waiting on him in silent contemplative and meditative prayer. He speaks to us in prayer, not just through Bible reading, and in many other ways, such as godly counsel (including spiritual direction), providential circumstances, sanctified common sense, inner witness and peace (although not always or immediately), prophecy and words of knowledge or wisdom, visions and dreams, nature, and heavenly visitation or the "hand of the Lord."[12]

To "pray continually" (1 Thess. 5:17) can include not just flash prayers throughout the day but also the practice of the daily office in which we pause at fixed hours of the day (or the divine hours) to pray and attend more intentionally to God's presence through Scripture and other readings.[13] We also learn to pray the Scriptures and let God's Word guide and direct us in our prayers for ourselves, others, the world, and creation.[14]

Prayer should also include corporate prayer with a prayer partner or with several or many others in a group prayer meeting. A pastor's own spiritual life can be deeply strengthened by leading church members in corporate prayer meetings or prayer groups. By making prayer together with others a top priority in church life and ministry, we follow the apostles and early disciples, who devoted themselves to prayer and the Word (Acts 6:4; see also Acts 2:42). Daniel Henderson, with Margaret Saylar, has written a wonderful book, *Fresh Encounters*, on experiencing transformation through united worship-based corporate prayer in groups led by pastors in local churches.[15] We who are pastors need to make prayer a top priority not only in our individual spiritual lives but also in the corporate spiritual life of the local churches we are shepherding. Pastors need to lead worship-based prayer meetings, because spiritual power is released through prayer. The Korean church is an inspiring model for all of us. Korean Christians have a long tradition of gathering daily for early morning (4:00 or 4:30 a.m.) prayer meetings under pastoral leadership to pray and intercede together for one another, for the church, and for the world. Most American churches have only one weekly prayer meeting, and it is often poorly attended. I have made it a top priority to regularly attend the Wednesday night prayer meeting of the English congregation at my church, usually led by a pastor, including myself. All our pastoral staff and church board meetings include prayer, our church periodically holds prayer and fasting meetings that last an entire day, and we have an all-church prayer meeting for all our congregations (English, Mandarin, and Cantonese) a few times a year. I am convicted by the Lord to make prayer, individually as well as corporately, an even bigger priority and occupation in my own spiritual life and in our church life together.

We cannot cover every aspect of prayer in this chapter, but one more significant area we need to focus on is what Peter Wagner has called the prayer shield,[16] which involves interceding in prayer for pastors and Christian leaders. There is spiritual warfare going on (Eph. 6:10–12), and prayer covering, or a prayer shield, is needed for the protection of pastors and church leaders, especially since they are under the strongest spiritual attacks from the evil one. We pastors need to have intercessors from our churches and elsewhere diligently and daily praying for us and our families, for protection against the attacks of the evil one and for empowerment and anointing from the Holy Spirit so we can grow in our spiritual lives to become more like Jesus and do the works of Jesus in faithful and fruitful ministry. I am deeply thankful that in my life and ministry as a pastor and a professor I have a group of intercessors at my church and through the Renovaré ministry started by Richard Foster, who provide prayer covering for me. I send them quarterly updates of prayer requests and praises too.

Having a prayer partner or two to regularly and frequently pray with is also very helpful for a pastor. I have several special friends as prayer partners, including Jeffrey Bjorck, who has been my faculty colleague, close friend, and prayer partner for almost thirty years now. We meet regularly for prayer and often for lunch. A more recent faithful prayer partner and close friend from a distance in Singapore is John Abisheganaden, who intercedes and prays for me daily, as I do for him.

E. M. Bounds, in his well-known classic, *Power through Prayer*, emphasized that God is not looking for better methods but for better men and women—people mighty in prayer. The Holy Spirit works through people, not through structures or methods. He anoints people, not plans—people of prayer.[17]

To close this section on prayer in the spiritual life of the pastor or church leader, here is a benediction from Richard Foster: "May you now, by the power of the Holy Spirit, receive the spirit of prayer. May it become, in the name of Jesus Christ, the most precious occupation of your life. And may the God of all peace strengthen you, bless you, and give you joy—Amen."[18]

Scripture

We have just covered prayer as a key priority in the spiritual life of the pastor. Scripture, as God's inspired Word, is another key priority in the pastor's spiritual life, just as it was in the early church (see Acts 2:42; 6:4). Although God can speak to us through other means, the Bible is the primary way God communicates with us, and everything else needs to be tested to see if it is in line with the truth of Scripture (John 17:17; 1 Thess. 5:21; 2 Tim. 3:16).

The Holy Spirit inspired the writing of Scripture through individuals guided by him (2 Tim. 3:16), and he works powerfully through God's Word, the Bible. The sword of the Spirit is the Word of God (Eph. 6:17), our spiritual offensive weapon to use against the devil and his spiritual attacks, deceptions, and temptations. Hebrews 4:12 states, "For the word of God is alive and active. Sharper than any double-edged sword, it penetrates even to dividing soul and spirit, joints and marrow; it judges the thoughts and attitudes of the heart." In Matthew 4:4, we read about Jesus being tempted in the wilderness by the devil and how he responded by using Scripture as the sword of the Spirit against the devil: "Jesus answered, 'It is written: "Man shall not live on bread alone, but on every word that comes from the mouth of God."'" Jesus emphasized the crucial and essential role that the Word of God has in sustaining our very lives. We need to uphold the Bible as God's inspired Word in our lives, in pastoral ministry, and in our churches—to keep the Bible and to keep to the Bible, as J. I. Packer challenged us in *Truth and Power*.[19] John Piper has more recently inspired us to read the Bible supernaturally, with its peculiar glory in its complete truthfulness.[20] We need to approach Scripture personally, reading the Bible as God's love letter to us. This is a book that God inhabits and therefore is infused with the very living and real presence of God. When we read it, we meet God on holy ground and experience "the fire of the Word," as Chris Webb has described it,[21] with our minds and our hearts captivated and transformed by the power of the Spirit through the Word.

The Holy Spirit ministers life to us through the Word in various ways. For example, the Word equips us (2 Tim. 3:16–17), cleanses us (Ps. 119:9, 11; John 15:3), feeds us (Heb. 5:12–13; 1 Pet. 2:2), guides and leads us (Ps. 119:105), and produces and deepens our faith or trust in God (Rom. 10:17; 1 Pet. 1:23).[22]

We can hear the Word, read the Word, study the Word, memorize the Word, and meditate on the Word, which is the crucial means of understanding and applying the Word that we hear, read, study, and memorize.[23] *Lectio divina*, or devotional (divine, sacred) reading of Scripture in an attentive way to prayerfully meet or experience God in Scripture and surrender to him, can be a particularly helpful way to get into God's Word. It involves four phases: reading, meditating on, praying, and contemplating Scripture.[24]

Reading Spiritual Classics

There is also much that we as pastors and church leaders can and need to learn from church history,[25] (including historical and systematic theology and biblical theology), especially from the early church fathers and mothers (*abbas* and *ammas*) in the first five hundred to seven hundred years of church history, called the patristic period. They spent much time (years) literally in the desert or the wilderness in prayer and in the Word, in solitude and silence. Spiritual and devotional reading of their writings, gleaning from their deep wisdom and authentic spiritual lives in Christ, will immensely and substantially bless and grow our own spiritual lives.[26] There is also much to gain from reading the Christian spiritual classics from later in church history, including the medieval, Reformation, Puritan, and pietistic traditions.[27] The *Philokalia*, a classic text from the Orthodox tradition, also has substantial spiritual depth and wisdom to help us nurture our spiritual lives. First compiled by St. Macarios and St. Nicodemos in 1777 on Mount Athos, it contains, in five volumes, the spiritual writings of about thirty church fathers from the fourth to the fifteenth centuries.[28]

Spiritual Disciplines

The traditional spiritual disciplines, from an ancient tradition of using spiritual activities or practices as means of grace, create time and space for God to work deeply in us, by the power of the Holy Spirit, to transform us to become more like Jesus in our character and our ministries. There are now many books about the traditional spiritual disciplines, including the two classics, *Celebration of Discipline* by Richard Foster and *The Spirit of the Disciplines* by Dallas Willard.[29] Foster described twelve spiritual disciplines involving both individual and group life: the inward disciplines of meditation, prayer, fasting, and study; the outward disciplines of simplicity, solitude, submission, and service; and the corporate disciplines of confession, worship, guidance, and celebration. Willard offered two major categories of spiritual disciplines: disciplines of abstinence (solitude, silence, fasting, frugality, chastity, secrecy, and sacrifice) and disciplines of engagement (study, worship, celebration, service, prayer, fellowship, confession, and submission).

There are actually at least seventy-five spiritual disciplines, and they have been described by Adele Calhoun in her very comprehensive and helpful handbook of practices that can transform us. She grouped them under seven major categories:

1. Worship: celebration, gratitude, holy communion, rule for life, Sabbath, *visio divina*, and worship
2. Open myself to God: contemplation, examen, iconography, journaling, pilgrimage, practicing the presence, rest, retreat, self-care, simplicity, slowing, teachability, and unplugging
3. Relinquish the false self: confession and self-examination, detachment, discernment, mindfulness/attentiveness, secrecy, silence, sobriety, solitude, spiritual direction, submission, and waiting
4. Share my life with others: accountability partner, chastity, community, covenant group, discipling, face-to-face connection, hospitality, mentoring, service, small group, spiritual friendship, unity, and witness
5. Hear God's Word: Bible study, *lectio divina* or devotional reading, meditation, and memorization
6. Incarnate the love of Christ: blessing others/encouragement, care of the earth, compassion, control of the tongue, forgiveness, humility, justice, solidarity in Jesus's sufferings, stewardship, and truth telling
7. Pray: breath prayer, centering prayer, contemplative prayer, conversational prayer, fasting, fixed-hour prayer, inner-healing prayer, intercessory prayer, labyrinth prayer, listening prayer, liturgical prayer, prayer of lament, prayer partners, praying Scripture, prayer of recollection, prayer walking, and welcoming prayer[30]

These spiritual disciplines are not only for deepening our own internal or personal spiritual lives but also for transforming us into Christlike, loving people who will reach out to our external world and bless others too. Spiritual formation into deeper Christlikeness is ultimately for the sake of others: it leads to loving God and loving others as Jesus taught in the greatest commandment (Matt. 22:37–40; Mark 12:30–31).[31] And it involves practicing the presence of God in everything, including the ordinary, mundane routines and activities of our daily lives, not just in our quiet times or retreats or church worship services.[32]

Growing spiritually as pastors, not just individualistically in our inward spirituality but also in community with others, especially in the church, is important, and, therefore, being in a small group or fellowship group is crucial.[33] More specifically, being involved in spiritual direction, in both giving and receiving spiritual direction, is an important part of growing spiritually as pastors or church leaders. We can receive spiritual direction formally with a spiritual director or more informally with a spiritual companion or close friend in Christ, with whom we can also give spiritual direction or guidance. Both involve discerning and obeying the will of God in our lives in a prayerful context.[34] My wife and I meet regularly with a small group of twelve to fifteen people at our home every other week for a light meal, sharing, study of the Bible or a good Christian book, and prayer. I also meet regularly with my prayer partner and spiritual companion at Fuller Seminary to share and pray together, receive and give informal spiritual direction, and support each other. These have been precious relationships for years that have helped me grow spiritually in Christ as a person and as a pastor. I therefore highly recommend regular participation in a small group and in spiritual direction to every pastor and church leader for growing their spiritual lives. This can also be described as deep connecting with others in spiritual community by engaging in soul talk, as Larry Crabb described it.[35]

The traditional spiritual disciplines covered so far can be helpful in our growth into deeper Christlikeness. However, they can also be potentially dangerous if they are used in a legalistic, performance-based way by self-effort. They can actually harm our spiritual lives if our practice of them leads to self-sufficiency, self-righteousness, spiritual pride, and arrogance in our lives and ministries. The authentic disciplines, as Gary Thomas described them (e.g., selflessness, waiting, suffering, persecution, social mercy, forgiveness, mourning, contentment, sacrifice, hope, and fear), are therefore a crucial addition to the traditional spiritual disciplines: "They turn us away from human effort—from men and women seeking the face of God—and turn us back toward God seeking the face of men and women."[36] These authentic disciplines, or circumstantial spiritual disciplines, so crucial for the development of authentic faith or a fire-tested life, are usually initiated or allowed by God outside of us and our choice: "God brings them into our life when he wills and as he wills. . . . This is a God-ordained spirituality, dependent on his sovereignty—There's no pride left when God takes me through a time of suffering. There's no self-righteousness when I am called to wait. . . . This is a spirituality I can't control, I can't initiate, I can't bring about. It is a radical dependence on God's husbandry. All I can do is try to appreciate it and learn from it."[37] Ultimately, we learn, through undergoing the authentic disciplines, "to love with God's love and to serve with God's power."[38]

Both the traditional and the authentic spiritual disciplines are essential in our spiritual lives. They can be more clearly understood in the context of brokenness in our lives. In Psalm 51:16–17 we read about how brokenness is precious to God and essential for us: "You do not delight in sacrifice, or I would bring it; you do not take pleasure in burnt offerings. My sacrifice, O God, is a broken spirit; a broken and contrite heart, you, God, will not despise." Alan Nelson has defined brokenness as "reduced to submission, tamed." Through this taming of the soul, we deny ourselves and become less so that Christ can become more in us (John 3:27–30), knowing that without Christ we can do nothing (John 15:5).[39] Brokenness is a crucial part of our progressive sanctification,[40] the process of becoming more like Jesus over time by the power of the Holy Spirit. We learn to humble ourselves, die more to our old self or false self, and grow in our new self or true self in Christ (Eph. 4:22–24). We learn to "let go and let God" take more control of our lives by the power of the Holy Spirit, but not in a quick-fix, instant, total sanctification way that has been strongly critiqued by J. I. Packer and more recently by Andrew Naselli.[41] We let go and let God lead and control us more and more, over time, throughout the course of our entire lives on earth, in our progressive growth or sanctification in Christ.

Brokenness is often associated with painful experiences of suffering, but it is not synonymous or the same as suffering. While we need to have a biblical theology of redemptive suffering that is ultimately good for us,[42] we need to avoid glorifying suffering per se. Actually, whatever tames our souls and leads us to deeper humility and surrender to God is an experience of brokenness, even if there is little or no suffering. It may be an experience of deep contentment or joy, with awe and worship and thanksgiving from the heart, for example, seeing the beauty and majesty of God in some part of his creation, such as a brilliant sunset, or his miraculous power in the healing of a terminally ill person with cancer.

Nelson has also helpfully differentiated between voluntary and involuntary brokenness. Involuntary brokenness involves experiences that just pop up that are not under our control and we did not choose. The authentic disciplines are good examples. With voluntary brokenness, we choose to engage in the practice of a traditional spiritual discipline or a behavior of brokenness that can help us surrender and submit to God more through the taming and tenderizing of our souls.[43] Both voluntary brokenness, through the practice of the traditional spiritual disciplines in a grace-filled, nonlegalistic way, and involuntary brokenness, experienced through the authentic disciplines, are crucial in deepening our spiritual lives and becoming more like Jesus. However, ultimately, it is by God's grace and the Holy Spirit's work in a sovereign way that we are transformed into deeper Christlikeness. God can work in any way or any how or any time he wants. We are humbly at his mercy and his grace. We can rest and rejoice in him, because he is good and faithful (2 Thess. 3:3), and "he who began a good work in you will carry it on to completion until the day of Christ Jesus" (Phil. 1:6).

RECOMMENDED READINGS

Allison, Gregg R. *Historical Theology: An Introduction to Christian Doctrine*. Grand Rapids: Zondervan, 2011.

Barton, Ruth Haley. *Invitation to Retreat: The Gift and Necessity of Time Away with God*. Downers Grove, IL: InterVarsity, 2018.

Benner, David. *Sacred Companions: The Gift of Spiritual Friendship and Direction*. Downers Grove, IL: InterVarsity, 2002.

Bennett, Kyle David. *Practices of Love: Spiritual Disciplines for the Life of the World*. Grand Rapids: Brazos Press, 2017.

Calhoun, Adele Ahlberg. *Spiritual Disciplines Handbook: Practices That Transform Us*. Rev. ed. Downers Grove, IL: InterVarsity, 2015.

Chryssavgis, John. *In the Heart of the Desert: The Spirituality of the Desert Fathers and Mothers*. Rev. ed. Bloomington, IN: World Wisdom, 2008.

Coniaris, Anthony M. *A Beginner's Introduction to the Philokalia*. Minneapolis: Light & Life Publishing, 2004.

Fadling, Alan. *An Unhurried Life: Following Jesus' Rhythms of Work and Rest*. Downers Grove, IL: InterVarsity, 2013.

Ferguson, Sinclair B. *Devoted to God: Blueprints for Sanctification*. Carlisle, PA: Banner of Truth Trust, 2016.

Foster, Richard J. *Celebration of Discipline: The Path to Spiritual Growth*. Special anniversary ed. New York: Harper, 2018.

———. *Prayer: Finding the Heart's True Home*. New York: HarperSanFrancisco, 1992.

Goggin, Jamin, and Kyle Strobel, eds. *Reading the Christian Spiritual Classics: A Guide for Evangelicals*. Downers Grove, IL: IVP Academic, 2013.

Griffin, Emilie. *Wilderness Time: A Guide for Spiritual Retreat*. San Francisco: HarperSanFrancisco, 1997.

Grudem, Wayne. *Systematic Theology: An Introduction to Biblical Doctrine*. Grand Rapids: Zondervan, 1994.

Hansen, Gary Neal. *Kneeling with Giants: Learning to Pray with History's Best Teachers*. Downers Grove, IL: InterVarsity, 2012.

Harney, Kevin G. *No Is a Beautiful Word: Hope and Help for the Overcommitted and (Occasionally) Exhausted*. Grand Rapids: Zondervan, 2019.

Hartman, Dayton. *Church History for Modern Ministry: Why Our Past Matters for Everything We Do*. Bellingham, WA: Lexham Press, 2016.

Henderson, Daniel, with Margaret Saylar. *Fresh Encounters: Experiencing Transformation through United Worship-Based Prayer*. Colorado Springs: NavPress, 2004.

Hudson, Trevor. *Discovering Our Spiritual Identity: Practices for God's Beloved*. Downers Grove, IL: InterVarsity, 2010.

Johnson, Jan. *Meeting God in Scripture: A Hands-On Guide to Lectio Divina*. Downers Grove, IL: InterVarsity, 2016.

Keller, Timothy. *Walking with God through Pain and Suffering*. New York: Dutton, 2013.

Lawrence, Michael. *Biblical Theology in the Life of the Church: A Guide for Ministry*. Wheaton: Crossway, 2010.

Ortberg, John. *The Life You've Always Wanted: Spiritual Disciplines for Ordinary People*. Reprint ed. Grand Rapids: Zondervan, 2015.

———. *Soul Keeping: Caring for the Most Important Part of You*. Grand Rapids: Zondervan, 2014.

Piper, John. *Reading the Bible Supernaturally: Seeing and Savoring the Glory of God in Scripture*. Wheaton: Crossway, 2017.

Shigematsu, Ken. *Survival Guide for the Soul: How to Flourish Spiritually in a World That Pressures Us to Achieve*. Grand Rapids: Zondervan, 2018.

Smith, Gordon T. *Spiritual Direction: A Guide to Giving and Receiving Direction*. Downers Grove, IL: InterVarsity, 2014.

Stump, Eleonore. *Wandering in Darkness: Narrative and the Problem of Suffering*. Oxford, UK: Oxford University Press, 2010.

Swoboda, A. J. *Subversive Sabbath: The Surprising Power of Rest in a Nonstop World*. Grand Rapids: Brazos Press, 2018.

Tan, Siang-Yang. *Rest: Experiencing God's Peace in a Restless World*. Vancouver: Regent College Publishing, 2003.

Wagner, C. Peter. *Prayer Shield: How to Intercede for Pastors and Christian Leaders*. Rev. ed. Bloomington, MN: Chosen, 2014.

Warren, Tish Harrison. *Liturgy of the Ordinary: Sacred Practices in Everyday Life*. Downers Grove, IL: InterVarsity, 2016.

Whitney, Donald S. *Praying the Bible*. Wheaton: Crossway, 2015.

———. *Spiritual Disciplines for the Christian Life*. Rev. ed. Colorado Springs: NavPress, 2014.

Willard, Dallas. *The Spirit of the Disciplines*. San Francisco: HarperSanFrancisco, 1988.

4

The Personal and Family Life of the Pastor

The pastor is called on to fill many roles, with various images of what a pastor is or should be, in today's church and world. This is why some have concluded that the pastor's job or ministry is an impossible one! However, what is impossible with men and women is possible with God (Luke 18:27; see also Matt. 19:26). *Portraits of a Pastor*, edited by Jason Allen, describes nine essential roles for a pastor serving in church leadership: pastor as shepherd, pastor as husband and father, pastor as preacher, pastor as theologian, pastor as church historian, pastor as evangelist, pastor as missionary, pastor as leader, and pastor as man of God.[1] In an earlier "painting" of the portrait of a pastor as preacher, based on some New Testament word studies, John Stott described the preacher as a steward (the preacher's proclamation and appeal), a herald (the preacher's message and authority), a witness (the preacher's experience and humility), a father (the preacher's love and gentleness), and a servant (the preacher's power and motive).[2] The following are some of the major ministerial metaphors of our time provided by William Willimon: media star, political negotiator, therapist, manager, resident activist, preacher, servant, and rebel.[3] This chapter focuses more on the person of the pastor and his or her personal and family life, including the pastor as husband and father or wife and mother, and the pastor as man or woman of God.

The Personal Life of the Pastor

A wholistic model of the pastor as a person includes viewing the pastor as a physical person, a thinking person, a feeling person, a relating person, and a choosing person but integrated as a whole person.[4] Before looking in more detail at the pastor as a person and his or her personal life, we first need to cover a crucial truth about the essential identity or new nature of a Christian, including a pastor. This new nature involves union with Christ or being in Christ (or with Christ, through Christ, and into Christ) and Christ being in us. Andrew Purves some years ago wrote a book emphasizing this truth as a Christological foundation in reconstructing pastoral theology.[5] More recently, Rankin Wilbourne's *Union with Christ* has become particularly helpful for a general audience.[6]

Our union with Christ is a biblical truth that is essential for us to understand and apply to ourselves as persons. John Ortberg, in his foreword to Wilbourne's book, pointed out that the word *Christian* occurs only three times in the New Testament, but Paul, in his letters, used the phrase "in Christ" about 165 times.[7] Wilbourne provided several meanings of union with Christ,[8] which is the basis of our salvation. Union with Christ means we are in Christ: "crucified with Christ" (Gal. 2:20), "buried with him" (Rom. 6:4), "raised with Christ" (Col. 3:1), and "seated . . . with him in the heavenly realms in Christ Jesus" (Eph. 2:6). More specifically, union with Christ means we are hidden in Christ, especially as stated in Galatians 2:20: "I have been crucified with Christ and I no longer live, but Christ lives in me. The life I now live in the body, I live by faith in the Son of God, who loved me and gave himself for me." Union with Christ is not about improving the old self but having a new self in Christ: "Therefore, if anyone is in Christ, the new creation has come: The old has gone, the new is here!" (2 Cor. 5:17).

Union with Christ also means Christ is in us. We have "Christ in [us], the hope of glory" (Col. 1:27). Paul emphasized this truth in many of his letters, including 2 Corinthians: "Do you not realize that Christ Jesus is in you?" (13:5). And he explained how this works in our personal lives and experiences through the power and presence of the Holy Spirit, who is given to us to dwell within us: "Do you not know that you are God's temple and that God's Spirit dwells in you?" (1 Cor. 3:16 ESV), and "Do you not know that your bodies are temples of the Holy Spirit, who is in you, whom you have received from God? You are not your own" (1 Cor. 6:19). Paul also stated that if we do not have the Spirit, then we do not have Christ and do not belong to Christ (Rom. 8:9). Wilbourne concluded that union with Christ means we have the Spirit of Christ, or the Holy Spirit, within us: "The Spirit is the real, living bond between Jesus and us."[9] Union with Christ, meaning that we are in Christ and Christ is in us by the presence and power of the Holy Spirit within us, is our basic identity as human persons who are Christians. It is by faith, or trust in Jesus, that this truth of union with Christ becomes powerfully real in our lives. Faith can therefore be defined as "finding your identity in Christ."[10]

Knowing that we are united with Christ and live by faith in him, we need to pay attention to our personal lives as pastors, not as self-improvement projects or by self-effort but by continuing to abide in Christ (John 15:5) with the help and power of the Holy Spirit. There are various ways of dealing with the personal life of the pastor and different areas on which to focus. Some very helpful material is already available.[11] This chapter summarizes some of it and also provides additional reflections.

As mentioned earlier, viewing the pastor wholistically as a person means we see the pastor as a physical or biological person who also thinks, feels, relates to God and others, and chooses. The pastor is an embodied soul, so to speak. The spiritual life of the pastor, in union with Christ, is the most important dimension of the pastor's personal life. This was covered in some detail in the previous chapter. The pastor as a man or woman of God is one of the nine essential roles of a church leader, and Donald Whitney has provided some helpful guidelines for what this should look like in a pastor's personal life.[12] A pastor needs to be a man or woman of God because God commands pastors to be so: "Watch your life and doctrine closely. Persevere in them, because if you do, you will save both yourself and your hearers" (1 Tim. 4:16). A pastor is to be an example to the flock (1 Pet. 5:3), especially to "set an example for the believers in speech, in conduct, in love, in faith and in purity" (1 Tim. 4:12). A pastor can faithfully be a man or a woman of God in these ways: flee sin and pursue holiness (1 Tim. 6:11), as specifically as possible; become a Bible-controlled person (John 17:17; 2 Tim. 3:16) by hearing, reading, studying, memorizing, and meditating on the Bible regularly and then applying it continually in obedience to the Word; and practice the disciplines of godliness or the spiritual disciplines (1 Tim. 4:7).

Whitney raised two crucial questions for a pastor in regard to becoming a man or a woman of God: "*First, do you recognize the intentionality necessary to cultivate and sustain godliness in ministry?*" and "*Second, will you resolve to make the pursuit of pastoral holiness a top priority?*"[13] However, it must be emphasized again that being a godly or holy man or woman as a pastor is ultimately the work of the Holy Spirit in us, in union with Christ, and not a result of our own effort.

Cameron Lee and Kurt Fredrickson have written a helpful book for pastors on understanding and coping with the challenges of pastoral ministry so "that their work will be a joy" (Heb. 13:17) and not a burden. Addressing the personal life of the pastor, they suggested five major principles for pastors to follow: cultivate a Sabbath heart (including taking a Sabbath day off once a week to rest, worship, and cease from work); take care of the body God gave you (including getting enough sleep, exercising regularly, and eating a healthy diet); embrace wise limits (including setting proper boundaries); nurture healthy relationships (including using good conflict resolution); and make one's family a priority (including spending time with one's spouse and children, with appropriate expectations).[14] These principles are especially important to follow since research that Lee and Fredrickson reviewed shows that pastors now have higher rates of obesity, hypertension, and depression than most Americans, take more antidepressants, and have a lower life expectancy than in the past.[15]

Bob Burns, Tasha Chapman, and Donald Guthrie have written a book titled *Resilient Ministry* based on research with seventy-three pastors and their spouses over a six-year period.[16] Five themes of resilient ministry over the long haul emerged from the data obtained:

1. Spiritual formation (1 Tim. 4:7, 16) (focusing on growth in spiritual maturity over time, including the practice of spiritual disciplines)
2. Self-care (practicing self-denying self-care that may include going to bed on time to get enough sleep, saying no to work so as to have time for Sabbath and sabbatical, engaging in regular exercise, and eating a nutritious and balanced diet[17])
3. Emotional and cultural intelligence (learning to identify one's feelings accurately and to wisely manage them, and to be aware of ethnic, generational, socioeconomic, geographical, and educational contexts or differences and to understand how they may affect oneself and others)
4. Marriage and family (having enough time and good communication with a spouse, children, and extended family)
5. Leadership and management (embracing the challenging truth that pastors need to learn leadership and management skills, accepting responsibility to do so, and practicing leadership and management in efficient and effective ways)[18]

Peter Scazzero is well known for his writings and teaching on the emotionally healthy church, emotionally healthy spirituality, and the emotionally healthy leader (including the pastor).[19] He writes with great clarity and vulnerability, based on biblical truth and wisdom and the hard lessons he learned in the trenches of pastoral ministry and the crucible of life's painful experiences. His recent book on the emotionally healthy leader reveals how transforming our inner lives as pastors or church leaders can deeply transform our churches, our teams, and ultimately the world. There are four main characteristics of the emotionally unhealthy leader: having low self-awareness, prioritizing ministry over marriage or singleness, doing more activity for God than their relationship with God can sustain, and lacking a good rhythm of work and Sabbath.[20] There are also four unhealthy and often unspoken commandments of church leadership: something is not a success unless it is bigger and better, what one does is more important than who one is, superficial spirituality is okay, and don't rock the boat as long as the work gets done.[21]

Regarding the outer life and ministry of the pastor or church leader, including the four main areas of planning and decision making, culture and team building, power and wise boundaries, and endings and new beginnings,[22] Scazzero emphasized the primacy of paying attention first to the inner life of the pastor or church leader. To minister and lead from a transformed and deep inner life, the emotionally healthy leader needs to engage in four practices over a lifetime:

1. Face your shadow (by naming your feelings so you can tame them, exploring the impact of your past, identifying negative scripts handed down to you, and seeking feedback from sources and others who are trustworthy).

2. Lead out of your marriage or singleness (if you are married, make marriage your first ambition, your first passion, and your loudest gospel message that points others to Christ; if you are single, be clear and intentional about the kind of single you are called by God to be—as a vowed celibate for life or as a dedicated celibate for now—and make a healthy singleness your first ambition and your loudest gospel message pointing people to Christ).

3. Slow down for loving union with God (by finding your "desert" with God, establishing a rule of life for ordering your life in which God is present in your everything, and learning to relax and rest in the journey of being an imperfect leader, knowing that deep spiritual and personal growth in loving union with God is a process that takes a lifetime).

4. Practice Sabbath delight (by taking a full day off once a week to cease from work, rest, practice delight, and contemplate and worship God).[23]

In the busyness that often characterizes the life and ministry of a pastor, it is also essential to learn to rest in the Lord, to experience God's peace in a restless and driven world. In an earlier book I described nine ways of experiencing rest in the Lord and from the Lord: Shepherd-centeredness in Christ;

Spirit-filled surrender; solitude and silence; simplicity; Sabbath; sleep; spiritual community; servanthood; and stress management from a biblical perspective that emphasizes love, faithfulness, and humility rather than competition, drivenness, and pride, and cognitive restructuring of negative, unbiblical, extreme irrational thinking into more biblical, realistic, and reasonable thinking coupled with prayer and thanksgiving.[24]

Learning to rest in the Lord is part of self-care from a biblical perspective. As mentioned earlier, self-care is one of the five major themes of resilient ministry over the long haul. Self-care is not selfish care. It is actually an ethical imperative for counselors as well as pastors because the well-being of the counselor or pastor essentially benefits and blesses the clients or parishioners and enhances their well-being too.[25] In fact, self-care can be seen as a way of denying oneself that is biblically consistent. As the authors of *Resilient Ministry* put it:

> The idea of self-care involves the pursuit of physical, mental, and emotional health. While just as important as spiritual formation, self-care may initially sound selfish. After all, didn't Jesus say that those who follow him must give up all rights to themselves (Mark 8:34)? How does our Lord's call to self-denial square with the idea of self-care? In truth, responsible self-care is actually a way to deny oneself. The old life may have included slothful or obsessive activities such as inconsistent sleep habits, crazy work hours, poor or neurotic exercise, and an unhealthy diet. Self-denying self-care, on the other hand, may include getting to bed on time, saying no to work by setting aside periods for Sabbath and sabbatical, getting responsible exercise, and eating a balanced diet.[26]

There are many lists of self-care activities,[27] but they usually include the following recommendations provided by psychologist Michael Mahoney:

1. Be gentle with yourself; honor your own process.
2. Get adequate rest.
3. Make yourself comfortable.
4. Move your body often.
5. Develop a ritual of transition for leaving work at the office.
6. Receive a regular professional massage.
7. Cherish your friendship and intimacy with family.
8. Cultivate your commitment to helping; honor the privilege of our profession.

9. Ask for and accept comfort, help, and counsel (including personal therapy).
10. Create a support network among your colleagues.
11. Enjoy yourself.
12. Follow your heart and embrace your spiritual seeking.[28]

However, there is a tendency in self-care, even if appropriate and biblically consistent, to emphasize or overemphasize balance in our lives. It is not always possible to have balance in our lives, nor is it appropriate in certain seasons of our lives. Sally Canning has critiqued this balance emphasis in self-care, noting that there are times or seasons in our lives when God may allow certain experiences, including suffering, to stretch us or knock us out of balance. Stewardship and sanctified suffering may be more appropriate at such times than balanced self-care.[29] We need to go beyond self-care to God's care for us and others caring for us in Christian community: "Beyond self-care—or beyond our abilities to care for ourselves—is God's desire to care for us through friendship with Christ and through friendships with others in Christian community. Beyond self-care is 'God-care' for us, and 'we-care' or 'community-care' in the body of Christ for one another."[30]

To conclude this section on the personal life of the pastor, here are some soul-searching questions from *Resilient Ministry* by Burns and his colleagues that can serve as a personal evaluation of the various aspects of our lives:

1. Emotional life: What feelings are you experiencing? How do you deal with the loneliness of leadership?
2. Intellectual life: What are you doing to understand the cultural trends in your country and the broader cultural trends in the world? With whom do you share your ideas?
3. Physical life: Reflect on your current diet. What are you eating and why? How do you exercise regularly and adequately? When was your last physical exam? What are your sleep patterns?
4. Sexuality: How and with whom do you process your sexual issues as a pastor? How do you deal with the temptation of internet pornography?
5. Social/relational life: Name two persons or couples you would describe as safe and trustworthy in your life. How do you manage the tension between the competing demands of ministry and family?
6. Spiritual life: How would you describe your walk with God over the past year? Does someone hold you spiritually accountable? When did you last get away for a spiritual and ministry planning time?[31]

The Family Life of the Pastor

The family life of the pastor is another key priority. Much has been written recently in this area that will be a blessing and a help to pastors, many of whom are married and may also have children.[32] This section also briefly covers the family life of the single or unmarried pastor, without any implication that this is a second-class or inferior position to be in. Both marriage (e.g., see Heb. 13:4) and singleness (e.g., see 1 Cor. 7:8) are equally honored in the Bible, with God's will being the most important thing to follow and obey, whether we are addressing singleness and celibacy or marriage between a man and a woman.

Family issues are a common reason pastors leave the ministry. A clergy family faces many challenges, including boundaries and time, frequent moves, insufficient income, and the need for pastoral care for the family.[33] It is therefore crucial for a pastor who is married and has children to make the family a priority. This includes scheduling regular time to be with them each week unless he or she is traveling.

In a helpful chapter on the pastor as husband and father (or wife and mother), Daniel Akin emphasized two main aspects: a pastor will love his wife, and a pastor will train up his children. Based on Ephesians 5:25–33, a pastor will love his wife in a sacrificial (5:25), sanctifying (5:26–27), sensitive (5:28), satisfying (5:29–30), and specific (5:31–33) way. He will serve as a spiritual leader, affirm and appreciate his wife, express personal affection or romance his wife, engage in intimate conversation, always be honest and open, provide home stability and support, and show family commitment.[34] Based on Ephesians 6:1–4, a pastor will train up his children by educating them (vv. 1–3) and encouraging them (v. 4). Akin provided ten ideas based on practical theology for good parenting of children by a pastor: try to understand life from their perspective; work at being a good husband (or wife); exercise loving discipline; use your eyes (nonverbal) and words (verbal) to express love to them; realize that love is sometimes spelled T-I-M-E; regularly hold, hug, and kiss your children (appropriately of course!); let your home be a fun place; when appropriate, encourage your children to be out of the nest of home and allow them to grow and spread their wings; regularly use seven magical words whenever necessary: "I am sorry. Will you forgive me?"; and pray for them and their salvation, and regularly talk with them about Jesus and God.[35]

Servanthood in the home[36] is another way of looking at the family life of a pastor who is married and has children. Jesus commands us to love our neighbor as ourselves (Mark 12:31), and we can easily forget that this includes loving our closest neighbor—our spouse, our children, our parents, and our siblings.

Servanthood in marriage[37] means giving 100 percent of our commitment and effort, with God's help, to loving and serving our spouse and remaining faithful, regardless of the response (or lack of response) from our spouse. This involves sacrifice and giving to our spouse (except in the case of domestic abuse, which should not be tolerated). Gary Thomas has written one of the most substantial books on marriage from a biblical perspective that emphasizes sacrificial and Christlike love for our spouse, or what he has called sacred marriage. The book focuses on the question, "What if God designed marriage to make us holy more than to make us happy?" According to this view, marriage is first a spiritual discipline that is more about you and God than about you and your spouse.

> Marriage calls us to an entirely new and selfless life. . . . Any situation that calls me to confront my selfishness has enormous spiritual value, and I slowly began to understand that the real purpose of marriage may not be happiness as much as it is holiness. . . . If we view the marriage relationship as an opportunity to excel in love, it doesn't matter how difficult the person is whom we are called to love; it doesn't matter even whether that love is ever returned. We can still excel at love. We can still say, "Like it or not, I'm going to love you like nobody ever has." . . . Marriage creates a situation in which our desire to be served and coddled can be replaced with a more noble desire to serve others—even to sacrifice for others. . . . Each day we must die to our own desires and rise as a servant. Each day we are called to identify with the suffering Christ on the cross, and then be empowered by the resurrected Christ. We die to our expectations, our demands, and our fears. We rise to compromise, service, and courage.[38]

Sacred marriage involves dying to self on a daily basis, by the power of the Holy Spirit, in union with Christ, because we cannot do this on our own.

Years ago, Paul Stevens shared a touching and hilarious story about visiting the Wedding Church in Cana of Galilee with his wife, Gail, on their twenty-fifth wedding anniversary. Brother Joseph, who was the resident Roman Catholic clergyman there, when told about the anniversary exclaimed, "Mama mia, twenty-five years of martyrdom!" Gail's parents were with them, just after celebrating their fiftieth wedding anniversary, and Brother Joseph said to them, "Mama mia, a fifty-year martyrdom!"[39] We who are pastors need to embrace sacred marriage and such daily martyrdom to grow in our relationship with God and then in our marital relationship with our spouse, cherishing and deeply loving our spouse in a faithfully committed, lifelong marriage.

In order to minister deeply and effectively to our spouse's needs—realizing that ultimately only the Lord can fulfill our deepest longings, which are God shaped—three elements are necessary, as Larry Crabb has pointed out: a decision to minister to our spouse; an awareness of our spouse's deepest needs (which must be communicated and clarified); and a conviction that we are God's chosen instrument to minister to our spouse's deepest needs.[40] We also need to learn the love language or languages that our spouse prefers and in which he or she can understand and receive our love and care. The five major love languages that Gary Chapman has described are (1) words of affirmation (encouragement or appreciation), whether verbal or written; (2) quality time during which we give full and undivided attention to our spouse; (3) gifts or gift giving, which can take various forms, such as companionship and engaging in activities for our spouse's sake; (4) acts of service in which we do concrete things that our spouse particularly appreciates—(e.g., taking out the trash, washing the dishes, or mowing the lawn); and (5) physical touch, such as a hug or a kiss.[41] We need to use the love language preferred by our spouse, showing sensitivity and caring, and not our own preferred love language. For example, my wife, Angela, really appreciates acts of service, such as when I take out and bring in the trash cans or wash the dishes, whereas I prefer words of affirmation and physical touch. We have had to sacrificially and lovingly serve each other, meeting each other's deepest needs, using the appropriate love language or languages our spouse prefers rather than our own.

Research has shown that servanthood in marriage, involving sacrifice for a spouse's sake, leads to some benefits and blessings for the couple and the marriage. For example, those most comfortable with the idea of sacrificing for their spouse were the ones most committed to each other, the happiest together, and the most self-disclosing in their marital relationship. Sacrificial attitudes and actions have also been found to be more likely in happy, committed people.[42]

The special blessings and struggles of being a pastor's wife have been recently shared by Kay Warren, wife of Rick Warren, the pastor of Saddleback Church in Lake Forest, California, in *Sacred Privilege*. This should be essential reading for any pastor's spouse as well as for the pastor. Many churches expect a pastor's spouse to also be involved in church ministry. This two-for-one spoken or unspoken demand is often present when hiring a pastor. We need to let go of such unrealistic expectations in our churches, and pastors need to protect their spouses and children.

Parenting is another major part of servanthood in the home. It involves sacrificial love for our children and focusing not so much on what we can do to teach and influence our children as on how God can use them to teach and influence us.[43] Examples of how we can sacrificially love our children include making time just to hang out with them, attending their sports events, playing board games with them rather than watching TV, and intentionally getting home in time to have dinner with them rather than working late at the office. Paul Stevens has pointed out that the Bible emphasizes raising godly parents through the influence of children more than raising godly children through parenting them.

> Children are God's gifts to immature people to help them grow up. They are also God's gifts to help parents go deep with God. . . . Parenting is not *for* anything. It is not a contract with God in which one gives countless hours in order to turn out good children that rise up and call us blessed. It is a covenant experience of belonging in which God meets us and forms us in the nitty-gritty of family life. The big question in the end is not how the kids turn out, but how the parents turn out![44]

Children can be used by God to help us parents grow up in Christ, and in this paradoxical sense, children actually end up raising parents. We need to be careful not to parent our children in such a way as to make them successful and perfect kids. There is no such thing as perfect parenting or perfect children. Instead, we need to let go of such pressure and prayerfully trust God more. Our children are known as PKs, or pastors' kids. We need to learn about their special struggles, especially concerning their identity, the unique pressures they face to be perfect kids, and the often unrealistic expectations of church members.[45] We need to listen carefully to our children and discern what God is teaching us through them and their struggles as well as their joys. Deeply and lovingly listening to our children is a crucial part of servanthood in parenting and learning from them.[46] We also need to know how to honor our children, siblings, and parents (especially if they are aging or aged).[47]

Concerning single pastors, Peter Scazzero has provided several helpful guidelines for how they can lead out of their singleness. Single pastors first need to decide if God has called them to be vowed celibates for life, with the gift of celibacy, or to be dedicated celibates who will remain single for as long as God wants. The first ambition then should be to have a healthy singleness that includes engaging in appropriate and good self-care, investing in community and developing at least one or two deep friendships for the journey, and practicing hospitality on a consistent basis by inviting all kinds of people over, including family members and members of the larger family of God in the church community. Then single pastors need to let their singleness be their loudest gospel message, pointing to Jesus as the secret and source of their fulfillment in healthy singleness.[48]

Whether we are married or single, as pastors we have much to attend to in our personal and family lives. Our pastoral ministry should flow out of our spiritual lives and our personal and family lives. We need to ultimately live our personal and family lives and conduct our pastoral ministry with ethical integrity based on moral theology and pastoral ethics[49] by the power and with the help of the Holy Spirit. One particular area of struggle for many people is pornography, which is now so rampant and easily accessible on the internet. The church has also been affected, with recent surveys showing that at least 50 percent of Christian men and 20 percent of Christian women are addicted to pornography or view it on a regular basis. The same statistics have been found concerning pastors and church leaders.[50] However, these may be under-estimates, since Carol Archebelle, in an advertisement in *Christianity Today*, reported that, based on a five-year national survey of churches, 68 percent of churchgoing men and 30 percent of churchgoing women view pornography on a regular basis.[51] Pastors need to deal with this area of lust and sexual sin more honestly, taking necessary steps to resist pornography and to pursue sexual purity in order to be holy servants of God in pastoral ministry.[52]

We end this chapter with the following tough questions from H. B. Charles Jr. Whether the questions are used for self-evaluation or for account-ability with a small group, may they help us live and minister with ethical integrity in Christ:

Are you having a daily quiet time with the Lord?

How is your prayer life?

Are you being faithful to your wife?

Are you making time for your children?

Are you practicing sexual purity?

Are you handling your finances properly?

Do you need to seek reconciliation with anyone?

Are you keeping any secrets that can ruin your family or ministry down the road?[53]

The last question is particularly crucial in light of the many sex scandals, extramarital affairs, and child sexual abuse cases that have emerged in recent years, even among clergy and pastors. As pastors, we need the help and purify-ing power of the Holy Spirit to be holy men and women of God, for we are only imperfect vessels, jars of clay in whom God has placed the treasure of

Jesus Christ and the gospel in order "to show that this all-surpassing power is from God and not from us" (2 Cor. 4:7).

RECOMMENDED READINGS

Allen, Jason K., ed. *Portraits of a Pastor: The 9 Essential Roles of a Church Leader*. Chicago: Moody, 2017.

Burns, Bob, Tasha D. Chapman, and Donald C. Guthrie. *Resilient Ministry: What Pastors Told Us about Surviving and Thriving*. Downers Grove, IL: InterVarsity, 2013.

Chapman, Gary. *The Five Love Languages: How to Express Heartfelt Commitment to Your Mate*. Chicago: Northfield Publishing, 1992.

Crabb, Larry. *The Marriage Builder*. Grand Rapids: Zondervan, 1982.

Croft, Brian, and Cara Croft. *The Pastor's Family: Shepherding Your Family through the Challenges of Pastoral Ministry*. Grand Rapids: Zondervan, 2013.

Fernando, Ajith. *The Family Life of a Christian Leader*. Wheaton: Crossway, 2016.

Harbaugh, Gary L. *Pastor as Person*. Minneapolis: Augsburg, 1984.

Piper, Barnabas. *The Pastor's Kid: Finding Your Own Faith and Identity*. Colorado Springs: David C. Cook, 2014.

Purves, Andrew. *Reconstructing Pastoral Theology: A Christological Foundation*. Louisville: Westminster John Knox, 2004.

Stevens, Paul. *Marriage Spirituality: Ten Disciplines for Couples Who Love God*. Downers Grove, IL: InterVarsity, 1989.

Thomas, Gary. *Sacred Marriage: What If God Designed Marriage to Make Us Holy More Than to Make Us Happy?* Grand Rapids: Zondervan, 2000.

———. *Sacred Parenting: How Raising Children Shapes Our Souls*. Grand Rapids: Zondervan, 2004.

Warren, Kay. *Sacred Privilege: Your Life and Ministry as a Pastor's Wife*. Grand Rapids: Revell, 2017.

Wilbourne, Rankin. *Union with Christ: The Way to Know and Enjoy God*. Colorado Springs: David C. Cook, 2016.

PART 2

AREAS
OF PASTORAL
MINISTRY

5

Preaching and Teaching

D. Martyn Lloyd-Jones was a medical doctor and assistant to the famous Lord Horder before he became a world-renowned preacher and pastor of Westminster Chapel in London. He wrote these powerful words about preaching in his 1971 classic, *Preaching and Preachers*: "To me the work of preaching is the highest and the greatest and the most glorious calling to which anyone can ever be called. If you want something in addition to that I would say without any hesitation that the most urgent need in the Christian Church today is true preaching; and as it is the greatest and the most urgent need in the Church, it is obviously the greatest need of the world also."[1] He described preaching as "Logic on fire! Eloquent reason! . . . It is theology on fire. . . . Preaching is theology coming through a man who is on fire. . . . What is the chief end of preaching? . . . It is to give men and women a sense of God and His presence."[2] He highlighted the need for the anointing, unction, or power of the Holy Spirit in true preaching:

Seek this power, expect this power, yearn for this power; and when the power comes, yield to Him. Do not resist. Forget all about your sermon if necessary. Let Him loose you, let Him manifest His power in and through you. . . . Nothing but a return of this power of the Spirit on our preaching is going to avail us anything. This makes true preaching, and it is the greatest need of all today—never more so. Nothing can substitute for this. . . . This "unction," this "anointing," is the supreme thing. Seek it until you have it; be content with nothing less. Go on until you can say, "And my speech and my preaching was not with enticing words of man's wisdom, but in demonstration of the Spirit and of power" (1 Cor. 2:4). He is still able to do "exceeding abundantly above all that we can ask or think" (Eph. 3:20).[3]

A pastor has many roles, but the pastor as preacher is the primary one and the top priority. Preaching has been described as the pastor's "preeminent responsibility . . . indispensable task, permanent duty and . . . most conse-quential and urgent job assignment—priority number one."[4] Others have said, "The first and most important responsibility of the pastor is to preach the Word of God,"[5] and "Preaching is indispensable to Christianity."[6]

Therefore, part 2 of this book on the areas of pastoral ministry begins with preaching and teaching. Although preaching is not synonymous with teach-ing, they overlap quite a bit and are covered here together. On the one hand, a good teacher may not necessarily be a good preacher, because preaching requires the special unction from the Holy Spirit to enable a pastor to preach powerfully, passionately, and effectively so that lives are deeply touched and transformed. Teaching should also be anointed by the Spirit, but it may not be as intense or forceful in its presentation. It should, however, be clear and insightful based on Scripture. A good preacher, on the other hand, is usually also a good teacher, but this is not always the case. A sermon or message of a good preacher may be powerful and effective in touching lives deeply, but it may not have as much content as in systematic teaching. However, an anointed preacher is often also a gifted teacher.

J. I. Packer has differentiated preaching from teaching this way:

> To pass on biblical content, unapplied, is only to teach, not to preach. A lecture, as such, is not a sermon; preaching is teaching plus. Plus what? Plus applica-tion of truth to life. One's adequacy as a preacher, interpreting God's Word to God's people, is finally determined not by the erudition of one's exegesis but by the depth and power of one's application. . . . I lecture on a regular basis as well as preach, and find preaching to be far and away the more draining of the two activities. And no wonder! For whereas one lectures to clear heads and ripen minds, one preaches to change lives and save souls.[7]

In the end, good and true biblical preaching also includes a great degree of good and true biblical teaching. A pastor as preacher needs to be a theolo-gian[8] or a pastor-theologian[9] to preach God's Word and truth, and a pastor as church historian[10] is actually part and parcel of being a pastor as theologian.

There are numerous books available today on preaching, but several classics are essential and helpful to the pastor as preacher. They include Lloyd-Jones's *Preaching and Preachers* (as already mentioned), James Stewart's *Heralds of God* (originally published in 1946), Haddon Robinson's *Biblical Preaching*,

John Stott's *Between Two Worlds*, John Piper's *The Supremacy of God in Preaching* and *Expository Exultation*, and Jerry Vines and Jim Shaddix's *Power in the Pulpit*.[11] Many other helpful books on preaching have been published in recent years, most of which cover expository or expositional preaching, which is based on the very texts of Scripture and is often called biblical preaching.[12]

What Is Preaching?

There are various definitions of preaching. To preach, in New Testament language, is to cry out, herald, or exhort. Robinson made this challenge: "Preachers should pour out the message with passion and fervor in order to stir souls."[13] Packer has stated, "A sermon, then, is *an applicatory declaration, spoken in God's name and for his praise, in which some part of the written Word of God delivers through the preacher some part of its message about God and godliness in relation to those whom the preacher addresses.*"[14] He further asserted, "Holy Scripture . . . may truly be described as God preaching."[15]

Abraham Kuruvilla has proposed a vision or ideal for preaching that is broader than a categorical definition of preaching: "Biblical preaching, by a leader of the church, in a gathering of Christians for worship, is the communication of the thrust of a pericope of Scripture, discerned by theological exegesis, and of its application to that specific body of believers, that they may be conformed to the image of Christ, for the glory of God—all in the power of the Holy Spirit."[16] Preaching is therefore biblical, pastoral, ecclesial, communicational, theological, applicational, conformational, doxological, and spiritual.[17]

Jason Meyer has written a substantial and comprehensive biblical theology of preaching and provided a succinct definition of preaching, or the ministry of the Word: "The ministry of the word in Scripture is *stewarding and heralding God's word in such a way that people encounter God through his word.*"[18] There are three components or phases in preaching, which is a dynamic process. Stewarding, the first phase, is when the preacher faithfully receives God's Word entrusted to him or her. Heralding God's Word, the second phase, is when the preacher or herald provides a human voice to express the divine Word, which can then be heard by others. Encountering God through his Word, the third phase, is when the people, having heard the Word preached, are now responsible to steward the Word by making a response to God's Word.[19] Meyer's more specific definition of expository preaching is this: "Preaching must (1) re-present the word of God in such a way that the preacher (2) represents the God of the word (3) so that people respond to God."[20]

A very well-known definition of expository preaching was given by Robinson in his widely used text *Biblical Preaching*: "Expository preaching is the communication of a biblical concept, derived from and transmitted through a historical, grammatical, and literary study of a passage in its context, which the Holy Spirit first applies to the personality and experience of the preacher, then through the preacher applies to the hearer."[21]

Jerry Vines and Jim Shaddix, in the first edition of another widely used text, *Power in the Pulpit*, defined preaching as "the oral communication of a biblical truth by the Holy Spirit through a human personality to a given audience with the intent of enabling a positive response."[22] More recently, in the second edition of their book they provided this definition of expository preaching: "The process of laying open the biblical text in such a way that the Holy Spirit's intended meaning and accompanying power are brought to bear on the lives of contemporary listeners."[23] They further divided expository preaching into two types: general exposition, which has to do with expository preaching on selected and specific Bible texts, and systematic exposition, which has to do with expository preaching of books of the Bible, chapter by chapter and paragraph by paragraph (or verse by verse), in a sequential and exhaustive way.[24]

Expository preaching has been equated with all true, biblical preaching. For example, Lloyd-Jones asserted that "a sermon should always be expository."[25] Similarly, Stott wrote that "all true Christian preaching is expository preaching."[26] And Albert Mohler stated, "According to the Bible, exposition is preaching. And preaching is exposition."[27] However, there are various definitions of expository preaching, and this term can be loosely used with many imprecise meanings. Jason Allen has suggested at least four essential features of expository preaching, or biblical exposition (sometimes also called expositional preaching): accurate interpretation of the text; derivation of the central point of the sermon and the sermon's main points from the text; application of the sermon that comes from the text and is brought to bear on the congregation or hearers; and more tenuously, the priority of sequential, verse-by-verse exposition, also called *lectio continua*.[28] He then simply and minimally defined biblical exposition as "*accurately interpreting and explaining the text of Scripture and bringing it to bear on the lives of the hearers.*"[29]

Not all preaching is expository preaching. Other forms or ways of preaching (some of which may overlap) include topical (subject based), textual, evangelistic, narrative, biographical, dramatic monologue, theological or doctrinal, apologetic, and ethical or devotional.[30] However, as Vines and

Shaddix have concluded, "Our conviction . . . is that all preaching should be expositional in nature. . . . We believe all sermon forms can and should be subjected to the expositional process."[31]

Why Preach?

Preaching is the primary task of the pastor for two reasons: the Bible calls for it, and church history supports such an emphasis.

The preaching of God's Word runs throughout the Bible, and the biblical foundation for preaching is that God's Word is authoritative and inspired, true, and the source of life eternal and abundant (e.g., see 2 Tim. 3:16; 1 Pet. 1:23–25; James 1:18; see also Matt. 4:4; Heb. 4:12). In fact, God is the God who speaks, and he can be described as the first preacher.[32] And Jesus was definitely a preacher during his ministry on earth (e.g., see Mark 1:14 NASB). The prophets in the Old Testament were sent by God to proclaim and preach his truth and his Word. John the Baptist was in the wilderness "preaching a baptism of repentance" (Mark 1:4 NASB). The early apostles devoted themselves to prayer and the ministry of the Word (Acts 6:4). Paul instructed Timothy in 1 Timothy 4:13, "Until I come, devote yourself to the public reading of Scripture, to preaching and to teaching." He gave his final charge to Timothy in 2 Timothy 4:2: "Preach the word; be prepared in season and out of season; correct, rebuke and encourage—with great patience and careful instruction." Paul's challenge to preach the gospel or good news of salvation to the lost was powerfully captured in Romans 10:13–15: "'Everyone who calls on the name of the Lord will be saved.' How, then, can they call on the one they have not believed in? And how can they believe in the one of whom they have not heard? And how can they hear without someone preaching to them? And how can anyone preach unless they are sent? As it is written: 'How beautiful are the feet of those who bring good news!'"[33] The Bible has a high view of elders (or pastors) in the church who preach and teach, describing them as being worthy of double honor: "The elders who direct the affairs of the church well are worthy of double honor, especially those whose work is preaching and teaching" (1 Tim. 5:17).

Church history also supports the Bible's emphasis on preaching God's Word. David Dunn-Wilson has reviewed preaching in the first five centuries of church history. He covered the missionaries and the pastors in the early New Testament church, and after the apostles, the early fathers, the apologists, the ascetics and mystics, the liturgists, the theologians (including Eastern theologian-preachers such as Basil of Caesarea, Gregory of Nyssa, and

Gregory of Nazianzus, and Western theologian-preachers such as Hilary of Poitiers and Leo the Great), and the homileticians (such as Ambrose, Augustine of Hippo, and John Chrysostom).[34] Similarly, Michael Pasquarello III has emphasized the need for us to engage in preaching in communion with the preachers in church history, in the story of sacred rhetoric. He examined an even wider segment of church history, including monastic voices (such as Gregory the Great, St. Benedict, and Bernard of Clairvaux), medieval voices (such as Bonaventure and Thomas Aquinas), late medieval voices (such as Erasmus and Hugh Latimer), and Reformation voices (such as Martin Luther and John Calvin).[35] Packer, referencing preachers from church history to the more recent past, stated, "Anyone acquainted with the preaching career and sermonic legacy of such as (for instance) John Chrysostom, Augustine, Martin Luther, Hugh Latimer, John Knox, Richard Baxter, John Bunyan, George Whitefield, John Wesley, Jonathan Edwards, Charles Simeon, Robert Murray M'Cheyne, Charles Spurgeon, John Charles Ryle, Martyn Lloyd-Jones, and Billy Graham knows, first that their goal in preaching was to become the means of God's encounter with their hearers, and second, that it was by focusing God's teaching in Scripture that they sought to achieve this purpose."[36]

How to Preach

On the topic of how to preach, James Bryant and Mac Brunson, in *The New Guidebook for Pastors*, provided some guidelines for biblical preaching: the priority of prayer and asking for the Holy Spirit's guidance and illumination; taking enough time to read through the text carefully and slowly, noting whatever is observed in the text; consulting books or commentaries on the background and context of the text for the sermon; and beginning to do the work of exegesis, or interpretation of the text.[37] They also provided five basic steps for exegeting the text:

Step One
1. Begin at the paragraph level and move to the sentence and clause level.
2. Identify the verbs, participles, infinitives, and so forth.
3. Parse the verbs and take special notice of their tenses, voice, and mood, and decline the nouns (if your knowledge of Greek and Hebrew is good enough to do this; otherwise, consult an exhaustive concordance or other helpful books).
4. Identify the meaning of the words by use of a Hebrew or Greek dictionary.

5. Diagram the paragraph and the sentences. This can be done in English, but it is best if you are able to do it in the original language.

6. What is the primary thought and what are the secondary ideas or thoughts? Diagramming will help with this.

7. How do these sentences and ideas relate to one another?

Step Two

1. Identify phrases in the paragraph.

2. Determine the syntax and the structure of the paragraph.

3. Are there certain phrases that stand out?

Step Three

1. Conduct word studies of particular words that are significant, using concordances and lexicons.

2. Take note of how many times a word is used in the Bible or if there are several different words used to describe the same thing.

Step Four

1. Consult various translations.

2. Consult good sound commentaries.

Step Five

1. Determine the main idea of the text and be able to write this in a present tense sentence. If you cannot do this, you are not ready to write the message and you are certainly not ready to preach the message.

2. Develop the points based on the main idea of the text.

3. Each point should reflect three elements: exposition, illustration, and application.

4. The introduction should capture the attention of the congregation.

5. The conclusion should be thoughtful, moving, and reflective of the sermon. . . . When you approach the conclusion, you are preaching for a response, not just a conclusion. . . . Always preach for decision. Be sure that you use the second person personal pronoun *you* often.

6. Type the sermon out in full, complete with introduction and conclusion. . . . One of the best things to do . . . is to include footnotes, especially on the illustrations.[38]

I need to comment on some of the steps Bryant and Brunson have recommended because I do not fully agree with them. First, like Bryant and Brunson, Lloyd John Ogilvie in *A Passionate Calling* also emphasized the importance of an effective and good introduction in a sermon because we need to capture our hearers' attention in the first three minutes or risk losing them for the rest of the sermon.[39] However, he did note that some well-known preachers did not spend much time or effort crafting a really good introduction—for example, Robert Murray M'Cheyne, G. Campbell Morgan, and Dietrich Bonhoeffer. Every preacher is unique and different, and we need to develop our own preaching style that fits our unique personality. Phillips Brooks in 1877 said, "Preaching is the bringing of truth through personality."[40] I personally do not spend much time preparing a polished and captivating introduction to my sermons. This allows more time for prayer, careful interpretation of the text, and putting together a good outline of the sermon, with appropriate illustrations that do not distract from the main message and helpful and practical applications for life change and transformation that come from the text being preached. I usually state my text in the Bible and announce the title of my sermon, making a few brief comments, and then go directly to expounding the text.

Second, the concept of determining the one main idea in the text, which Robinson in *Biblical Preaching* and others have emphasized, while helpful, needs some qualification. Sometimes we may be preaching from a text in Scripture that does not lend itself simply to one big idea or one main point (e.g., preaching from several verses from the book of Proverbs that may contain several points, or preaching from the book of James, which covers diverse issues and topics). Timothy Keller concluded that the concept of a big idea within a text of Scripture can be somewhat artificial. It may be true for some biblical passages but not for others. The Bible has many genres, and its richness may not lend itself to such reduction for every text. As a result, he warned against a certain kind of "expository legalism."[41] We need to be more flexible, and I agree with him.

Third, the directive to type out the sermon in full also needs to be qualified and nuanced. Ogilvie similarly advocated writing out a complete fifteen-page manuscript of a sermon,[42] but with an ending that does not include four forbidden words in preaching with passion: "And now, in conclusion."[43] He suggested that, to finish well, a preacher should keep the ending more open so that the listeners are longing for more.[44] I do not think it is necessary for every preacher to write out or type out a full manuscript of a sermon, word for word. Then the temptation is for the preacher to depend too much on the manuscript and to even read it in a boring way. Packer has much wisdom to share on this topic:

> How much preparatory writing do I do? As much as is necessary to ensure that I know my message and have words at my command to make all my points, both expository and applicatory. . . . How much writing is needed . . . varies . . . from preacher to preacher. . . . How much written material do

I take with me to the pulpit? As much as I need to be exact, as well as free and spontaneous, in the way that I speak. This, for me, means a half sheet of paper, with skeletal notes in abbreviations of my own devising, for each half hour of talk. Some preachers need less, some more. Some need to have a complete script with them, not to read word for word, but to give them confidence as they speak.[45]

I use index cards to write out the text I am preaching on, with other translations inserted where necessary to clarify meanings of words or phrases, and brief notes and abbreviations. I also have several quotations on index cards from helpful commentaries or books that are relevant to the text and points I am making. I do not usually refer to them or read them, except for a good and relevant quotation or two sometimes. I always mention my sources when needed to avoid plagiarism. I therefore preach extemporaneously, or without notes.[46] I have my index cards in the pulpit with me, but I seldom look at them. I am not advocating that my style is the only or better way. Each preacher is different, and we must choose what is best for our personality and style, depending also on the graces and gifts the Holy Spirit sovereignly grants us. We need not view writing out a full manuscript of our sermons as a requirement, but some or many of us may find doing so helpful.

As pastors, we need to prayerfully and humbly depend on the Holy Spirit for our sermons and in preaching them, even when we run out of time in a particular week full of crises and emergencies in the church, the family, or elsewhere. We must never plagiarize by preaching someone else's sermon or by not giving credit to our sources of sermon material. In our weakness and struggles, we preach, but always with God's grace and help and the power of the Spirit, as the apostle Paul did (1 Cor. 2:1–5; see also 2 Cor. 3:5; 4:7; 12:9–10). Some of my best sermons God used to bless many lives were preached in a week of emergencies when my sermon preparation time was drastically reduced. Only by the grace of God and the anointing of the Holy Spirit were lives touched. May we all be reminded that effective preaching is ultimately God's work.

Fourth, in regard to the thoroughness of the process of preparing an expository sermon and exegeting the text, Ogilvie is even more exact and definitive about how much time we should spend in sermon preparation. He is well known for this directive: "Great preaching is the result of one hour of specific preparation for each minute in the pulpit delivering the sermon!"[47] Or put another way: "An hour in the study for every minute in the pulpit."[48] He sees no alternative but to hold preachers to such a high standard. While I appreciate his desire to challenge us in this way so that we are thoroughly prepared to passionately preach for the glory of God and the blessing of many lives,

I find his directive not applicable or practical in many pastoral situations. It therefore has to be qualified and nuanced.

First of all, some of us do not preach twenty-minute sermons that should take twenty hours to prepare. Some of us preach forty-minute sermons, which means we would have to spend forty hours in sermon preparation! This is, of course, unrealistic and impractical, because, as pastors, we have many other responsibilities besides preaching. Second, I am especially empathic toward my fellow Korean or Korean American pastors who usually have prayer meetings almost daily at 4:30 in the morning. They are already very sleep deprived, which is not good for their physical, mental, and spiritual lives. They definitely cannot follow the rule of one hour in the study for every minute in the pulpit, especially if they preach forty-minute sermons. I teach a Korean DMin class every two years as a summer one-week intensive at Fuller Theological Seminary. I have humbly and lovingly told my students, who have been mainly pastors in the trenches, *not* to follow such a rule. And to get more sleep. At the same time, we do need to spend enough time thoroughly preparing our sermons (e.g., ten to fifteen hours) and including time for prayer. We cannot and should not wait until Saturday night to prepare a sermon for Sunday morning. Starting sermon preparation early in the week is best. I usually take up to ten hours or so for my sermon preparation each week, but I have been preaching for fifty years. The Lord has graciously given me certain giftings, including good facility with the English language, so reading, comprehension, and writing are much quicker to come by. He has also graciously given me the spiritual gift of preaching or pastor-teacher (1 Cor. 12:28, 29; Eph. 4:11), which he has used in my life and ministry here and abroad. Third and finally, we are reminded again that every preacher is unique and differently gifted by God, and that the amount of time needed to prepare a sermon varies. For example, I know of a well-known and gifted preacher who needs about twenty hours of sermon preparation time, whereas another gifted preacher needs only about eight hours.

At the beginning of this chapter, I quoted Lloyd-Jones and his plea for preachers to get an anointing from the Holy Spirit so they can preach with fire from above. This sacred anointing is crucial for sermon preparation. However, there is no secret formula or guaranteed method to get this unction from the Holy Spirit.[49] It is a sovereign act of God, and we need to simply rest in him and trust him to provide in whatever way he wills at a particular time. We simply need to leave the results in God's good hands, as Dallas Willard used to remind us. We should not focus on doing great things for God, including trying to be great preachers. Instead, we should focus on doing things, including preaching, for a great God. He is the One who is great and who does great things, and to him alone be the glory! Jeremiah 45:5 is a good challenge for us all: "Should you then seek great things for yourself? Do not seek them." We need to be "dying to preach," as Steven Smith put it, by embracing the cross in the pulpit: to die to self, to die for others, and to die in Christ that others, including our congregations, may live.[50]

Preaching and Reading

In reading the biblical text and carefully exegeting it, we need the help of solid and sound commentaries as well as substantial books for general reading. We need to read widely to properly exegete the culture and interpret the times in which we are living so that we can make relevant and effective applications in our sermons for our listeners. John Evans has written *A Guide to Biblical Commentaries and Reference Works*,[51] which is of great benefit in choosing the best commentaries and reference works to use in sermon preparation. Keller has suggested that perhaps the best online reference tool is www.biblestudytools.com and the best tools to buy are Logos Bible Software and BibleWorks.[52]

With regard to reading in general, Cornelius Plantinga Jr. has written a helpful guide, *Reading for Preaching*,[53] to help preachers be in conversation with storytellers, biographers, poets, and journalists. Eugene Peterson provided an annotated list for spiritual reading in *Take and Read*.[54] His classic books on pastoral ministry[55] and spiritual theology[56] are also excellent reading for pastors and preachers.

Although reading is crucial in the preparation of good, biblical messages, we also need to know our diverse hearers well and listen to them[57] so that our preaching feeds them in deep and relevant ways with cultural intelligence.[58] As pastors, we need to be in regular contact with our parishioners and others who attend our church services. I schedule time each week to visit with or call several people from my church. However, we must always get permission to use the details of someone's life in a sermon, even if we do not mention the person's name. We need to do this even, or especially, with our spouses and family members.

How to Listen

Whether a sermon deeply touches and transforms lives is not up to just the preacher and the preaching—it is also up to the listener. Of course, it is ultimately up to the Holy Spirit to anoint both the preacher and the listener. Packer has summarized what Richard Baxter wrote in 1673 in *A Christian Directory* about how we should listen to sermons, including directions for understanding the Word we hear, directions for remembering what we hear, directions for holy resolutions and affections in hearing, and directions for putting what we hear into practice. Packer concluded, "Baxter's discipline of expecting, focusing, memorizing (writing notes if need be), discussing, praying, and applying is at the opposite extreme from our modern habit of relaxing at sermon time, settling back in our seats to see if the preacher's performance will interest and entertain us, and if anything he says will particularly strike us—and if not, then to forget the sermon and to say if asked that we got nothing out of it."[59] He recommended, following Baxter, that preachers encourage listeners to engage in a routine of serious listening to sermons. We as pastors also need to learn to preach to ourselves first.[60]

Learning from Past Preachers: Jonathan Edwards and Gardner C. Taylor

H. B. Charles Jr., in his helpful and practical book *On Preaching*, described the "preaching crisis" he experiences once a year when he feels frustrated with his preaching and wants to work harder to become a better preacher[61] (although I must add that he is already an excellent preacher). We all can improve and grow in our preaching, but we need to guard against perfectionism and being driven to perform. We should focus on being our unique selves and developing our own styles of preaching under the guidance of the Holy Spirit. However, we can still learn from other preachers, including many gifted preachers throughout the centuries. Here are two wonderful examples to learn from: Jonathan Edwards (1703–58) and Gardner C. Taylor (1918–2015).

John Piper listed ten things Edwards did as a preacher that made God supreme: (1) stirred up holy affections, (2) enlightened the mind, (3) saturated with Scripture, (4) employed analogies and images, (5) used threat and warning, (6) pleaded for a response, (7) probed the workings of the heart, (8) yielded to the Holy Spirit in prayer, (9) was broken and tenderhearted, and (10) was intense.[62] Piper also emphasized that "the goal of all preaching is the glory of God reflected in the glad submission of the human heart,"[63] which can be fully satisfied only in and with the glory, goodness, and greatness of God. "God is glorified *by* our enjoying him."[64]

The second example is the well-known preacher and pastor Gardner C. Taylor, who has been called America's last pulpit prince. He died in 2015 at the age of ninety-six. Jared Alcántara has penned a wonderful book, *Learning from a Legend*, on what Taylor can teach us about preaching. He described six main lessons we can learn, summarized using the acrostic PREACH: pain, redemption, eloquence, apprenticeship, context, and holiness. Alcántara concluded, "P. R. E. A. C. H.! That's what we are called to do. Dr. Taylor was a preacher's preacher, preaching through pain, pointing to a Redeemer, setting a standard for pulpit eloquence, apprenticing himself to others, caring about context, and striving toward holiness. P.R.E.A.C.H.! That's what he did because that's who he was."[65]

We would be remiss not to mention the many examples of gifted women preachers throughout church history up to the present. Well-known contemporary women preachers include Barbara Brown Taylor, Fleming Rutledge, Anne Graham Lotz, and Joyce Meyer.

Preaching and Mental Health

There is a need for pastors to preach messages related to mental health and mental illness. This is an area that has not been adequately developed in the local church context. In 2013 the suicide death of Matthew Warren, son of Rick and Kay Warren, made headlines in America.[66] Yet his death was by no means an isolated incident. Suicide was the cause of death of more than forty-four thousand Americans in 2015, and about one suicide takes place every twelve minutes according to the US Department of Health and Human Services. Some have called suicide a new public health crisis, as the overall suicide rate in the United States has increased by almost 30 percent in the past fifteen years.[67] Suicide is only one of many mental health issues that need to be addressed by pastors and churches, including in sermons.

The American Association of Christian Counselors (AACC) has launched a number of "The Struggle Is Real" conferences in the last few years, focusing on the church, mental health, and counseling. The goal is to help pastors and churches, as well as professional and lay Christian counselors, deal more effectively with mental health needs in the church and to overcome the stigma of mental illness. I have presented a plenary address, titled "Psychology Collaborating with the Church: A Pastor-Psychologist's Perspective and Personal Experience," covering the areas of preaching and teaching, pastoral care, leadership, community outreach, premarital counseling, and organizational research.[68] Psychological research and scholarship can be helpful to a pastor, especially when preaching on psychology related topics such as mental illness and psychological disorders. However, a biblical perspective should always be primary, and the biblical texts used in preaching and teaching must never be compromised or "psychologized." They should be carefully and soundly interpreted.

There are many good books available on mental health issues written from a Christian perspective. They include, for example, *The Struggle Is Real: How* to *Care for Mental and Relational Health Needs in the Church* and Gary Collins's well-known book *Christian Counseling: A Comprehensive Guide*,[69] which contains material on over thirty major issues people can have, including what the Bible says (if anything) about each one. He has done the concordance search for us so that ample biblical (and psychological) material is available to use in our preaching on problems such as anxiety, anger, abuse and neglect, addictions, depression, guilt and forgiveness, loneliness, marital difficulties, and so forth.

Finally, much psychological literature and research has been produced in recent years in the field of positive psychology regarding the more positive aspects of human functioning. Such literature and research focuses on happiness and human flourishing and virtues such as wisdom, forgiveness, gratitude, humility, hope, and grace. Mark McMinn has written *The Science of Virtue: Why Positive Psychology Matters to the Church*,[70] which is of great benefit when preaching on these virtues and related topics. Ellen Charry's *God and the Art of Happiness*[71] helps us think theologically about happiness and flourishing and realize that the Bible does encourage the happiness and flourishing that are associated with loving obedience to God. Goodness and happiness can go together in our Christian lives, although we experience pain and suffering in this fallen world.

Preaching and teaching are crucial and primary areas of pastoral ministry. Dallas Willard has emphasized the calling and ministry of pastors as teachers of the nations.[72] Preaching regularly from one Sunday to the next is challenging for pastors. Gardner C. Taylor actually referred to preaching as "the sweet torture of Sunday morning."[73] However, there is also "the romance of preaching," so called by D. Martyn Lloyd-Jones: "Now let us hurry on to something much more important—the romance of preaching! There is nothing like it. It is the greatest work in the world, the most thrilling, the most exciting, the most rewarding, and the most wonderful."[74] Perhaps Darrell Johnson described preaching best: "A Chinese pastor has said, 'Dare to preach . . . and watch what happens.' Something always happens."[75]

RECOMMENDED READINGS

Alcántara, Jared E. *Learning from a Legend: What Gardner C. Taylor Can Teach Us about Preaching*. Eugene, OR: Cascade Books, 2016.

Byassee, Jason, and L. Roger Owens, eds. *Pastoral Work: Engagements with the Vision of Eugene Peterson*. Eugene, OR: Cascade Books, 2014.

Chapell, Bryan. *Christ-Centered Preaching: Redeeming the Expository Sermon*. 2nd ed. Grand Rapids: Baker Academic, 2005.

Charles, H. B., Jr. *On Preaching: Personal and Pastoral Insights for the Preparation and Practice of Preaching*. Chicago: Moody, 2014.

Clinton, Tim, and Jared Pingleton, eds. *The Struggle Is Real: How to Care for Mental and Relational Health Needs in the Church*. Bloomington, IN: WestBrow Press, 2017.

Dunn-Wilson, David. *A Mirror for the Church: Preaching in the First Five Centuries*. Grand Rapids: Eerdmans, 2005.

Evans, John F. *A Guide to Biblical Commentaries and Reference Works*. 10th ed. Grand Rapids: Zondervan, 2016.

Gibson, Scott M., ed. *The Worlds of the Preacher: Navigating Biblical, Cultural, and Personal Contexts*. Grand Rapids: Baker Academic, 2018.

Glynn, John, and Michael H. Burer, eds. *Best Bible Books: New Testament Resources*. Grand Rapids: Kregel, 2018.

Heisler, Greg. *Spirit-Led Preaching: The Holy Spirit's Role in Sermon Preparation and Delivery*. Rev. ed. Nashville: B&H Academic, 2018.

Hiestand, Gerald, and Todd Wilson. *The Pastor Theologian: Resurrecting an Ancient Vision*. Grand Rapids: Zondervan, 2015.

Johnson, Darrell W. *The Glory of Preaching: Participating in God's Transformation of the World*. Downers Grove, IL: IVP Academic, 2009.

Keller, Timothy. *Preaching: Communicating Faith in an Age of Skepticism*. New York: Viking, 2015.

Kim, Matthew D. *Preaching with Cultural Intelligence: Understanding the People Who Hear Sermons*. Grand Rapids: Baker Academic, 2017.

Lloyd-Jones, D. Martyn. *Preaching and Preachers*. Grand Rapids: Zondervan, 1971.

McMinn, Mark R. *The Science of Virtue: Why Positive Psychology Matters to the Church*. Grand Rapids: Brazos Press, 2017.

Merida, Tony. *The Christ-Centered Expositor: A Field Guide for Word-Driven Disciple Makers*. Nashville: B&H Academic, 2016.

Ogilvie, Lloyd John. *A Passionate Calling*. Eugene, OR: Harvest House, 2014.

Packer, J. I. *Truth and Power: The Place of Scripture in the Christian Life*. Downers Grove, IL: InterVarsity, 1996.

Pasquarello, Michael, III. *Sacred Rhetoric: Preaching as a Theological and Pastoral Practice of the Church*. Grand Rapids: Eerdmans, 2005.

Piper, John. *Expository Exultation: Christian Preaching as Worship*. Wheaton: Crossway, 2018.

———. *The Supremacy of God in Preaching*. Rev. ed. Grand Rapids: Baker Books, 2015.

Plantinga, Cornelius, Jr. *Reading for Preaching: The Preacher in Conversation with Storytellers, Biographers, Poets, and Journalists*. Grand Rapids: Eerdmans, 2013.

Richard, Ramesh. *Preparing Evangelistic Sermons: A Seven-Step Method for Preaching Salvation*. Grand Rapids: Baker Books, 2005.

Robinson, Haddon. *Biblical Preaching: The Development and Delivery of Expository Messages*. 3rd ed. Grand Rapids: Baker Academic, 2014.

Smith, Steven W. *Dying to Preach: Embracing the Cross in the Pulpit*. Grand Rapids: Kregel, 2009.

Stewart, James S. *Heralds of God: A Practical Book on Preaching*. Vancouver: Regent College Publishing, 2001.

Stott, John. *Between Two Worlds: The Art of Preaching in the Twentieth Century*. Grand Rapids: Eerdmans, 1982.

Taylor, Barbara Brown. *The Preaching Life*. Lanham, MD: Cowley Publications, 1993.

Vines, Jerry, and Jim Shaddix. *Power in the Pulpit: How to Prepare and Deliver Expository Sermons*. Rev. ed. Chicago: Moody, 2017.

6

Corporate Worship

Gathering God's people together in corporate worship, especially on Sundays (or Saturdays) for worship services, is both a sacred privilege and a responsibility of the pastor. Although a worship leader or worship pastor may be responsible for leading a worship team in a time of corporate singing, the senior or lead pastor of a church still needs to oversee the entire process of corporate worship. However, the degree of involvement the senior pastor has in corporate worship can vary. Bob Kauflin shared in *Worship Matters* that as a worship leader, he has worked with a lead pastor who was very involved in planning the worship service weeks ahead of time, another pastor who went over the song set on Sunday morning, and still another pastor who wanted to know the plan only by email. Some lead pastors are much less involved, or even uninvolved, glad to let the worship leader take care of all the details of corporate worship, especially the singing, so that they can focus mainly on preaching. Kauflin has found that the pastors who are easiest to minister with are the ones who are willing to work together as a team but still take ultimate responsibility for the eventual outcome.[1]

As pastors, we may oversee corporate worship with varying degrees of involvement, but we need to take ultimate responsibility for the worship services in our churches. We should work closely with the worship leader or worship pastor if there is one but let him or her have some freedom in the planning and the process of leading worship. However, the worship service is more than just singing,[2] or worship in song. Corporate worship, especially during Sunday (or Saturday) services, encompasses the entire worship service and usually includes many of the following components provided by Bryan Chapell:

- Calls (scriptural, pastoral, choral, unison, responsive, songs and hymns, etc.)
- Prayers (pastoral, unison, responsive, corporate, elder-led, congregant-offered, personal, silent, collect, scriptural, extemporaneous, ancient or contemporary form, hymn)
- Scripture Readings (pastoral, unison, individual, choral, antiphonal, responsive)
- Music (hymns, psalms, solos, choral anthems, choral-congregational responses)
- Offerings and Collections
- Creeds and Affirmations (Apostles', Nicene, Athanasian, catechisms, historical and contemporary writings)
- Benedictions and Charges (scriptural, historical, extemporaneous)
- Rubrics (i.e., explanations and transitions between worship aspects)
- Sermon
- Sacraments
- Expressions of Fellowship
- Testimonies and Ministry Reports
- Oaths and Vows
- Ordinations and Commissionings
- Church Discipline
- Fasting
- Other[3]

Variations exist, and Sunday services may not include all these components. Most services, however, include the central practices or elements of worship, which are "the preaching of God's word, the public reading of God's word, praying in accordance with God's word, singing what coheres with God's word, and seeing God's word through the ordinance (baptism and the Lord's Supper or Holy Communion)."[4]

Before going into more detail about the pastor's role in worship, we need to understand the meaning of worship from a biblical perspective, including a biblical theology of worship.[5]

What Is Worship?

John Piper, in *Let the Nations Be Glad!*, wrote these powerful words about worship and missions: "Missions is not the ultimate goal of the church. Worship is. Missions exists because worship doesn't. Worship is ultimate, not missions, because God is ultimate, not men. When this age is over, and the countless millions of the redeemed fall on their faces before the throne of God, missions will be no more. It is a temporary necessity. But worship abides forever."[6] He went on to point out that the New Testament actually contains little explicit teaching about corporate worship and how it should be conducted (i.e., worship services). Corporate worship is therefore not worship services or worship singing per se. These are examples of possible expressions of worship, but they are not the essence of true biblical worship. What, then, is worship or the true essence of worship from a biblical perspective? Piper concluded, after reviewing the New Testament and its teaching on worship, that

> the essential, vital, indispensable, defining heart of worship is the experience of *being satisfied with God in Christ*. This experience magnifies his worth, and such magnifying is what worship is. This is why Jesus and the apostles were so stunningly indifferent to external forms and so radically intent on inward, spiritual, authentic worship. . . . Worship is not first an outward act; it is an inner spiritual treasuring of the character and the ways of God in Christ. It is a cherishing of Christ, or being satisfied with all that God is for us in Christ. When these things are missing, there is no worship, no matter what forms or expressions are present.[7]

Piper also drew out four major implications of this biblical view of worship as satisfaction in God: our highest duty is to pursue joy in God; worship is radically God centered; worship is an end in itself; and all of life should be our expression of worship (as Paul taught).[8]

There are other definitions of worship from a biblical perspective. Ralph Martin defined worship thus: "*Worship is the dramatic celebration of God in his supreme worth in such a manner that his 'worthiness' becomes the norm and inspiration of human living.*"[9] Daniel Block wrote, "*True worship involves reverential human acts of submission and homage before the divine Sovereign in response to his gracious revelation of himself and in accord with his will.*"[10] And according to Gerrit Gustafson, "Worship is the act and attitude of wholeheartedly giving yourself to God—spirit, soul, mind and body."[11]

Doug Gregg and I have described worship as "'lovemaking' with God. The most common New Testament word for worship—*proskuneo*—literally means to 'step towards to kiss.' We can bow and prostrate ourselves before

God from a distance, but we must be close, intimate, trusting, and vulnerable if we are to step forward into God's loving embrace and receive his kiss of life, his Holy Spirit. Worship . . . is our response of love to the God who has reached out in love to us."[12] A. W. Tozer has written, "It is quite impossible to worship God without loving Him, and the inward operations of the Holy Spirit will enable us . . . to offer Him such a poured-out fullness of love."[13]

Through worship, the Holy Spirit transforms us in at least five ways. First, the Holy Spirit helps us to focus on God and not ourselves. Second, the Holy Spirit enables us to experience God's mercy and love in fresh ways. Third, the Holy Spirit provides clearer direction regarding God's will for our future. Fourth, the Holy Spirit, through powerful praise and worship of God, exposes the schemes of the devil, reveals his presence, and breaks demonic bondages and strongholds in our lives. Fifth, and finally, the Holy Spirit transforms our hearts and empowers us to engage in obedient lifestyles according to God's Word and will. Surrendering to God in true worship ultimately changes us.[14]

Piper concluded:

> The ultimate goal of God in all of history is to uphold and display his glory for the enjoyment of the redeemed from every tribe and tongue and people and nation. His goal is the gladness of his people, because God is most glorified in us when we are most satisfied in him. Delight is a higher tribute than duty. The chief end of God is to glorify God and enjoy his glory forever. Since his glory is magnified most in the God-centered passions of his joyful people, God's self-exaltation and our jubilation are one. The greatest news in all the world is that God's ultimate aim to be glorified and our aim to be satisfied are not at odds.[15]

A Biblical Theology of Worship

It is important for us to have an overall understanding of what the Bible, in both the Old and the New Testaments, actually teaches about worship: a biblical theology of worship.[16] Brian Croft and Jason Adkins have provided a brief but helpful overview of this.[17] With regard to worship in the Old Testament, they stated, "A reiterated theme of the Old Testament is God's regard for himself. He is committed steadfastly to his glory and honor and seeks to make himself known through the key Old Testament events of creation, exodus, exile, and the promise of a new covenant. God's devotion to the glory of his name provides a foundation for other Old Testament phenomena, including worship regulations in the law, penalties for violating these regulations, and the frequent commands for God's people to praise him."[18] They based this summary on a number of Old Testament passages (Gen. 15:12–16; Exod.

7:15; 8:10, 22; 9:14, 29–30; 10:2; 14:4, 18; 25–30; 36–40; Lev. 10:1–2; Josh. 4:24; 6:16; Judg. 7:2; 1 Kings 18:36; 20:13; Pss. 19:1; 29:2; 50:6; 95:6; 149:1; Isa. 43:7; Ezek. 36:21–22).[19]

With regard to worship in the New Testament, they emphasized that God takes great care to instruct Christians on what worship is and also how to worship, especially in the Gospels and Paul's writings. They reviewed a number of New Testament passages (Matt. 28:19–20; John 4:12, 20, 23–24; Acts 2:41–42; 5:12; 6:4; 1 Cor. 11:26; 14:15, 33, 40; Eph. 2:18; 5:18–21; Col. 3:15–16; 4:3, 16; Heb. 10:25; James 5:14; 1 Tim. 2:1–2; 4:13; 2 Tim. 4:1–2) and stated that Christian worship is truthful and spiritual, purposeful, congregational, and specific, with guidelines and commands regarding what God expects in Christian worship.[20] They made this conclusion about a biblical theology of worship and how to apply it: "A summary of the Old Testament's teaching on worship is that God cares deeply how he is worshipped, and a summary of the New Testament's teaching on worship is that God has specifically instructed believers on how to worship him. Christian ministers must understand and apply these principles as they oversee their local congregations."[21]

Although the New Testament provides specific guidelines for how to worship God, it does not spell out all the concrete components of a worship service, as Piper has already pointed out. The biblical aspects of worship need to be present, and the focus of real worship should always be adoration of the Triune God. But there is space for creative expressions of worship contextualized to each local church and culture.

The Pastor's Role in Corporate Worship

The pastor's role in corporate worship can vary from almost noninvolvement to total involvement. However, the ultimate oversight or responsibility for corporate worship, especially on Sundays (or Saturdays) in worship services, belongs to the pastor. As pastors, we should not just narrowly focus on the sermon part of a corporate worship service. We need to oversee the entire service to ensure that, with the Holy Spirit's help, it is truly an expression of real worship in spirit and in truth that involves each member's entire being (heart, soul, mind, and strength).

As a senior pastor, I have focused, over the years, on these elements of a Sunday worship service: preaching (which is my major responsibility); pastoral prayer; Scripture reading; announcements; leading the open sharing time; conducting Holy Communion, with times for silence and meditation on God's Word and the meaning of the atonement (or what Jesus did on the cross for us); conducting baptisms and baby dedications; doing commissioning of mission teams; conducting ordination services when needed; doing the closing of the service, usually with an invitation to come forward for prayer ministry; and pronouncing the benediction. I have left the worship in song time to the worship leader of a particular worship team and more recently to the worship minister who has joined our pastoral staff. Although I am not as involved in the worship in song part of the service, the worship minister and worship team know my sermon topic and text in advance so they can select songs in line with my preaching topic. Other pastors may want to be more involved in the worship in song part by helping to select the songs, including a song of preparation before the sermon and a closing song of response after the sermon. I sometimes select a closing song of response.

Pastors do not just lead their congregations in corporate worship with their sermons. They need to provide pastoral and spiritual oversight, as shepherds of God's people, to feed them, nurture them, and take care of them throughout the worship service so that they are engaged in true worship that transforms them to be more Christlike. Ultimately, a pastor must first of all be a true worshiper. It is not easy, especially during a worship service, for a pastor to really focus on God and worship him, because he or she has so many other concerns, including preaching the sermon. It is a regular struggle for me as a senior pastor on Sundays to prayerfully focus on God rather than on all the details of the worship service. But when we as pastors are most satisfied in God alone and thereby see him most glorified in us, then we can lead our congregations to truly love, adore, and worship God and be most satisfied and most joyful in him.

Kauflin provided the following definition of a worship leader that can also be applied to the pastor, who is ultimately responsible for overseeing corporate worship and the worship service: "A faithful worship leader magnifies the greatness of God in Jesus Christ through the power of the Holy Spirit by skillfully combining God's Word with music, thereby motivating the gathered church to proclaim the gospel, to cherish God's presence, and to live for God's glory."[22]

Worship That Transforms Lives

Alexis Abernethy has edited a helpful book on worship that transforms lives, with six major implications for the practice of worship.[23] First is the role of suffering. While worship is adoration of God based on our covenantal relationship with him, we need his help in our worship of him, which he does provide, especially in our struggles with pain, suffering, and sadness. We need to be vulnerable as pastors to share our struggles and to encourage our parishioners to do likewise. We need to provide time for open sharing or testimonies that include our struggles with pain, suffering, and sadness and to pray with lament over them.

Second, the role of the Holy Spirit is essential and crucial in worship, including corporate worship. We need to pray for his anointing and for his power and presence to be with us all during the worship service. The Spirit, however, can work spontaneously and also cumulatively over time in our worship services as well as in our daily walk with the Lord, including as we practice the spiritual disciplines.

Third, the posture of the worship leader is crucial. The worship leader, whether a worship team leader or a worship pastor, needs to lead the congregation in worship, and not just worship in song. The pastor leads by worshiping and not just by singing praise.

Fourth, corporate worship, which involves worshiping God with other members of the body of Christ, needs to be fleshed out. It needs to go beyond individual worship that simply happens with other people around in a worship service. We need to be more aware of other members of God's family in Christ and to worship together in a spirit of community and family. We can pray together in small groups, with hands joined if we are comfortable with this practice, during a service. Open sharing times with brief testimonies and prayers for one another can also help us experience corporate worship. We need to look around us as we worship together in Sunday services. The pastor especially needs to keep his or her eyes and ears open, to be sensitive to how the congregation is responding or not responding and how the Spirit is moving. Pastors must not get lost in their own individual experience of worship and lose touch with the people they are leading in worship.

Fifth, the sacraments need to be given more attention and focus in true corporate worship. Holy Communion, or the Lord's Supper, needs to be conducted meaningfully and tied to real life outside the local church—for example, to global issues and creation.

Sixth, and finally, the role of the arts in worship needs further clarification and development. Some parishioners may not be comfortable with incorporating more of the arts (e.g., dance, sculpture, paintings) into corporate worship services. We can learn from churches in other cultures and countries that may have more expressive and bolder styles of worship. For example, worship in dance, singing together with clapping, holding hands, lifting up of our arms and hands, and swaying to the music can help us worship God with our bodies and whole beings. The arts is a crucial area that we need to attend to, develop, and incorporate more into our worship services.[24]

As Piper has emphasized, worship is ultimate because God is ultimate. We will worship God forever. We need to learn to worship him well now on earth. To God be the glory, and praise be to the Lord!

RECOMMENDED READINGS

Abernethy, Alexis D., ed. *Worship That Changes Lives: Multidisciplinary and Congregational Perspectives on Spiritual Transformation*. Grand Rapids: Baker Academic, 2008.

Block, Daniel I. *For the Glory of God: Recovering a Biblical Theology of Worship*. Grand Rapids: Baker Academic, 2014.

Chapell, Bryan. *Christ-Centered Worship: Letting the Gospel Shape Our Practice*. Grand Rapids: Baker Academic, 2009.

Cherry, Constance M. *The Worship Architect: A Blueprint for Designing Culturally Relevant and Biblically Faithful Services*. Grand Rapids: Baker Academic, 2010.

Croft, Brian, and Jason Adkins. *Gather God's People: Understand, Plan, and Lead Worship in Your Local Church*. Grand Rapids: Zondervan, 2014.

Hicks, Zac. *The Worship Pastor: A Call to Ministry for Worship Leaders and Teams*. Grand Rapids: Zondervan, 2016.

Kauflin, Bob. *Worship Matters: Leading Others to Encounter the Greatness of God*. Wheaton: Crossway, 2008.

Peterson, David G. *Engaging with God: A Biblical Theology of Worship*. Downers Grove, IL: IVP Academic, 2002.

Ross, Allen P. *Recalling the Hope of Glory: Biblical Worship from the Garden to the New Creation*. Grand Rapids: Kregel, 2006.

Rutledge, Fleming. *The Crucifixion: Understanding the Death of Jesus Christ*. Grand Rapids: Eerdmans, 2015.

Van Opstal, Sandra Maria. *The Next Worship: Glorifying God in a Diverse World*. Downers Grove, IL: InterVarsity, 2016.

Witvliet, John D. *Worship Seeking Understanding: Windows into Christian Practice*. Grand Rapids: Baker Academic, 2003.

7

Intentional Disciplemaking and Spiritual Formation

Another major area of pastoral ministry is intentional disciplemaking and spiritual formation of God's people into deeper Christlikeness. Dallas Willard, in *Renovation of the Heart*, asserted that spiritual formation in Christlikeness (Rom. 8:29) should be the exclusive primary goal of the local church or congregation.[1] Similarly, intentional disciplemaking, which is almost synonymous with spiritual formation, has been emphasized as the key priority of the local church and the people of God because Jesus, in the Great Commission in Matthew 28:18–20, commanded us to make disciples of all nations: "Then Jesus came to them and said, 'All authority in heaven and on earth has been given to me. Therefore go and make disciples of all nations, baptizing them in the name of the Father and of the Son and of the Holy Spirit, and teaching them to obey everything I have commanded you. And surely I am with you always, to the very end of the age.'"

In 1999 at the First International Consultation on Discipleship, John Stott lamented that while the church was growing very quickly around the world, there was great superficiality, reflecting growth with no depth. He concluded, "No doubt God is not pleased with superficial discipleship. The apostolic writers of the New Testament declare . . . that God wants His people to grow up and to grow into maturity in Christ."[2] Since then, many Christian leaders and pastors have advocated for intentional disciplemaking, and a voluminous number of books on the subject have been published, especially

in the past two decades or so.[3] Edmund Chan is the founder of the Global
Alliance of Intentional Disciplemaking Churches (IDMC Global Alliance)
and the author of several key books on intentional disciplemaking.[4] He was
the senior pastor of Covenant Evangelical Free Church (CEFC) in Singapore
for twenty-five years until 2012, when he successfully handed this influential
disciplemaking church of several thousand people over to the two successors he had mentored for over two decades. His church holds an Intentional
Disciplemaking Church Conference every year that has blessed more than
five thousand pastors, leaders, and others from over four hundred churches
and thirty-five nations. In May 2013 his church initiated and helped to host
the Global Discipleship Congress in Manila, in the Philippines, which was
attended by over seventy-four hundred participants from sixty-one nations.[5]
He is a personal friend, and my church has adapted some of his strategies for
becoming more of an IDMC.

Definitions of Disciplemaking and Spiritual Formation

We first need to clarify what disciplemaking is and what spiritual formation
is and the relationship between these two often-used terms.

Chan, in *A Certain Kind*, defined disciplemaking as "the process of bringing people into right relationship with God, and developing them to full maturity in Christ through intentional growth strategies, that they might multiply
the entire process in others also."[6] This definition has four major components:
(1) bringing people into right relationship with God through Christ in responsible evangelism; (2) developing them to full maturity in Christ by responsibly
following up with new believers so that they may grow in their newfound faith
in Christ; (3) through intentional growth strategies using a core curriculum
that is biblically based for different levels of discipling; (4) that they might
repeat the entire process in others so that there is spiritual multiplication of
disciples who make other disciples who also make other disciples.[7]

He also defined an IDMC using eight major characteristics: (1) purpose
driven, with disciplemaking as the core mission of the church; (2) responsible
evangelism, in which people are being led to Christ and conscientiously followed up with; (3) intentional growth strategies, through which people are
being developed to be equipped for ministry according to each one's spiritual
gifts; (4) leadership commitment, in which church leaders are committed to
model disciplemaking and not just agree to it; (5) vision casting, especially
by a disciplemaking pastor who clearly, with the leaders of the church, ar-
ticulates and adopts the disciplemaking vision and strategy for the whole

church; (6) vision concretizing, in which concrete and specific means are being implemented to facilitate the purpose of disciplemaking, including mentoring relationships in the church, systematic follow-up programs for new believers, and training programs for disciplemakers; (7) small group infrastructure, in which small groups are formed to function as essential intentional disciplemaking units; (8) and spiritual multiplication, in which people's lives are being transformed into deeper Christlikeness and spiritual multiplication is actually occurring, extending to several generations.[8]

Jim Putman and Bobby Harrington with Robert Coleman, in *DiscipleShift*, defined a disciple, based on Matthew 4:19 ("Follow me, and I will make you fishers of men" [KJV]), as a person who "(1) is following Christ (head); (2) is being changed by Christ (heart); (3) is committed to the mission of Christ (hands)."[9] Greg Ogden, in *Discipleship Essentials*, provided the following definitions of discipling (or disciplemaking) and a disciple: "Discipling is an intentional relationship in which we walk alongside other disciples in order to encourage, equip, and challenge one another in love to grow toward maturity in Christ. This includes equipping the disciple to teach others as well. . . . A disciple is one who responds in faith and obedience to the gracious call to follow Jesus Christ. Being a disciple is a lifelong process of dying to self while allowing Jesus Christ to come alive in us."[10]

What is spiritual formation? It is almost synonymous with disciplemaking. Spiritual formation into deeper Christlikeness is a phrase that is frequently used today, whereas disciplemaking is an older term that recently has also received much attention. Willard has defined spiritual formation as "the intentional process to shape a person's inner being to be like the inner being of Christ: God-connected, self-denying, joyful, easily obedient. While spiritual formation is always dependent upon the leadership of the Spirit and the provision of God's grace, it is founded on intentional human efforts."[11] These intentional human efforts, still empowered by the Holy Spirit and God's grace, have to do with the regular practice of the spiritual disciplines. Putman and Harrington with Coleman have pointed out that spiritual formation focuses on the use of spiritual disciplines to grow into deeper Christlikeness, whereas disciplemaking focuses more on the relationships that the Holy Spirit uses to help people become more Christlike.[12] Spiritual formation, while it involves the individual, includes relational aspects as well—for example, when it involves corporate spiritual disciplines such as worship, fellowship, and even guidance and confession.

Both spiritual formation and disciplemaking are ultimately for the sake of others and for the glory of God. They overlap and are almost synonymous. The goal of both spiritual formation and disciplemaking is to become more like Jesus: to be conformed to the image of Christ (Rom. 8:29), which is the will of God for all of us as his people, or so that Christ may be formed in us (Gal. 4:19). As Jack Hayford has put it, we will be Spirit-formed in both the purity (character or being) and the power (ministry or doing) of Jesus Christ (John 14:12).[13]

Intentional Disciplemaking and Spiritual Formation in the Church

Willard has strongly critiqued the contemporary church in America for making discipleship optional by focusing on making converts rather than disciples. In *The Great Omission*, Willard pointed out two omissions from the Great Commission Jesus gave in Matthew 28:18–20 that Christian institutions and churches of our day commit: omitting the making of disciples and then omitting the training of converts, which is needed to enable them to do more of what Jesus commanded.[14] He described a disciple of Jesus as someone who continuously "grow[s] in the grace and knowledge of our Lord and Savior Jesus Christ" (2 Pet. 3:18) and stated, "A disciple is a learner, a student, an apprentice—a *practitioner*, even if only a beginner. . . . [D]isciples of Jesus are people who do not just profess certain views as their own but apply their growing understanding of life in the Kingdom of the Heavens to every aspect of their life on earth."[15] He challenged the prevailing view of many professing Christians that we can be Christians forever and never become disciples. In fact, Willard pointed out that the word *disciple* occurs 269 times in the New Testament, whereas the word *Christian* occurs only three times and was first used to refer to disciples of Christ (Acts 11:26). He wrote, "The New Testament is a book about disciples, by disciples, and for disciples of Jesus Christ."[16] A true Christian is a disciple of Jesus Christ, having received him as Savior and Lord and having decided to follow him as his disciple or apprentice. Matthew Bates has emphasized that salvation by faith alone through God's grace should be understood as salvation by allegiance alone to Jesus Christ the King.[17]

Willard has also described a simple plan for a local church or congregation to pursue its primary and exclusive goal of spiritual formation in Christlikeness. It is called the VIM model for transforming every area of our being into deeper Christlikeness: mind, will (heart or spirit) and character, body, social dimension, and soul. The acronym VIM stands for vision of life in the kingdom of God (that is the range of God's effective will, where what God wants done is done) now and forever; intention to be a kingdom person (we can and need to decide to live life in the kingdom, completely relying on Jesus and intending to obey him); and means of spiritual transformation into Christlikeness or maturity in Christ, including the practice of spiritual disciplines.[18] He concluded, "No special talents, personal skills, educational programs, money, or possessions are required to bring this to pass. We do not have to purify and enforce some legalistic system. Just ordinary people who are apprentices, gathered in the name of Jesus and immersed in his presence, and taking steps of inward transformation as they put on the character of Christ: this is all that is required. . . . Let that be our only aim, and the triumph of God in our individual lives and our times is ensured."[19]

A more specific tool that can be of great help in the spiritual formation of people in local churches is a Renovaré resource: A *Spiritual Formation Workbook* by James Bryan Smith with Lynda Graybeal.[20] It can be used in a Renovaré spiritual-formation small group, usually with two to eight members. A more detailed description of this type of small group aimed at spiritual formation into Christlikeness will be provided in a later chapter on small groups and fellowships. Smith has also written an excellent trilogy, *The Good and Beautiful God*, *The Good and Beautiful Life*, and *The Good and Beautiful Community*, that can be very helpful to use as a curriculum for spiritual formation.

Diane Chandler has described Christian spiritual formation in a comprehensive way as an integrated approach for personal and relational wholeness in Christ, with seven dimensions: formation of the spirit (foundational), emotional formation, relational formation, intellectual formation, vocational formation, physical health formation, and resource formation (i.e., wise stewardship of finances, material possessions, time, and the earth). Christian spiritual formation of the whole person in Christlikeness should include all seven dimensions.[21]

Kenneth Boa has described twelve major biblical and practical approaches to spiritual formation, each focusing on a particular emphasis of Christian spirituality:

1. Relational spirituality focuses on loving God completely, ourselves correctly, and others compassionately.
2. Paradigm spirituality focuses on cultivating an eternal versus a temporal perspective.
3. Disciplined spirituality focuses on engaging in the historical (spiritual) disciplines.
4. Exchanged life spirituality focuses on grasping our true identity in Christ.

5. Motivated spirituality focuses on a set of biblical incentives.

6. Devotional spirituality focuses on falling in love with God.

7. Holistic spirituality focuses on every component of life under the lordship of Christ.

8. Process spirituality focuses on process versus product, being versus doing.

9. Spirit-filled spirituality focuses on walking in the power of the Spirit.

10. Warfare spirituality focuses on overcoming the world, the flesh, and the devil.

11. Nurturing spirituality focuses on a lifestyle of evangelism and discipleship.

12. Corporate spirituality focuses on encouragement, accountability, and worship.[22]

While acknowledging that there are diverse descriptions of Christian spiritual maturity, Gordon Smith has defined spiritual maturity as "union with Christ and, in and through him, it is a dynamic participation in the life of the triune God."[23] He further described spiritual maturity as having four distinct but interdependent expressions: wisdom, good work, ability to love others, and joy.[24] He offered four ways a pastor or church leader can lead parishioners into spiritual formation and maturity in Christ: the church as a liturgical community called to worship, the church as a teaching-learning community called to the renewal of the mind, the church as a missional community called to witnessing in word and deed to the reign of Christ, and finally personal pastoral care and spiritual direction for the church.[25]

There are now many books available on discipleship and disciplemaking, with various models and programs for use in the local church. Bill Hull, in *The Disciple-Making Pastor*, emphasized the role of the pastor as coach in leading and pastoring a disciplemaking church, because the pastor's main task is to equip people to do ministry (Eph. 4:11–12) and to grow them up to maturity in Christ (Eph. 4:13). He described a disciple—based on Jesus's teaching on discipleship—as someone who "is willing to deny self, take up a cross daily, and follow Him (Luke 9:23), puts Christ before self, family, and possessions (Luke 14:25–35), is committed to Christ's teachings (John 8:31), is committed to world evangelism (Matt. 9:36–38), loves others as Christ loves (John 13:34–35), and abides in Christ, is obedient, bears fruit, glorifies God, has joy, and loves the brethren (John 15:7–17)."[26] The pastor as coach (trainer or equipper) can follow Jesus's method of teaching his disciples by using the following six steps: "tell them what, tell them why, show them how, do it with them, let them do it, and deploy them."[27]

Glenn McDonald, in *The Disciple Making Church*, focused on asking the right questions concerning six relationships that are essential for developing a church that is characterized by disciples who make disciples: (1) Who is your Lord? (loving and treasuring Jesus as Lord); (2) Who are you? (God's deeply loved servant and disciple); (3) Who is your Barnabas? (a spiritual mentor); (4) Who is your Timothy? (someone to disciple, mentor, and bless); (5) Where is your Antioch? (Christian community with a few other disciples); and (6) Where is your Macedonia? (a mission field just outside your comfort zone, locally or abroad).[28] He also described the six marks of a disciple: "a heart for Christ alone, a mind transformed by the word, arms of love, knees for prayer, a voice to speak the good news, and a spirit of servanthood and stewardship."[29]

McDonald emphasized the need for a disciplemaking church to have seven habits for how to be and do church: (1) to stay centered by means of prayer and discernment; (2) to have discipleship as a singular focus; (3) to shift to a strategy of relationships from a strategy of programs; (4) to focus on the six marks of a disciple instead of external behaviors; (5) to develop a practice of personal discipline; (6) to effectively use a personal-development plan for spiritual growth; and (7) to get the church board to shift from focusing on attendance, building, and cash (ABCs) to focusing on reproducible relationships, permission to do ministry, and a master plan for discipleship (RPMs).[30]

Randy Pope's book *Insourcing: Bringing Discipleship Back to the Local Church*, written with Kitti Murray, is a must-read for pastors wanting to help their churches be disciplemaking churches. He has provided a more detailed and ideal description of the kind of disciple we want to produce and reproduce: a mature and equipped believer who

- is living consistently under the control of the Holy Spirit, the direction of the Word of God, and the compelling love of Christ;
- has discovered, developed, and is using his or her spiritual gifts;
- has learned to effectively share his or her faith, while demonstrating a radical love that amazes those it touches;
- gives evidence of being a faithful member of God's church, an effective manager of life, relationships, and resources, a willing minister to others, including "the least of these," and an available messenger to nonkingdom people; and
- demonstrates a life characterized as gospel driven, worship focused, morally pure, evangelistically bold, discipleship grounded, family faithful, and socially responsible.[31]

Pope shared the five important emphases in their small groups, which are called Life-on-Life Missional Discipleship (LOLMD) groups: truth, equipping, accountability, mission, and supplication (or TEAMS).[32] The specific characteristics of LOLMD groups, as compared to traditional small groups, are life transformation; everyone prepares; high commitment, high cost; leader selects members; truth, equipping, accountability, mission, and supplication; size of four to ten; produces mature and equipped followers of Christ; composed of Christians, men with men, women with women; leader is a disciple, coach, and mentor; missional experience; and leader development.[33] LOLMD has three major components: (1) helping people move from unbelief to belief, so personal evangelism and public preaching are crucial; (2) coaching a new believer to grow from belief to maturity, with small-group Bible studies, Sunday school classes, seminars and sermons playing a role but with LOLMD groups as key to a deeper and longer-lasting maturity; and (3) equipping a disciple to go from maturity to leadership.[34] Pope also provided a curriculum for three years, covering gospel living (the first six weeks of each annual curriculum), grace commitments, knowing God, healthy marriage, biblical worldview, and God-honoring parenting.[35] He has recently started Life-on-Life Ministries to help churches worldwide establish LOLMD groups (www .lifeonlife.org/insourcing).

Putman and Harrington with Coleman, in *DiscipleShift*, have described five key shifts needed in disciplemaking: from reaching to making, from informing to equipping, from program to purpose, from activity to relationship, and from accumulating to deploying.[36] In implementing discipleship in a local church and making this "discipleshift," a pastor and his or her team of leaders need to develop the biblical vision for the church; create a common language, with clear definition of terms; develop the process of disciplemaking and let it be used by those serving in the front lines of ministry in the church; consistently live out the biblical vision of discipleship and disciplemaking and consistently recast the vision; and regularly assess, make course corrections, and encourage.[37]

Bobby Harrington and Alex Absalom have emphasized the central role of relationships in disciplemaking in the church. In *Discipleship That Fits*, they described five kinds of relationships that God uses to help us grow into spiritual maturity in Christ. They are (1) divine (alone with God in our inner world and personal walk with him), based on Jesus's relationship with the Father; (2) transparent (with two to four people in our deepest friendships, including marriage), based on Jesus's relationship with the three; (3) personal (with four to twelve people in small groups), based on Jesus's relationship with the Twelve; (4) social (with twenty to seventy people in missional communities), based on Jesus's relationship with the seventy; and (5) public (with hundreds of people on Sundays at church services), based on Jesus's relationship with the crowds. The outcomes of the divine relationship are focused on identity, destiny, and truth. The outcomes of the transparent relationship are focused on intimacy, openness, and impact. The outcomes of the personal relationship are focused on closeness, support, and challenge. The outcomes of the social relationship are focused on community, mission, and practice. The outcomes of the public relationship are focused on inspiration, momentum, and preaching.[38] Comprehensive disciplemaking must include all five relationships that God uses to grow people into deeper Christlikeness and not focus on just one or two. The authors stated, "God disciples us through relationships differently in different relational contexts."[39]

While Harrington defined a disciple as someone who is following Jesus, is being changed by Jesus, and is committed to Jesus's kingdom mission, Absalom focused on a disciple as an intentional learner from Jesus who should ask two crucial questions: What is Jesus saying? and What am I doing in response?[40] Members of discipleship small groups need to repeatedly ask these questions in order to truly grow in discipleship and obedience to Jesus, by his grace and the power of the Holy Spirit. Another way of posing these two crucial questions is: What is the Holy Spirit telling me? and What am I doing about what the Holy Spirit is telling me? These two questions have been used in discipleship small groups of four to six people in one of the fastest-growing and largest churches in England.[41]

Bobby Harrington and Josh Patrick, in *The Disciple Maker's Handbook*, made these conclusions based on best practices of pastors and church planters who make disciplemakers: (1) the pastor or leader needs to make disciplemaking the top priority of the church; (2) there should be a focus on mobilizing everyday Christians; (3) disciplemaking must be kept simple and reproducible (e.g., by repeatedly asking the two crucial questions of discipleship); (4) practical tools for making disciplemaking doable need to be created and implemented; and (5) the entire pastoral staff of a church should focus on the top priority of disciplemaking, equipping members as disciples who make other disciples.[42]

Ogden, in *Transforming Discipleship*, emphasized the importance of making disciples a few at a time. He especially advocated a discipleship group of three and up to four people with the same gender and put forth three necessary ingredients for life transformation into greater Christlikeness: transparent trust, the truth of God's Word, and mutual accountability. They "converge to release the Holy Spirit to bring about a rapid growth toward Christlikeness. . . . When we (1) open our hearts in transparent trust to each other (2) around the truth of God's Word (3) in the spirit of mutual accountability, we are in the Holy Spirit's hot house of transformation."[43] Ogden has also written *Discipleship Essentials*, a book widely used as the core curriculum for discipleship groups of three or four members. It has enough biblically based material for twenty-five sessions of one and a half hours each, covering one topic at a time. The twenty-five topics are divided into four parts: "Part 1: Growing Up in Christ" (making disciples, being a disciple, quiet time, Bible study, prayer, and worship); "Part 2: Understanding the Message of Christ" (the three-person God, made in God's image, sin, grace, redemption, justification, and adoption); "Part 3: Becoming Like Christ" (filled with the Holy Spirit, fruit of the Holy Spirit, trust, love, justice, and witness); and "Part 4: Serving Christ" (the church, ministry gifts, spiritual warfare, walking in obedience, and sharing the wealth). Topic twenty-five is a bonus section on money,[44] and Ogden has provided a disciple's covenant to be signed at the first session so that participants take this training seriously with a high level of commitment.[45]

My church adopted this book for use in our intentional disciplemaking program with small groups of three or four members (sometimes six if three couples were involved) in 2012, when we started an intentional discipleship-training program adapted from Edmund Chan's model. We now require all those serving in leadership and ministry positions in our church to go through this program. Church members not serving in leadership positions have also participated in the training.

David Platt, in *Follow Me*, provides six primary questions intended to help formulate a personal disciple-making plan:

1. How will I fill my mind with truth?
2. How will I fuel my affections for God?
3. How will I share God's love as a witness in the world?
4. How will I show God's love as a member of the church?
5. How will I spread God's glory among all peoples?
6. How will I make disciplemakers among a few people?[46]

Each of these primary questions are followed by more specific questions as a way to further clarify each point.

Based on Jesus's Sermon on the Mount in Matthew 5–7, Chan has described eight biblical fundamentals of a core curriculum for disciplemaking in an IDMC:

1. Biblical theology: This asks the question, Who is God?
2. Biblical allegiance: This asks the question, Who is my Master in life?

3. Biblical identity: This asks the question, Who am I?

4. Biblical purpose: This asks the question, What am I called to do?

5. Biblical values: This asks the question, What is of ultimate importance in my life?

6. Biblical priorities: This asks the question, What are the things I must put first?

7. Biblical empowering: This asks the question, How can I keep on keeping on?

8. Biblical foundation: This asks the question, What should I anchor my life upon?[47]

According to Chan, these eight questions are the most important questions for a disciple of Christ to answer. Whatever specific materials are used in discipleship groups, these biblical fundamentals must be kept uppermost in intentional discipleship training in an IDMC.

Chan described five basic building blocks needed to establish an IDMC, in addition to prayer and the work of the Holy Spirit, which are crucial. They are as follows:

1. Establish biblical foundations. His book *Roots and Wings*, written with his wife, Ann Chan, is a helpful discipleship Bible study based on the core curriculum for discipleship. It covers What is a disciple? Why is disciplemaking important? Who is to make disciples? and How are we to make disciples?

2. Champion a compelling disciplemaking vision. This needs to be done first by prayerfully receiving a compelling vision from God, then by preaching or casting the vision.

3. Launch a prototype or early model of a concrete plan that starts small to build deep, although we may still think big.

4. Establish specific action steps so church members can see the vision in concrete ways. For example, read and discuss disciplemaking books among the church leadership, conduct an initial consecration weekend retreat, have a leadership development program for disciplemaking leaders, and prioritize disciplemaking in the church calendar—for example, by setting up and scheduling discipleship small groups.

5. Establish the infrastructure. The entire church needs to be organized around disciplemaking as its core mission and key priority. This involves developing a specific plan for establishing an IDMC; creating

policies supporting a disciplemaking church (e.g., requiring all pastors and pastoral staff to be involved in the personal mentoring of others); creating ministries that are coordinated with disciplemaking as a common goal; offering a sermon series on disciplemaking; using funds in the church budget for sending leaders or pastors to a disciplemaking conference or to visit an IDMC elsewhere; creating a church calendar that prioritizes disciplemaking activities and programs; dialoguing on disciplemaking at pastoral staff meetings and church board meetings; and creating a discipleship culture in the church that facilitates further growth in disciplemaking.[48]

My Personal Experience as a Senior Pastor with Intentional Disciplemaking and Spiritual Formation in the Church

I have reviewed much material on intentional disciplemaking and spiritual formation in a local church context to help pastors who want to obey the Great Commission of Jesus Christ to make disciples of all nations (Matt. 28:18–20). I have been involved for over twenty-five years as a ministry team member (and earlier as a board member) with Renovaré, a spiritual renewal ministry and movement founded by Richard Foster with much involvement by Dallas Willard until his death in 2013. However, as much as I believe in the top priority of disciplemaking and spiritual formation in the church, I must admit that it is easy to get distracted by the many other responsibilities of a senior pastor and the ministries of a local church. The years 2017 and 2018 were particularly challenging years of transition for my church, with four new pastoral staff members and two who left because of a move and a retirement. We also had to make remodeling plans for our worship sanctuary, which is over thirty-five years old. In the midst of such things, the compelling vision of disciplemaking and spiritual formation needs to be continually and prayerfully renewed. I have been challenged and convicted afresh, in writing this chapter, to lead my church, with the Holy Spirit's power and help, to continue to be more of an IDMC.

My church adapted Chan's model for an IDMC by starting an Intentional Discipleship Training (IDT) program in 2012. One of our church deacons, originally from Singapore, knew Chan and his church and the IDMC model well and strongly challenged and encouraged me to start a more systematic discipleship and disciplemaking program in our church. I was initially reluctant to start another program because we were already busy with several other programs. I believed then that we were doing discipling through small groups and bigger fellowships, Sunday school classes, one-on-one mentoring and spiritual direction, pastoral care and counseling, special seminars, Sunday worship services, and preaching. However, after much prayer and dialogue, the pastoral staff and some key church leaders all agreed that we needed to start a more systematic program of disciplemaking. We decided to adapt Chan's program and work toward being more of an IDMC. Chan was able to speak a couple of times to our member churches of First Evangelical Church Association (FECA) on intentional disciplemaking and also preached at our church. We had some helpful discussions about his model. One of his senior pastors, Tony Yeo, was on sabbatical in the Los Angeles area a few years ago, and he kindly met with me and our pastoral staff to further discuss intentional disciplemaking. This was most helpful.

We started the IDT program with our first Breakthrough Weekend (BTW) retreat for church leaders in 2012. We have had several BTW retreats since then. However, we have recently modified the BTW retreat from a weekend retreat to a one-day retreat, and it has been held in my home because our church has only several hundred people, and BTW retreat attendees range in number from a dozen to two dozen people. This change has made the retreat more convenient and much less costly. I have been the main speaker at these retreats, which are the kick-off event to start a new series of IDT sessions in small groups of three to four people, sometimes six if the group contains three couples. We have been using Ogden's *Discipleship Essentials*, over a six-month period or longer, in these IDT small groups. We have had several rounds of IDT programs over the past few years. Most of our church leaders have gone through the program because it is mandatory for them, and some church members have also participated.

In addition to the more formal IDT small groups, we have started several informal discipleship groups in the last couple of years. These groups meet weekly over the course of a few months, and the two to three participants support one another in the three Rs of reading Scripture, resisting sin, and reaching out to non-Christians. These groups can start at any time, and members are not required to first attend a BTW retreat, as in the more formal IDT program. They follow an approach that has been adapted from Neil Cole's life transformation groups.[49]

We have also started a few new small groups called life groups that are intergenerational and made up of both men and women. These groups have a discipleship focus, but they are more informal, focusing on sharing and praying together.

Have the IDT and other groups made a difference in our church in producing more disciples who also make disciples who make disciples? Many leaders and church members who have participated in the groups have expressed deep appreciation for the experience and testified that their lives have been blessed and transformed. We have seen people grow in deeper maturity in Christ and go on short-term mission trips and participate in outreach events such as Alpha meetings. However, we have not seen a multiplication of disciples or discipleship groups in any significant way. We know seeing the multiplication effects of disciplemaking and discipleship training takes time. It is not easy for a typical church to become an IDMC that focuses on spiritual formation and disciplemaking as its top priority.[50]

It is also crucial to keep evangelism and missions as other priorities in church life and ministry. I will cover this topic in the next chapter of this book. We have seen conversions, but not many in recent years in our church. We need to prayerfully ask the Holy Spirit to touch more people so that they come to know Christ as new believers and disciples who can then be dis-cipled to grow in Christ, to disciple others, with more multiplication effects. I also know that vision can weaken. I need to continue to lead in the ways suggested by Edmund Chan, to keep the compelling vision of disciplemak-ing clear and alive as a top priority in our church and to help make it more of an IDMC. However, it is important for us to be reminded that ultimately the Holy Spirit is the One who transforms hearts and lives. We need to leave the results, including multiplication effects of disciplemaking, to him. Many of the marks of a true disciple are ideal. We need to realize that spirituality is often messy,[51] and we are all imperfect disciples.[52] We are also imperfect pastors who need to be vulnerable and embrace our limitations and human weaknesses.[53] Christ's power is made perfect in our weakness, and his grace is sufficient for us (2 Cor. 12:9–10). Let us depend on him.

We also need to keep disciplemaking in the church as simple as possible and not feel bound to any model, method, or program. For example, the BTW retreat is not mandatory, and many discipleship training programs do not include it. Whatever material we use is secondary. The most important thing is agape love: genuine godly love for the people we are discipling. To keep disciplemaking simple, remember to use the two crucial questions: What is Jesus saying? and What am I doing in response? Also, eventually, disciple-making involves life-on-life mentoring relationships,[54] whether one-on-one or in a small group, without any specific materials, after the basics have been covered.

As pastors, we are all called by Jesus to fulfill the Great Commission (Matt. 28:18–20) to make disciples of all nations—and not commit the great omission. As Platt has put it, "Every child of God has been invited by God to be on the front lines of the supreme mission in all of history. Every disciple of

Jesus has been called, loved, created, and saved to make disciples of Jesus who make disciples of Jesus who make disciples of Jesus until the grace of God is enjoyed and the glory of God is exalted among every people group on the planet. . . . This is a call worth dying for. This is a King worth living for."[55]

RECOMMENDED READINGS

Andrews, Alan, ed. *The Kingdom Life: A Practical Theology of Discipleship and Spiritual Formation*. Colorado Springs: NavPress, 2010.

Boa, Kenneth. *Conformed to His Image: Biblical and Practical Approaches to Spiritual Formation*. Grand Rapids: Zondervan, 2001.

Bonhoeffer, Dietrich. *The Cost of Discipleship*. New York: Touchstone, 1995.

Chan, Edmund. *A Certain Kind: Intentional Disciplemaking That Redefines Success in Ministry*. Singapore: Covenant EFC, 2013.

———. *Mentoring Paradigms: Reflections on Mentoring, Leadership and Discipleship*. Singapore: Covenant EFC, 2008.

Chandler, Diane J. *Christian Spiritual Formation: An Integrated Approach for Personal and Relational Wholeness*. Downers Grove, IL: IVP Academic, 2014.

Coleman, Robert E. *The Master Plan of Discipleship*. Grand Rapids: Revell, 1987.

Fernando, Ajith. *Discipling in a Multicultural World*. Wheaton: Crossway, 2019.

Foster, Richard J. *Streams of Living Water: Celebrating the Great Traditions of Christian Faith*. San Francisco: HarperSanFrancisco, 1998.

Harrington, Bobby, and Alex Absalom. *Discipleship That Fits: The Five Kinds of Relationships God Uses to Help Us Grow*. Grand Rapids: Zondervan, 2016.

Harrington, Bobby, and Josh Patrick. *The Disciple Maker's Handbook: Seven Elements of a Discipleship Lifestyle*. Grand Rapids: Zondervan, 2017.

Howard, Evan B. *A Guide to Christian Spiritual Formation: How Scripture, Spirit, Community, and Mission Shape Our Souls*. Grand Rapids: Baker Academic, 2018.

Hull, Bill. *The Disciple-Making Pastor: Leading Others on the Journey of Faith*. Rev. ed. Grand Rapids: Baker Books, 2007.

Marshall, Colin, and Tony Payne. *The Vine Project: Shaping Your Ministry Culture around Disciple-Making*. Youngstown, OH: Matthias Media, 2016.

McDonald, Glenn W. *The Disciple Making Church: From Dry Bones to Spiritual Vitality*. Grand Haven, MI: FaithWalk Publishing, 2004.

Ogden, Greg. *Discipleship Essentials: A Guide to Building Your Life in Christ*. Rev. ed. Downers Grove, IL: InterVarsity, 2007.

Platt, David. *Follow Me: A Call to Die. A Call to Live*. Carol Stream, IL: Tyndale, 2013.

Pope, Randy, with Kitti Murray. *Insourcing: Bringing Discipleship Back to the Local Church*. Grand Rapids: Zondervan, 2013.

Putman, Jim, and Bobby Harrington, with Robert E. Coleman. *DiscipleShift: Five Steps That Help Your Church to Make Disciples Who Make Disciples*. Grand Rapids: Zondervan, 2013.

Smith, Gordon T. *Called to Be Saints: An Invitation to Christian Maturity*. Downers Grove, IL: IVP Academic, 2014.

Smith, James Bryan. *The Good and Beautiful Community: Following the Spirit, Extending Grace, Demonstrating Love*. Downers Grove, IL: InterVarsity, 2010.

———. *The Good and Beautiful God: Falling in Love with the God Jesus Knows*. Downers Grove, IL: InterVarsity, 2009.

———. *The Good and Beautiful Life: Putting on the Character of Christ*. Downers Grove, IL: InterVarsity, 2009.

Wilhoit, James C. *Spiritual Formation as if the Church Mattered: Growing in Christ through Community*. Grand Rapids: Baker Academic, 2008.

Willard, Dallas. *The Great Omission: Reclaiming Jesus's Essential Teachings on Discipleship*. New York: HarperSanFrancisco, 2006.

———. *Renovation of the Heart: Putting on the Character of Christ*. Colorado Springs: NavPress, 2002.

Willard, Dallas, and Gary Black Jr. *The Divine Conspiracy Continued: Fulfilling God's Kingdom on Earth*. New York: HarperOne, 2014.

Wilson, Jared C. *The Imperfect Disciple: Grace for People Who Can't Get Their Act Together*. Grand Rapids: Baker Books, 2017.

Wright, N. T. *After You Believe: Why Christian Character Matters*. New York: HarperOne, 2010.

8

Evangelism, Missions, and Social Concern

Disciplemaking cannot be split from evangelism, and evangelism cannot be separated from disciplemaking. Jesus has called us to go and make disciples of all nations, or people groups (Matt. 28:18–20). He has not commanded us just to make converts, or to help people make decisions to accept Christ as Lord and Savior, but to make disciples who will follow him all the days of their lives. However, the first step to discipleship, or following Jesus, is conversion: receiving Christ into our hearts and lives as our personal Lord and Savior and committing ourselves to following him as disciples. Evangelism refers to witnessing: telling others about Jesus Christ through loving words and actions, in the power of the Holy Spirit, so that they may receive him as their Savior and serve him as their Lord in the fellowship of his church. In the New Testament, the Greek word *evangelize* means "to share or announce good news."[1] Howard Snyder has asserted, "Evangelism is the first priority of the church's ministry. . . . The church that fails to evangelize is both biblically unfaithful and strategically shortsighted."[2] Jesus himself, in Luke 19:10, told us his main reason and top priority for coming to earth: "For the Son of Man came to seek and to save the lost." Gary McIntosh and Charles Arn, in *What Every Pastor Should Know*, started with "Ministry Rules for Evangelism and Outreach" as their first chapter because these are such important topics. They warned, "Churches that do not focus on these ministries will die in just a few generations."[3]

In Acts 1:8, Jesus told the apostles, "But you will receive power when the Holy Spirit comes on you; and you will be my witnesses in Jerusalem, and in all Judea and Samaria, and to the ends of the earth." The Holy Spirit's presence and power are primarily to enable us to be witnesses for Christ locally in evangelism wherever we are living and then globally and cross-culturally in missions, spreading out until we reach the ends of the earth. Actually, missions are now happening in our own backyards because many people groups of diverse ethnicities and nationalities have become immigrants and even refugees, moving here to the United States. But he has also called us to go and reach out cross-culturally to other countries and places, all over the world in world missions.

This chapter covers evangelism, missions, and social concern. Sharing the good news of salvation through faith in Jesus Christ by God's grace alone involves sharing the whole gospel with the whole person in the whole world. This also involves social concern for the poor and suffering and justice for the oppressed. In other words, the Great Commission (Matt. 28:18–20) must be obeyed together with the greatest commandment, to love God and our neighbors as ourselves (Matt. 22:37–40; Mark 12:29–31). The Christian life and Christian ministry can be summed up as knowing Christ and making him known, and loving God and loving others.

Win Arn and Charles Arn have rightly tied together evangelism and disciplemaking in their well-known book *The Master's Plan for Making Disciples*, which discusses how every Christian can be an effective witness for Christ with the support and help of an enabling and equipping church and pastor.[4] However, evangelism is still often a low priority in the church and in a Christian's life. The pastor's roles as evangelist[5] and missionary[6] are therefore crucial in helping parishioners become faithful and winsome witnesses for Christ and ensuring that evangelism and missions, as part of disciplemaking and spiritual formation, are priorities in the church.

Evangelism

There are many helpful books available on evangelism, including a number of recent ones.[7] Jesus has given us the mandate to be his witnesses in the power of the Holy Spirit (Acts 1:8). Paul also instructed Timothy as a young pastor or church leader, "But you, keep your head in all situations, endure hardship, do the work of an evangelist, discharge all the duties of your ministry" (2 Tim. 4:5). These are wise and biblical words for all of us who are pastors and church leaders. One of our roles as a pastor is to do the work of an evangelist—but not to do all of it or to do it all. Our role is also to equip our parishioners for works of service (including evangelism), to build up the body of Christ (Eph. 4:12). Therefore, we first need to serve as examples in evangelism by prayerfully and regularly sharing Jesus with others who do not yet know him. We can do this in many ways: meeting with people over a meal; listening to and conversing with people in natural settings such as on a plane or in a shopping mall or grocery store; visiting with people in their homes, in the church office, or in hospitals; and, of course, by sharing the gospel in large and small ways in our sermons. We can then share stories of how the Lord touched lives with the gospel as we reached out to people in ways that were really divine appointments orchestrated by God.

As pastors, we also need to organize training programs or events to help our parishioners learn how to share the gospel in a simple and effective way. Many tools can be used, such as the Four Spiritual Laws, which Bill Bright popularized for many years through Campus Crusade for Christ, now called Cru. In our postmodern context, contemporary methods have more recently been described, such as the four worlds or four circles diagram (designed for good, damaged by evil, restored for better, and sent together to heal) used by James Choung in *True Story*.[8] God uses all kinds of ways to bring people to Christ, and there is no one foolproof method.[9] I still use the Four Spiritual Laws and have seen people come to Christ through this older tool.

Recently, in a sermon and in my small group, I shared a true story of how the Lord gave me a divine appointment to lead someone to Christ on an airplane while flying to Denver for a Renovaré ministry team retreat in June 2017. I was hoping to be upgraded free to first class because of my frequent flyer status and was initially disappointed that it did not happen. However, I ended up sitting next to a man who had missed his flight on another airplane and was very stressed out. I had an opportunity to have a friendly and caring conversation with him and eventually felt led by the Spirit to share the Four Spiritual Laws with him, and he accepted Christ right then and there on the plane. Not being upgraded to first class quickly paled in comparison to the sacred privilege and joy of sharing the gospel with someone ready to receive the good news and leading him to Christ by the power of the Holy Spirit.

As pastors, we can also organize and run evangelistic events to share the gospel with others. This can be done in a more indirect and less confrontational way—for example, through a church picnic or a harvest festival in place of Halloween (to reach out to the neighborhood kids). It can also be done in a more direct way, such as through an outreach concert, a drama presentation, Vacation Bible School for kids, or an evangelistic message with an altar call at the end to challenge people to receive Christ as Lord and Savior and to follow him as his disciples. A well-known evangelistic outreach program called Alpha (www.alpharesources.org) has been used worldwide to touch millions of lives.

It combines a powerful DVD message with food, fellowship, discussions in small groups, and an eventual challenge to believe in Jesus and follow him. Our church has used many of these evangelistic methods, including Alpha. My wife, Angela, and I have had the wonderful opportunity of helping to lead several people to Christ through the Alpha program.

More recently, an intergenerational group of our church members, led by our youth minister, minister of family life ministries, and minister of discipleship and missions, has gone out to the neighboring community and a shopping mall to do "treasure hunting." They simply approach people to strike up a friendly and warm conversation and offer to pray for them and whatever needs they have. When appropriate, they share very briefly their testimony and the gospel in a nutshell and ask if anyone would be open to accepting Christ. We have had up to forty-two people do this, and a few people have come to Christ as a result. This has emboldened people, especially some who were initially afraid, to simply reach out to people in friendly conversations. The Holy Spirit is always present to empower us to be witnesses for Christ, in small or big ways, in direct or indirect ways, in traditional or contemporary ways, and in introverted or extroverted ways.

Those of us who are more introverted, with a quiet type of personality, can still engage in what Adam McHugh has called introverted evangelism, which involves more listening to people and these steps: narrow your focus, ask questions, ask for time, don't accept the premise (of the question posed by someone), find a comfortable environment, and know your role.[10] A similar approach has been described by Randy Newman in *Questioning Evangelism* that focuses on asking good questions and listening to others and their needs in the context of engaging them in meaningful spiritual conversations.[11] Michael Simpson, in *Permission Evangelism*, emphasized hanging out with unbelievers and letting them give us permission to share our faith: listening to them rather than talking so much, telling stories rather than aggressively defending our faith, and depending on the Holy Spirit rather than on formulas or methods of evangelism.[12] Elaine Heath has also described a more contemplative approach to Christian outreach in *The Mystic Way of Evangelism*.[13] These more contemporary approaches to evangelism can be used by a pastor to train and encourage more parishioners in the church to overcome their fears of and struggles with evangelism of the more traditional and assertive style. We can all participate in evangelism and witnessing as Jesus has called us to do in the power of the Holy Spirit, who is sensitive to our different personalities and preferred styles.

While we all, as Christians, have been called by Jesus to be his witnesses through evangelism, some of us may have the gift of evangelism or the evangelist (Eph. 4:11). Peter Wagner has defined the gift of the evangelist as "the special ability that God gives to certain members of the Body of Christ to share the gospel with unbelievers in such a way that men and women become Jesus' disciples and responsible members of the Body of Christ."[14] Those of us who have this gift need to be regularly engaged in evangelism and sharing Christ with people. The pastor as evangelist does not necessarily mean that every pastor has this gift. It does mean, however, that every pastor must be involved in giving some leadership to the church concerning evangelism and serving as an example of a faithful witness to Christ for the church he or she is pastoring.

In the area of evangelism, the pastor needs to reflect the heart and heartbeat of God for the lost. Two crucial verses stand out from Scripture: "This is good, and pleases God our Savior, who wants all people to be saved and to come to a knowledge of the truth" (1 Tim. 2:3–4); and "The Lord is not slow in keeping his promise, as some understand slowness. Instead he is patient with you, not wanting anyone to perish, but everyone to come to repentance" (2 Pet. 3:9). Evangelism should be a top priority for every pastor and every church.

Evangelism as a Spiritual Discipline

In writing about evangelism as a spiritual discipline of the Holy Spirit, Doug Gregg and I emphasized that "God wants us to depend on him, not on a method or strategy of evangelism. The key is not a method but a relationship. The way, the truth, and the life is a Person. We are to look to Jesus and depend on the Holy Spirit as we enter the discipline of witness."[15] Jesus modeled six characteristics of witnessing in the Spirit in his reaching out to the woman at the well in Samaria (John 4:1–42): be focused on God, be humble and vulnerable, see people for who they really are, enter into the lives of those we encounter, welcome others into our lives, and be honest and direct in our challenge.[16]

In making evangelism a way of life for every Christian, a pastor, through his or her preaching, teaching, and personal example, can encourage parishioners to put into practice the following ideas:

- ask the Holy Spirit to bring two people to mind who need to know Jesus as their Lord and Savior and pray for them and their salvation;
- spend time with the people being prayed for and engage in meaningful spiritual conversations with them, asking good questions and listening well to them while being sensitive to the Holy Spirit's work;

- invite these people individually for a meal at a restaurant or at home and gently share one's testimony and the gospel with them;
- depending on the Holy Spirit, challenge them to receive Christ and pray with them to accept Christ personally as Lord and Savior, if they are ready.

Pastors can also encourage parishioners to pray for divine appointments from the Lord so they can share Jesus with people using a tool such as the Four Spiritual Laws or the four circles; share their burden for the lost with a few Christian friends in a small group; and pray together for the salvation of family members, relatives, friends, and acquaintances who are not yet believers in Christ and for the joy and power of the Holy Spirit to be present in their witness.[17]

Servant Evangelism

Steve Sjogren, in *Conspiracy of Kindness*, years ago described a unique approach to evangelism that he called servant evangelism. It consists of deeds of love plus words of love plus adequate time.[18] Concrete examples of sharing the love of Jesus with others in servant evangelism include giving free car washes and cleaning toilets. It involves doing intentional acts of the fruit of the Holy Spirit (Gal. 5:22–23). We serve the Lord Jesus by serving others, and true servanthood includes servant evangelism.

In *Servant Warfare*, Sjogren defined kindness as "practical acts of mercy done by followers of Jesus who are inspired by the Holy Spirit to see others through the eyes of God,"[19] and concluded, "Small things done with great love can change the world."[20] He also defined servant warfare as "using the power of kindness to penetrate the spiritually darkened hearts of people with the love of God."[21] Evangelism does involve spiritual warfare because the devil hates our evangelistic efforts, including servant evangelism. We need to use the full armor of God in spiritual warfare against the devil and the demonic powers of evil (Eph. 6:10–18; 1 Pet. 5:8–9), especially prayer in the Spirit (Eph. 6:18) and the Word of God, which is the sword of the spirit (Eph. 6:17). We are assured that he who is in us is greater than he who is in the world (1 John 4:4). Sjogren has reminded us that Spirit-inspired kindness is also a powerful weapon against spiritual darkness and oppression. Evil is overcome and spiritual darkness is dispelled by such kindness and the powerful light of Jesus and his love and truth shining into the hearts of unbelievers and drawing them to himself.

We can be "graced" witnesses who have been deeply touched and blessed by the extravagant and even scandalous grace of God, which we do not deserve, given to us in Jesus Christ through his death and resurrection for us. Philip Yancey described such graced witnesses as "grace-full" Christians.[22] Evangelism ultimately needs to come from the very heart of God. It needs to be full of love and grace for lost people and based on kindness and compassion for others.

Seven Rules for Effective Evangelism

There are various approaches to evangelism, with different methods and styles. Our own personalities and spiritual gifts will also influence our particular approach to evangelism. There is no one right or best way. McIntosh and Arn have provided seven guidelines for effective evangelism that can be helpful in the local church. First is the Great Commission Conscience Rule: at least three out of every five elected church officers or leaders should have a Great Commission conscience, guiding the church to be outward-focused, with evangelism and disciplemaking as top priorities. Second is the Receptivity Rule: for the most effective outreach and evangelism, the church should focus on people who are open and receptive. Third is the Entry Event Rule: for effective community evangelism, the church should offer at least nine entry events each year (e.g., Christmas pageant, harvest festival, church picnic, trip to local sports game, special seminars on family and parenting issues and marital issues, kids' events such as a swimming party or Vacation Bible School). Fourth is the Side-Door Ministry Rule: a minimum of two side doors should be organized by the church each year. A side door is a church-sponsored program, event, or group in which a nonmember can be comfortably and regularly involved in order to build good relationships with church members. Some examples include events or groups for people who ride motorcycles, or are newlyweds, or are fishermen, or enjoy scrapbooking, or like camping and hiking, or are single dads. Fifth is the Unchurched Friends Rule: each parishioner should have an average of nine or more unchurched friends or family members in order for the church to grow. Sixth is the Evangelism Training Rule: churches that effectively reach their communities train at least 10 percent of their parishioners in friendship evangelism every year. The training should help parishioners answer four basic but crucial questions: (1) How has being a Christian impacted my life? (2) What does being a Christian mean? (3) Why would I want my friend to become a Christian and join my church? and (4) How does someone become a Christian or accept Christ? Seventh is the Number of Conversions Rule: about 12 percent of nonbelieving or unchurched friends and relatives come to Christ in churches that have training programs to help their members reach out to such contacts.[23]

It is therefore crucial to have a systematic program of evangelism training for our parishioners and also to organize events and groups for evangelistic outreach. Using friendship evangelism is a basic approach. Nevertheless, there is still a proper place for Christian apologetics[24] to help us provide reasonable answers to questions raised by non-Christians as we witness to them about Jesus, but it should always be used with gentleness[25] and respect (1 Pet. 3:15).

The Importance of Prayer in Evangelism

Since spiritual warfare is real and particularly relevant in the context of evangelism, prayer is crucial in this area, both for protection and for the salvation of the lost. Ed Silvoso has emphasized the importance of prayer in evangelism: "Prayer is the most tangible trace of eternity in the human heart. Intercessory prayer on behalf of the felt needs of the lost is the best way to open their eyes to the light of the gospel."[26] Both Søren Kierkegaard and John Calvin reportedly said that the most loving thing we can do for others is pray for them.

Evangelism and Church Planting

Evangelism through the local church will often lead to church planting, or starting new churches. Pastors need to be sensitive to the Spirit's leading in this area and be willing to take the risky and often painful steps to plant a new church. Church planting can be difficult and disruptive to the established local church, with its comfort zones and often inward-focused, consumeristic mentality and culture. However, the Lord has called us to partner with him to advance his kingdom, and this includes church planting, which is crucial to fulfilling the Great Commission. In fact, Peter Wagner has strongly asserted, *"The single most effective evangelistic methodology under heaven is planting new churches."*[27] Two important books on church planting are *Church Planting Movements* by David Garrison (see www.churchplantingmovements.com) and *T4T: A Discipleship Re-Revolution* by Steve Smith with Ying Kai.[28] The T4T, or "Training for Trainers," church-planting movement has been powerfully blessed by God since it began in Asia in 2001, with over 1.7 million baptisms and more than 150,000 new churches planted.

As the senior pastor of my church, I have been involved in a couple of church plants. Though full of challenges, and properly done only after much prayer and consultation with church leaders and other pastoral staff, church planting is an exciting and crucial part of evangelism. Our church association, First Evangelical Church Association (FECA), recently revised our vision statement to make church planting a key focus and priority: "God has called us to grow and plant life-transforming, holistic, sustainable and reproducing churches for the advancement of His kingdom and glory."[29] We have planted churches locally and abroad or globally. FECA member churches, including our church, which was a founding member in 1997, are committed to a joint and integrative ministry of spirituality, mission, and social concern, in satisfying our Father's heart. Church planting can therefore occur locally or abroad globally in other countries. We pastors need to be prayerfully open to church planting, not just locally but also globally, especially among unreached people groups in different parts of the world,[30] which leads us to the topic of missions.

Missions

Evangelism broadens to missions as we reach out cross-culturally and also globally to the ends of the earth to fulfill the Great Commission (Matt. 28:18–20; Mark 16:15; John 20:21; Acts 1:8). Much has also been written about missions, including some recent and significant books.[31]

The pastor as missionary or lead missionary[32] must first have a clear vision of what missions involves. Andrew Walls and Cathy Ross have listed five marks of missions:

1. to proclaim the Good News of the Kingdom
2. to teach, baptize, and nurture new believers
3. to respond to human need by loving service
4. to seek to transform unjust structures of society
5. to strive to safeguard the integrity of creation and sustain and renew the life of the earth[33]

John Piper, in *Let the Nations be Glad!*, emphasized the supremacy of God in missions—especially through worship, prayer, and suffering. He explained that God has ordained for the mission of his church to advance "not only by the fuel of worship and in the power of prayer but also at the price of suffering."[34] Piper's powerful and biblical conclusion (mentioned earlier in this book) on the supremacy of God in missions is this:

> The ultimate goal of God in all of history is to uphold and display his glory for the enjoyment of the redeemed from every tribe and tongue of his people, because God is most glorified in us when we are most satisfied in him. Delight is

a greater tribute than duty. . . . The greatest news in all the world is that God's ultimate aim to be glorified and our aim to be satisfied are not at odds. . . . Therefore, the church is bound to engage with the Lord of glory in his cause. It is our unspeakable privilege to be caught up with him in the greatest movement in history—the ingathering of the elect from every tribe and language and people and nation until the full number of Gentiles comes in and all Israel is saved and the Son of Man descends with power and great glory as King of kings and Lord of lords and the earth is full of the knowledge of his glory as the waters cover the sea forever and ever.[35]

Piper based his conclusion on four key biblical texts: "Declare his glory among the nations, his marvelous deeds among all peoples" (Ps. 96:3); "Let the peoples praise you, O God; let all the peoples praise you! Let the nations be glad and sing for joy" (Ps. 67:3–4 ESV); "After this I looked, and there before me was a great multitude that no one could count, from every nation, tribe, people and language, standing before the throne and before the lamb. They were wearing white robes and holding palm branches in their hands" (Rev. 7:9); and "This gospel of the kingdom will be preached in the whole world as a testimony to all nations, and then the end will come" (Matt. 24:14).

The pastor's role in missions should include knowing enough about missions to instruct parishioners on the following topics:

- Missionaries—differentiating between the Timothy-type missionary, who stays on the mission field in the same place even after churches have been planted, and the Paul-type missionary, who is more itinerant and moves on to other frontier areas
- Nations—we are called to reach more nations, or people groups, and not just more people; reached and unreached (people groups that are less than 2 percent Christian are unreached)
- The 10/40 window—an area of the world that spans from 10 degrees north of the equator to 40 degrees north of the equator, from Northwest Africa to East Asia, containing the majority of the world's unreached peoples
- The global south—a term referring to countries in Latin America, Africa, and parts of Asia where the largest numbers of evangelical Christians can now be found; they are sending more and more missionaries to the ends of the world[36]

In addition to educating parishioners about missions through preaching and teaching, the pastor can do a number of other things to lead the church in missions:

- Pray for missionaries and the lost in church worship services and prayer meetings
- Organize an annual missions conference with speakers who can encourage, instruct, and challenge parishioners to be "world Christians" with hearts and minds for missions even if they are senders and not full-time missionaries (though we all need to be full-time Christians wherever we are or work)
- Challenge the congregation to give financially for the support of missionaries from the church as well as others involved in the cause of missions, to regularly pray for missionaries and the world, and to go on short-term mission trips that the church organizes and supports and to give testimonies afterward in worship services and other meetings
- Encourage others to go as full-time missionaries if God calls and gifts them to serve in this capacity

The pastor can also help form and/or lead a missions committee to help the church focus on this area of church ministry.

God is a missional God, and he wants his people in the church to all be a missional people caught up with him and his world mission on earth and not just periodically think about missions. The mission of God becomes the mission of God's people, as Christopher Wright has so powerfully and biblically emphasized.[37] He has also pointed out that since 1910 the number of Christians in the world's population has hardly changed at all and has remained at about one-third of the population worldwide. Despite the recent tremendous growth of the church around the globe, especially in the global south, "there are still millions of individuals and thousands of peoples who have never yet even heard the name of the Lord Jesus Christ and the good news of what God has done through his cross and resurrection for the salvation of the world. Millions still wait for any portion of the Word of God to exist in their mother tongue."[38]

I received a form letter from Sam Metcalf, president of Church Resource Ministries, in which he shared a haunting statistic: in 1985, 24 percent of the world's population (1.1 billion) did not have access to the gospel; in 2017, that number was over 28 percent of the world's population or 2.1 billion people.[39] The task of missions to reach out to all the people groups of the world is still before us in a challenging and sobering way. God aches in his heart for the lost. May our hearts also ache with his, and may we live and go in obedience to make disciples of all nations. As mentioned earlier, members of some of these nations are actually in our backyards as immigrants or refugees. Missions can also be local as we reach out to people from different ethnicities and nationalities in cross-cultural ministry. But the call to be involved in global missions, especially to unreached people groups, is still loud and clear. Regular prayer, interceding for missionaries and for the lost worldwide, is a crucial part of this. *Operation World* by Jason Mandryk (www.operationworld.org) and *An Insider's Guide to Praying for the World* by Brian Stiller are helpful resources for engaging in such prayer.[40]

Wright raised several heart-searching and sobering questions for all of us as God's people to answer if we are going to fully and joyfully become God's missionary people: Where does my life fit into the great story of God's mission for all of creation (rather than where does God fit into my life story)? What would it mean to apply my life in obedience to the Bible (rather than trying to apply the Bible to fit my life)? What kind of church does God want us to be to fulfill his mission in all its fullness (rather than what can be included in the mission God expects from us as his church)? What kind of me does God want for his mission (rather than what kind of mission does God have for me)?[41] He stated, "*Fundamentally, our mission (if it is biblically informed and validated) means our committed participation as God's people, at God's invitation and command, in God's own mission within the history of God's world for the redemption of God's creation.*"[42]

God is a missional God, and he wants his people in the church to be missional people, to be involved in his mission on earth. The mission of God is the mission of God's people, as Wright has emphasized.[43] But what does it mean to be a missional church? Much has been written in recent years about the missional church.[44] Michael Frost and Alan Hirsch have provided this definition: "A missional church is one whose primary commitment is to the missionary calling of the people of God. As such, it is one that aligns with God's missionary purposes in the world. A missional leader is one who takes mission seriously and sees it as the driving energy behind all that the church does. The missional church is a sent church with one of its defining values being the development of a church life and practice that is contextualized to that culture to which it believes it is sent."[45] They pointed out that the traditional Christendom-mode church has three major flaws of being attractional (people being attracted or coming into the church), dualistic (splitting sacred from secular, holy from unholy, and in from out), and hierarchical (with a top-down, bureaucratic, and overly religious form of leadership).[46] In contrast, the missional church is incarnational (reaching out into the cracks and crevices of society), messianic (in its spirituality, seeing the world and God in a more integrated and holistic way, as Jesus the Messiah does), and apostolic (using a biblical practice of shared leadership based on the fivefold model

Paul described in Ephesians 4:1–16: apostle, prophet, evangelist, shepherd (pastor), and teacher (or APEST).[47]

Alan Roxburgh and Scott Boren defined a traditional or more typical church as a place we go to "worship, receive training in Christian life, have one's child baptized, bury someone, find community with other Christians, receive care and nurture from one another and from professional pastors, and equip one another in service and ministry."[48] In contrast, they defined a missional church as a church shaped by the mystery of its formation, the memory of its calling, and the mission of God in the world: "The church is God's missionary people. There is no participation in Christ without participation in God's mission in the world. The church in North America to a large extent has lost its memory to the point that mission is but a single element in multifaceted, programmatic congregations serving the needs of its members."[49]

Although the word *missionary* can be fraught with negative connotations and stereotypes, it is still appropriate to describe a missional church as a missionary entity. Lance Ford and Brad Brisco stated, "The church doesn't just send missionaries, the church *is* the missionary."[50] They went on to emphasize, based on John 17:15 and 20:21, "God is a missionary God who sends a missionary church. As Jesus was sent into the world, we too are sent into the world."[51] God is a missional God, and we as his people are a missional people, a sent people.

Kim Hammond and Darren Cronshaw emphasized the idea of sentness by contrasting two competing overarching postures that the people of God can assume and practice today. A typical church consists mainly of consumers who demand religious services and goods to be provided in the church and for church members. A missional church of missionaries, all sent and sending into the world, has sentness as its major characteristic.[52] They then provided helpful descriptions of six postures of missional Christians in elaborating on our sentness: "sent people, understanding that God has a mission and that mission has a church; submerged ministry, following Jesus and moving among places and people; shalom spirituality, seeking restoration for individuals, communities and all things; safe places, for people from diverse backgrounds to find faith and community; sharing life, forming teams around a common vision and strength of relationships; and standing in the gap, empowering pioneering leaders and missional experiments."[53]

In emphasizing sentness and the missionary nature of a missional church and focusing on the scattering of God's people, we can make the mistake of forgetting that God also gathers his church. We are a people gathered and scattered by God. Ross Hastings has offered a corrective by pointing out that a theology of the missional church sees it as participational, with "union in and participation with the missional God, who is bidirectional in his missional nature. He *both sends and brings*. The church in union with God will therefore be a bidirectional, a sending and a bringing church. It will gather to press into that union. . . . Its outgoing mission as the scattered church is also a participation in the ongoing mission on earth that Christ began and then entrusted his people to finish (John 20:21; Acts 1:1). Its task is not to do mission but to join God in what he by the Spirit is already doing."[54] To those of us who understand and lead our churches to be missional churches, he offered a cautionary note: we should be humble and not think of ourselves as superior to other pastors and churches who may be struggling to move beyond traditional models of being church that cater more to consumeristic church members.[55] At the same time, we need to engage in missional preaching that focuses on equipping our members to become faithful witnesses of Jesus Christ, as God's missional people, in culturally relevant ways where they are.[56]

Social Concern

As mentioned earlier, sharing the good news of salvation involves social concern, as we obey both the Great Commission and the greatest commandment to love our neighbors as ourselves. One of the six postures of missional Christians mentioned earlier is shalom spirituality, through which we seek, in a Christlike way, to bring restoration or wholeness to individuals, communities, and all things. This includes social concern to help the poor and the suffering and social action to bring justice to the oppressed, locally and globally,[57] as we are empowered by the Holy Spirit to love God and our neighbors (Matt. 22:37–38; Mark 12:30–31). Micah 6:8 says, "He has shown you, O mortal, what is good. And what does the LORD require of you? To act justly and to love mercy and to walk humbly with your God."

It is therefore crucial to fill "the hole in our gospel," as Richard Stearns has put it,[58] with Christlike love manifested in concrete social concern and social action. Mark Labberton, president of Fuller Theological Seminary, has written challenging and helpful books on the dangerous act of living God's call to justice and the dangerous act of loving our neighbors by seeing them through the eyes of Jesus.[59] Both acts include caring for all of God's world through creation care,[60] culture care,[61] and even culture making.[62]

Some examples of concrete acts of social concern that our church has been involved in include the following: helping to build houses with Habitat for

Humanity, feeding the homeless, ministering to refugees abroad, reaching out to orphans and HIV patients in India, sending shoeboxes with gifts for children through Operation Christmas Child, tutoring immigrant children, and providing love offerings or gifts for those in financial need in our church and beyond. We had a Social Concern Committee that has been integrated into our Missions Committee.

Acts of social concern will stretch us beyond our comfort zones, especially those of us in the United States whose lives and cultures are characterized by self-absorption, self-fulfillment, and self-focused consumerism. The call to follow Jesus as his disciples, to reach out in a holistic, Christlike way, will cost us our time, our money, our talents and gifts, and sometimes even our lives, if need be. Let us follow Christ in union with him and by the power of the Spirit to be missional pastors leading missional churches to "become poor" and to show sacrificial love, that others may be enriched in Christ: "For you know the grace of our Lord Jesus Christ, that though he was rich, yet for your sake he became poor, so that you through his poverty might become rich" (2 Cor. 8:9).

RECOMMENDED READINGS

Arn, Win, and Charles Arn. *The Master's Plan for Making Disciples: Every Christian an Effective Witness through an Enabling Church*. 2nd ed. Grand Rapids: Baker, 1998.

Chan, Samuel. *Evangelism in a Skeptical World: How to Make the Unbelievable News about Jesus More Believable*. Grand Rapids: Zondervan, 2018.

Chatraw, Joshua D., and Mark D. Allen. *Apologetics at the Cross: An Introduction for Christian Witness*. Grand Rapids: Zondervan, 2018.

Chuong, James. *True Story: A Christianity Worth Believing In*. Downers Grove, IL: InterVarsity, 2008.

Coleman, Robert E. *The Master Plan of Evangelism*. Rev. ed. Grand Rapids: Revell, 2006.

Ford, Lance, and Brad Brisco. *The Missional Quest: Becoming a Church of the Long Run*. Downers Grove, IL: InterVarsity, 2013.

Frost, Michael, and Alan Hirsch. *The Shaping of Things to Come: Innovation and Mission for the 21st Century Church*. Rev. ed. Grand Rapids: Baker Books, 2013.

Garrison, David. *Church Planting Movements: How God Is Redeeming a Lost World*. Monument, CO: WIGTake Resources, 2004.

Labberton, Mark. *The Dangerous Act of Loving Your Neighbor: Seeing Others through the Eyes of Jesus*. Downers Grove, IL: InterVarsity 2010.

———. *The Dangerous Act of Worship: Living God's Call to Justice*. Downers Grove, IL: InterVarsity, 2007.

Mandryk, Jason. *Operation World: The Definitive Prayer Guide to Every Nation*. Downers Grove, IL: InterVarsity, 2010.

McDowell, Josh, and Sean McDowell. *Evidence That Demands a Verdict: Life-Changing Truth for a Skeptical World*. Rev. ed. Nashville: Thomas Nelson, 2017.

Mittleberg, Mark. *Becoming a Contagious Church: Revolutionizing the Way We View and Do Evangelism*. Grand Rapids: Zondervan, 2000.

Myers, Bryant L. *Engaging Globalization: The Poor, Christian Mission, and Our Hyperconnected World*. Grand Rapids: Baker Academic, 2017.

Piper, John. *Let the Nations Be Glad! The Supremacy of God in Missions*. 3rd ed. Grand Rapids: Baker Academic, 2010.

Roxburgh, Alan J., and M. Scott Boren. *Introducing the Missional Church: What It Is, Why It Matters, How to Become One*. Grand Rapids: Baker Books, 2009.

Silvoso, Ed. *Prayer Evangelism*. Ventura, CA: Regal, 2000.

———. *That None Should Perish*. Ventura, CA: Regal, 1994.

Sjogren, Steve. *Conspiracy of Kindness: A Unique Approach to Sharing the Love of Jesus*. Rev. ed. Grand Rapids: Bethany House, 2008.

Stearns, Richard. *The Hole in Our Gospel*. Nashville: Thomas Nelson, 2010.

Sunquist, Scott W. *Understanding Christian Mission: Participation in Suffering and Glory*. Grand Rapids: Baker Academic, 2013.

Teasdale, Mark R. *Evangelism for Non-Evangelists: Sharing the Gospel Authentically*. Downers Grove, IL: IVP Academic, 2016.

Wagner, C. Peter. *Church Planting for a Greater Harvest: A Comprehensive Guide*. Ventura, CA: Regal, 1990.

Walls, Andrew F., and Cathy Ross, eds. *Mission in the Twenty-First Century: Exploring the Five Marks of Global Mission*. Maryknoll, NY: Orbis, 2008.

Woodward, J. R. *Creating a Missional Culture: Equipping the Church for the Sake of the World*. Downers Grove, IL: InterVarsity, 2012.

Wright, Christopher J. H. *The Mission of God's People: A Biblical Theology of the Church's Mission*. Grand Rapids: Zondervan, 2010.

9

Leadership

L eadership is another crucial responsibility for the pastor or church leader.[1] The literature available on leadership in general, as well as on Christian leadership in particular, is voluminous.[2] Bernice Ledbetter, Robert Banks, and David Greenhalgh have written a second edition of *Reviewing Leadership*,[3] which is a comprehensive Christian evaluation of current approaches to leadership. It is of great help and benefit to pastors, especially in their role as leader in the church. I have previously written on servant-hood and leadership in *Full Service*[4] and in a chapter in *The Three Tasks of Leadership*, edited by Eric Jacobsen,[5] a book I highly recommend to pastors. This present chapter discusses the concept of servant leadership, secular and biblical approaches to leadership, and the role of vision in leadership.

Servant Leadership and Servanthood

Many books have been written on a biblical approach to leadership, and most of them emphasize the concept of servant leadership. However, servant leadership has also been critiqued as an approach that is not necessarily biblical or distinctively Christian.[6] Robert Greenleaf first popularized the concept of servant leadership in 1977 in his now classic and well-known book, *Servant Leadership*.[7] Although he emphasized that leaders are first of all servants, many authors who use this concept put leadership first and see servanthood only as a means or approach to advance leadership functions and roles. A biblical perspective on this topic, however, affirms that servanthood is more foundational and essential in Christian life and ministry than leadership, even servant leadership. Jesus has first and foremost called us all, as Christians, to be his beloved servants, following his own example as the Master Servant (John 13:14–17; Phil. 2:5–11; see also Matt. 20:28; Luke 22:26–27). Only some of us may also be called and gifted to serve as leaders in him and for him.

Steve Hayner, when he was president of InterVarsity Christian Fellowship USA, years ago in 1998 wrote the following powerful words, emphasizing the need for true, loving, and humble Christlike servanthood rather than leadership per se or even servant leadership:

> There is a growing amount of modern literature on servant leadership. But I'm not sure I agree with leadership as the fundamental concept and servanthood as the modifier. Jesus gives an unmodified call to us to be servants—serving God and serving one another. Along the way, God may call us into specific roles of leadership. But there are no indications that obtaining those roles should be a believer's ultimate ambition. . . . Our ambition is not leadership, but servanthood. Our task is not to grow leaders, but to make disciples who will follow Jesus. Our goal is not to get out there and get things done, but to listen and obey. Our call is not to exercise power but to be faithful to our Lord and the way of the servant.
>
> How God chooses to use his servants is his concern. We may be called to lead or to follow, to exert authority or to submit, to turn our God-given gifts in one direction or another. But that is God's business. Our identity, our meaning in life, our sense of significance, and our self-worth are not to be based on the roles we fill, the power we wield, or the numbers we lead. We play to an audience of one, who loves us, affirms us, and uses us. . . . We should long to hear from our God the words, "Well done, you good and faithful servant!"[8]

Banks and Ledbetter, in an earlier edition of *Reviewing Leadership*, made this observation: "The trouble with the phrase 'servant leadership' . . . is that though it moves away from inadequate views of leading others, it still gets the order of the words wrong. Leadership is the key term and servant is the qualifier. What we need today are not, as is so often suggested, more *servant leaders*, but properly understood, more *leading servants*."[9] Leading servants are first and foremost servants who have been called to be leaders and gifted with the spiritual gift of leadership (Rom. 12:8) so they can also serve in leading. *Leading servant* may be a better term to use than *servant leadership*, which still tends to emphasize leadership, or *servant leader*, which may describe a "corporate CEO in disguise," as Edward Zaragoza has claimed.[10]

Ultimately, servanthood is foundational and essential to biblical leadership. Leadership is therefore always secondary to servanthood, despite many claims today in the church that leaders and leadership are the most crucial hope for the church. I have asserted, from a biblical perspective, that "Jesus Christ, through the church, is the hope of the world, and servants are the hope of the church."[11] Leaders who have not learned to be humble, loving, obedient servants of Jesus Christ can actually be harmful to the church and the world. Due to ego, pride, arrogance, drivenness, and unsanctified ambition to quickly achieve results and numerical church growth, they can end up building their own kingdoms rather than the kingdom of God and thereby harm the people they are supposed to be shepherding. A great temptation for pastors and church leaders is to try to do great things for God. But in trying to do great things for God, we can end up trying to be great ourselves or to do great things more for ourselves or our churches than for God.

Biblical servanthood, however, focuses on doing things for a great God. In simply doing things for a great God in loving obedience by the power of the Holy Spirit, we can be content and joyful to do small things with great love for others or sometimes big or great things for God if he wills. It is all up to God, not us. We do not seek great things for ourselves (Jer. 45:5). We seek instead the great God himself and to be satisfied in him so he is most glorified in us. Therefore, servanthood 101 should be an essential and required course for any training program on leadership. *Full Service: Moving from Self-Serve Christianity to Total Servanthood* can be used as a basic text on biblical servanthood.

Leadership and Management

It is interesting to note that, even in the secular world, leadership and management have come under great scrutiny and attack. For example, Barbara Kellerman, who is well known for her pioneering work on leadership and followership, strongly critiqued the leadership industry (as a scholarly discipline and a set of practical skills) for its failures and extravagant claims without real results. She emphasized the need to teach good followership instead of good leadership, especially since much teaching on leadership does not have empirical evidence to back it up and is done by gurus with leadership mantras of all sorts. She concluded, "Leadership is in danger of becoming obsolete. Not leaders—there will always be leaders—but leadership as being more consequential than followership, leadership as learning we should pay to acquire, leadership as anything better than business as usual, leadership as a solution to whatever problems, and leadership as an agreement of which merit is a component."[12]

Similarly, Matthew Stewart, in *The Management Myth*, critiqued the field of management, focusing on why the so-called management experts and even

MBA programs keep getting it wrong. He pointed out that there is a great deal of pseudoscience in so-called scientific management or MBA programs and even suggested that an MBA (master's in business administration) usually amounts to a lot of rubbish! He came to this conclusion:

> What makes for a good manager? If we put all of their heads together, the great management thinkers at the end of the day give us the same, simple, and true answer. A good manager is someone with a facility for analysis and an even greater talent for synthesis; someone who has an eye for the details and for the one big thing that really matters; someone who is able to reflect on facts in a disinterested way, who is always dissatisfied with pat answers and the conventional wisdom, and who therefore takes a certain pleasure in knowledge itself; someone with a wide knowledge of the world and an even better knowledge of the way people work; someone who knows how to treat people with respect; someone with honesty, integrity, trustworthiness, and the other things that make up character; someone, in short, who understands oneself and the world around us well enough to know how to make it better. By this definition, of course, a good manager is nothing more or less than a good and well-educated person.[13]

These critiques of both leadership and management should make us pastors and church leaders think twice before we buy in to the latest fads and techniques of so-called great leadership and effective management, including the most up-to-date MBA mantras and methods. We must not wholeheartedly adopt secular approaches to leadership and management that are based on the CEO model of running and leading corporations. The church is a living organism more than an organization, and Christian leadership, led by the Holy Spirit in union with Christ, is different and unique. It should be cross shaped and discipleship centered, and the character and spirituality of the pastor should be of prime importance.[14]

Yet despite the strong critiques and sobering assessments of leadership approaches, leadership is still necessary, and we must not be so extreme in our negative reactions to secular approaches to leadership that we proverbially throw out the baby with the bathwater. We can still learn much from experts in the field.

Eric Yaverbaum has summarized the top fifteen leadership strategies of the world's most successful CEOs based on interviews with one hundred top CEOs. They are as follows:

1. Have a clear vision, a specific direction, and a goal for your organization.
2. Focus on the two or three things most important to your vision and goals. Don't spread your attention too thin.

3. Communicate your vision, strategy, goals, and mission to everyone involved.
4. Listen to what others tell you. Be willing to accept and act upon criticism and suggestions.
5. Surround yourself with the right people, a strong team.
6. Treat your employees exceedingly well. Help them become successful in their careers and their lives.
7. Apply the Golden Rule: Do unto others what you would have others do unto you.
8. Be in a business you love and are passionate about.
9. Constantly innovate to gain and sustain competitive advantage and serve your customers better.
10. Plan everything. Leave nothing to chance.
11. Be a leader and actually *lead*. Take responsibility. Make tough decisions.
12. Lead by example.
13. Listen to the people who are closest to the customers and marketplace. They will give you your best advice and input.
14. Set performance goals and establish metrics by which you can measure your performance and results.
15. Be service-oriented.[15]

In the well-known book *Winning*, Jack Welch, former CEO of General Electric, and Suzy Welch highlighted what successful leaders do:

Leaders relentlessly upgrade their team, using every encounter as an opportunity to evaluate, coach, and build self-confidence; leaders make sure people not only see the vision, they live and breathe it; leaders get into everyone's skin, exuding positive energy and optimism; leaders establish trust with candor, transparency, and credit; leaders have the courage to make unpopular decisions and gut calls; leaders probe and push with a curiosity that borders on skepticism, making sure that questions are answered with action; leaders inspire risk taking and learning by setting the example; leaders celebrate.[16]

Marcus Buckingham has pointed out that great leaders possess optimism and ego, both essential for rallying people to a better future. They also have the one thing that is crucial in great leadership: clarity, based on insight, discipline, and courage.[17]

In an interview published in *Leadership*, James Collins, author of the bestseller *Good to Great: Why Some Companies Make the Leap—and Others*

Don't,[18] said, "One of the things from *Good to Great* that really resonated with church leaders was the level 5 Leadership finding, that leaders who took companies from good to great are characterized by personal humility and by a fierce dedication to a cause that is larger than themselves."[19] More recently, in *How the Mighty Fall and Why Some Companies Never Give In*, Collins described five stages of decline in the fall of mighty companies: stage 1: hubris born of success; stage 2: undisciplined pursuit of more; stage 3: denial of risk and peril; stage 4: grasping for salvation; and stage 5: capitulation to irrelevance or death.[20] Based on a commencement speech given by Winston Churchill in 1941 in which he repeatedly echoed to never give in, Collins stated that we should never give in and never, ever give up on our core values: "Failure is not so much a physical state as a state of mind: success is falling down, and getting up one more time, without end."[21]

We as pastors and church leaders can learn some helpful lessons from the secular literature on leadership. However, some views we need to reject from a biblical perspective, such as those that emphasize ego; an obsession with success, greatness, self-effort, and self-sufficiency; and taking control, forgetting the sovereignty of God and his ultimate control over all things. Leadership without following Jesus and being guided by the Holy Spirit and God's Word is a very dangerous thing and can be sinful, self-centered, and ego-obsessed. Therefore, we need to have a biblical perspective on distinctively Christian leadership.

Christian Leadership

The literature on Christian leadership consists of two major types: books that incorporate ideas from leadership in general, and those that strongly critique secular leadership and provide biblical perspectives and alternatives to leadership that are more distinctively Christian.

An example of the first type is the well-known writings of Christian leadership expert John Maxwell. He distilled and summarized the literature on leadership in general in his book *The 21 Irrefutable Laws of Leadership*, concluding that if we follow them, then people will follow us.[22] He has also written *The 21 Indispensable Qualities of a Leader*, outlining what will help us become the person others will want to follow.[23] However, whether his twenty-one laws of leadership are really irrefutable or whether his twenty-one qualities of a leader are really indispensable is open to debate. We need to be careful and biblically astute before integrating so many laws or qualities from the literature on leadership into our own Christian approach to leadership.

In fact, some of his laws and qualities can be questioned and rejected from a biblical perspective.

Before we examine more biblical approaches to Christian leadership, we need to define and clarify leadership, because there are actually differing views. Walter Wright, former president of Regent College in Vancouver, British Columbia, defined leadership as follows: "Leadership is a relationship—a relationship in which one person seeks to influence the thoughts, behaviors, beliefs or values of another person."[24] He raised the question about whether every Christian is a leader and answered, "Yes, to the extent that we seek to influence others and make a difference in the lives around us."[25] Others have defined leadership or a leader in a narrower and more specific sense. For example, John Stott has pointed out that "a leader . . . is someone who commands a following. To lead is to go ahead, to show the way and inspire other people to follow."[26] Robert Clinton, in *The Making of a Leader*, provided this definition: "Leadership is a dynamic process in which a man or woman with God-given capacity influences a specific group of God's people toward His purposes for the group."[27] I believe that leadership is better defined in this narrower and more specific sense.

All Christians, however, are called to be followers, or disciples, of Jesus Christ. Therefore, followership is actually more crucial and foundational than leadership. Eugene Peterson has written, "Christian leadership is built on the foundation of followership—following Jesus. For those of us who are in positions of leadership—our following skills take priority over our leadership skills. Leadership that is not well-grounded in followership—following Jesus—is dangerous. . . . In our scriptures, following is far more frequently addressed than leading. The person we follow is the primary influence on the leader we become. Christians follow Jesus."[28]

Aubrey Malphurs defined leaders as servants with the capacity and credibility to influence people in a particular context to pursue their God-given direction. He emphasized that, from a biblical perspective, a Christian leader must be a Christian, be a committed Christ follower, have divine revelation as his or her source of truth, emphasize godly character, understand the importance of motives, serve through the power of the Holy Spirit, practice godly servant leadership, and preferably have the gift of leadership (though this is not mandatory).[29]

Among the Christian authors who are critical of the secular approaches to leadership and of Christian attempts to integrate so-called laws of leadership into Christian leadership and ministry is Lance Ford. In *Unleader*, he strongly critiqued secular ideas of leadership, especially those based on the CEO and MBA models. He described our contemporary obsession with leadership, even in the church, as "leaderoholism."[30] He advocated abandoning leadership of the wrong kind and instead embracing servantship based on biblical servanthood and discipleship, or followership, and involvement in discipling one another. He reported that a quick search on Amazon.com of books on the topics of Christian leadership and discipleship showed there were around twenty-four thousand books (in 2011), of which 65 percent were on Christian leadership and 35 percent were on discipleship, with only 2 percent on followership. He also found stunning results in a search of New Testament verses that mention "discipleship," "following," and "leadership": "disciple" is mentioned 260 times, "follow me" 23 times, and "lead" or "leader" only 7 times. The ratio of discipleship/followership to leadership is therefore forty to one![31]

Ford strongly advocated for true servants of Jesus Christ to lead in a non-hierarchical way as unleaders, mutually supportive and accountable to other servants. He criticized positions and titles such as senior pastor or lead pastor as being unbiblical because they are based on hierarchical models of pastoral leadership with a so-called pecking order in the church. He claimed that the only real senior pastor found in the Bible is Jesus Christ, the "Chief Shepherd" (1 Pet. 5:4).[32] He concludes with the following:

> Unleaders are followers of Jesus who invite others to follow them into a life of servantship. Unleaders shun titles and applause and find their greatest joy in shining the light on the supreme beauty and wonder of Jesus Christ. Unleaders refuse to touch, much less hijack, his glory. They serve God in humility and obscurity as much as possible. Unleaders treat their fellow servants with mutual honor and respect as peers and co-followers of Christ. They embrace the family of God as a covenant of kindred fellowship. Unleaders follow Jesus embracing the towel and basin of serving along the journey.[33]

Ford's radical emphasis on biblical servanthood and discipleship as the foundation of true Christian leadership, or unleadership, resonates deeply with me as I have similarly written *Full Service* as a biblical focus on moving from self-serve Christianity to total servanthood, and not servant leadership or leadership per se.[34]

In *Upside-Down Leadership*, Taylor Field challenged readers to rethink influence and success or leadership from a radically biblical perspective. Similar to Ford in *Unleader*, Field presented his version of Christian leadership as upside-down leadership, with ten radical principles: stop leading; forget results; make no plans; think small; associate with losers; get off the cutting edge; don't just do something, stand there; think inside the box; become a nobody; and embrace shame.[35] Upside-down leadership means learning to be unleaders who follow the upside-down Savior, in living out these ten radical principles of true biblical leadership founded on servanthood and followership.

Stott's biblical perspective on Christian leadership, based on the first four chapters of 1 Corinthians and Paul's example, emphasizes humility. His prayer is for Christian leaders to be characterized above all else by "the humility and gentleness of Christ" (2 Cor. 10:1).[36]

In redefining leadership from a more biblical perspective, Joseph Stowell has focused on these character-driven habits of effective Christian leaders: making character the primary goal in the leader's life; having the transformational identity of a follower of Jesus; leading from moral authority as a platform; leading as a shepherd; leading as a servant; leading with a heart that is pure in being reliant on God, repentant, meek, and righteous; and most of all living and leading as a Christian leader to magnify Christ, above all else.[37] He concluded: "Making Jesus large is the ultimate outcome of character-driven leadership—the ultimate outcome for leaders who say, 'For me, to lead is Christ!'"[38]

The Christian leader also needs to lead with conviction, based on passionate beliefs that are biblical or Bible saturated, fully convinced and convicted by God's Word, as Albert Mohler has advocated.[39] We as pastors need to lead from our union with Christ, led by the Holy Spirit as we abide in Christ (John 15:5). Our leadership and ministries must flow out of a deep spiritual and personal life in Christ as we follow him, our true Leader and Head of the church, thereby building up the church in love (Eph. 4:15).

The Role of Vision in Leadership

Vision has been touted as crucial in leadership, including Christian leadership. Much has been written on how a Christian leader should have a clear vision from God for his or her church, congregation, ministry, or organization, and then articulate and cast the vision clearly and repeatedly, with a mission that includes concrete plans and steps to implement and actualize the vision so that God's purposes can be achieved with tangible results.[40] The results or outcomes are usually measured by metrics and numbers such as church attendance, number of conversions and baptisms, size of budgets and buildings, number of church plants, and other markers of church growth in a local church context. Jeff Woods has pointed out the difference between vision and mission: "There is a clear distinction. Vision is about picturing. Mission is about prioritizing. Vision assumes a futuristic perspective. Mission begins with today and moves forward. Vision pulls. Mission pushes. Mission does and delivers, competes and completes, accomplishes and achieves, explores and executes. . . . Visions help organizations imagine what they could become, while mission statements help them narrow their range of activities in order to achieve that vision."[41]

Some would say it is imperative and essential for a pastor to prayerfully embrace a God-given vision for the church and cast the vision clearly and repeatedly before the parishioners, with mission statements that have concrete steps to achieve the vision. Others have strongly critiqued this emphasis on having vision and mission statements, reflecting too quick an acceptance of secular leadership principles and practices. For example, Zaragoza has been strongly critical of Greenleaf's idea of servant leadership because, he says of a servant leader: "He (or she) has a vision or goal, devises a plan that will realize that vision, and then puts that plan into action, thereby achieving the goal."[42] Zaragoza criticized a concept of servant leadership that still emphasizes individualism, having profound or extraordinary vision, maintaining one's leadership by winning or being competitive, and striving to stay in control of a person or situation.[43] He may have overstated his case and not fairly represented Greenleaf and his concept of servant leadership, which actually makes servanthood foundational and primary, but his strong critique has some validity.

Ford has also criticized the emphasis in leadership, including Christian leadership, on the greatness of the leader and his or her organizational and leadership skill sets, magnetic personality or charisma, exceptional talents and gifts, and vision and ability to get people to embrace or accept his or her vision. Vision for the church can be overemphasized, oversold, and overglorified as the key to effective pastoral leadership of the church. In regard to the obsession with crafting great vision and mission statements by so-called great and effective leaders, Ford stated, "We are to sell ourselves first and then we will get to the Jesus stuff? So what would happen if we just give people Jesus straightaway? What if we give people Jesus and his vision? At issue is Jesus. When do we get to him?"[44]

Max De Pree, who has emphasized servanthood in true leadership, is well known for this succinct summary of a leader from *Leadership Is an Art*: "The first responsibility of a leader is to define reality. The last is to say thank you. In between the two, the leader must become a servant and a debtor. That sums up the progress of an artful leader."[45] Having and casting a God-given vision for a church is part of defining reality, and so it is still an important part of Christian leadership. But it has to be a vision that comes from God, is anointed by the Holy Spirit, and is founded firmly on Scripture. It has to be prayerfully clarified and embraced by a plurality of Christian leaders and servants in the church and not just self-initiated or individualistically developed. Whatever vision is finally embraced, it must be biblical. It must obey the Great Commission (Matt. 28:18–20) and the greatest commandment (Matt. 22:37–40; Mark 12:29–31). It must prioritize knowing Christ and making him known (to the ends of the earth) and loving God and loving others. The rest is secondary. A vision from God can be clearly received only through the process and practice of discernment. This is often best done by pursuing God's will together in a leadership group with other pastoral staff and church leaders, with much prayer and silent waiting on the Lord.[46]

The Pastor as Leader

The pastor as leader in the church has to lead in the areas that are covered in this book as key aspects of pastoral ministry: preaching and teaching; corporate worship; intentional discipleship and spiritual formation; evangelism, missions, and social concern; mentoring of church staff and lay volunteer co-workers; pastoral care and counseling; church boards, budgets, and buildings; weddings and funerals; small groups and fellowships; integrity and ethics; and leaving and retiring. This is almost an impossible list of pastoral responsibilities and ministries. However, while the pastor needs to provide pastoral oversight and leadership in these various areas, he or she is not expected to be the point person or person in charge of every one of these aspects of pastoral and church ministry. The pastor can delegate the major responsibility for some of these areas to another staff member or lay volunteer leader. For example, corporate worship can be delegated to a worship pastor or a volunteer worship director who works closely with the senior pastor.

As we as pastors serve in Christian leadership in a distinctively biblical way, we will not blindly adopt secular principles or practices of leadership, especially those that are based on CEO and MBA models of corporate leadership and management. In our role as leader in the church, we need to follow Jesus in cross-shaped or upside-down leadership, as unleaders who are first and foremost humble and loving servants of Jesus Christ and devoted disciples of him. We lead, but only in the Jesus way that incorporates sacrificial suffering, as Jesus himself exemplified. As mentioned earlier, according to Stowell, the Christian leader will most of all magnify Christ and say, "For me, to lead is Christ!"

We end this chapter on the crucial topic of leadership with the following words from *Full Service*:

> The crucial need for true servanthood in the church today cannot be overemphasized, precisely because such a high premium has been put on a certain kind of strong, visionary leadership to change the church and turn it around. There is a certain danger to such an emphasis on strong leadership: It may not be founded on true servanthood and devoted discipleship that follows Jesus all the way. Strong leadership of the wrong kind, often based on secular CEO and business management models, can end up with much pride, self-sufficiency, and therefore sin. What the church needs in order to be transformed into an Acts 2 type of community of faith (Acts 2:42–47) is the presence of true servants of Jesus who are filled with the Spirit, manifesting his fruit of love, joy, peace, patience, kindness, goodness, faithfulness, gentleness, and self-control (Gal. 5:22–23). The church needs servants who engage in true service rather than self-righteous service and who will lead when called by God to do so, with humility and grace, in prayerful consultation with a plurality of other fellow servants also called to lead, in order to have a vision for the church that is God's, and not a vision born of human ambition or wanting to be great or to do great things.[47]

RECOMMENDED READINGS

Barton, Ruth Haley. *Pursuing God's Will Together: A Discernment Practice for Leadership Groups*. Downers Grove, IL: InterVarsity, 2012.

———. *Strengthening the Soul of Your Leadership: Seeking God in the Crucible of Ministry*. Downers Grove, IL: InterVarsity, 2008.

Berntsen, John A. *Cross-Shaped Leadership: On the Rough and Tumble of Parish Practice*. Herndon, VA: Alban Institute, 2008.

Clinton, J. Robert. *The Making of a Leader: Recognizing the Lessons and Stages of Leadership Development*. Rev. ed. Colorado Springs: NavPress, 2012.

De Pree, Max. *Leadership Is an Art*. New York: Currency Books, 2004.

Fadling, Alan. *An Unhurried Leader: The Lasting Fruit of Daily Influence*. Downers Grove, IL: InterVarsity, 2017.

Field, Taylor. *Upside-Down Leadership: Rethinking Influence and Success*. Birmingham, AL: New Hope Publishers, 2012.

Ford, Lance. *Unleader: Reimagining Leadership . . . and Why We Must*. Kansas City, KS: Beacon Hill Press, 2012.

Goggin, Jamin, and Kyle Strobel. *The Way of the Dragon or the Way of the Lamb: Searching for Jesus' Path of Power in a Church That Has Abandoned It*. Nashville: Thomas Nelson, 2017.

Hull, Bill. *The Christian Leader: Rehabilitating Our Addiction to Secular Leadership*. Grand Rapids: Zondervan, 2016.

Jacobsen, Eric O, ed. *The Three Tasks of Leadership: Worldly Wisdom for Pastoral Leaders*. Grand Rapids: Eerdmans, 2009.

Kellerman, Barbara. *The End of Leadership*. New York: Harper Business, 2012.

Ledbetter, Bernice M., Robert J. Banks, and David C. Greenhalgh. *Reviewing Leadership: A Christian Evaluation of Current Approaches*. 2nd ed. Grand Rapids: Baker Academic, 2016.

Malphurs, Aubrey. *Being Leaders: The Nature of Authentic Christian Leadership*. Grand Rapids: Baker Books, 2003.

McIntosh, Gary, and Samuel D. Rima Jr. *Overcoming the Dark Side of Leadership*. Grand Rapids: Baker, 1997.

Osborne, Larry. *Lead Like a Shepherd: The Secret to Leading Well*. Nashville: Thomas Nelson, 2018.

Roxburgh, Alan J., and Fred Romanuk. *The Missional Leader*. San Francisco: Jossey-Bass, 2006.

Scazzero, Peter. *The Emotionally Healthy Leader: How Transforming Your Inner Life Will Deeply Transform Your Church, Team, and the World*. Grand Rapids: Zondervan, 2015.

Stewart, Matthew. *The Management Myth: Why the Experts Keep Getting It Wrong*. New York: Norton, 2009.

Stott, John. *Basic Christian Leadership: Biblical Models of Church, Gospel, and Ministry*. Downers Grove, IL: InterVarsity, 2002.

Stowell, Joseph M. *Redefining Leadership: Character-Driven Habits of Effective Leaders*. Grand Rapids: Zondervan, 2014.

Tan, Siang-Yang. *Full Service: Moving from Self-Serve Christianity to Total Servanthood*. Grand Rapids: Baker Books, 2006.

Yaverbaum, Eric. *Leadership Secrets of the World's Most Successful CEOs*. New York: Barnes and Noble, 2006.

10

Mentoring of Church Staff and Lay Volunteer Coworkers

The pastor or church leader is also involved in building up other leaders.[1] A major part of this investment in others' lives involves mentoring. Therefore, another aspect of pastoral ministry is the mentoring of church staff and lay volunteer coworkers so that they become faithful and fruitful servants and leaders for Christ.

Brad Johnson and Charles Ridley, in *The Elements of Mentoring*, provided this description of mentoring relationships:

> Mentoring relationships (mentorships) are dynamic, reciprocal, personal relationships in which a more experienced person (mentor) acts as a guide, role model, teacher, and sponsor of a less experienced person (protégé). Mentors provide protégés with knowledge, advice, counsel, support, and opportunity in the protégé's pursuit of full membership in a particular profession. Outstanding mentors are intentional about the mentor role. They select protégés carefully, invest significant time and energy in getting to know their protégés, and deliberately offer the career and support functions most useful for their protégés.[2]

There are thousands of publications, including books and journal articles, on mentoring. Much of this literature has been succinctly summarized by Johnson and Ridley, who listed many key elements—covering the knowledge, attitude, and skills needed for effective mentoring—divided into six themes.

- The first theme covers what excellent mentors do, or matters of skill: select your protégés carefully, be there, know your protégés, affirm them often, provide sponsorship, be a coach and teacher, encourage and support, offer counsel in difficult times, protect when necessary, nurture creativity, provide correction even when painful, self-disclose when appropriate, accept increasing friendship and mutuality, be an intentional model, and display dependability.
- The second theme covers traits of excellent mentors, or matters of style and personality: exude warmth, listen actively, show unconditional regard, respect privacy and keep confidentiality, embrace humor, do not expect perfection, be trustworthy, respect values, and do not give in to jealousy.
- The third theme covers arranging the mentor-protégé relationship, or matters of beginning: clarify expectations; establish measurable goals; define relationship boundaries; consider protégé relationship style; delineate potential benefits and risks; be sensitive to gender, race, and ethnicity; plan for change at the beginning; and schedule periodic reviews.
- The fourth theme covers knowing oneself as a mentor, or matters of integrity: be aware of the consequences of being a mentor, engage in self-care, be productive, resist cloning, ensure that you are competent, hold yourself accountable, practice humility, respect the power of attraction, and never exploit protégés.
- The fifth theme covers when things go wrong, or matters of restoration: above all do no harm, slow down the process, tell the truth, seek consultation, carefully document, and challenge your own irrational thinking.
- The sixth and final theme covers welcoming change and saying good-bye, or matters of closure: welcome change and growth, accept endings, engage in helpful ways for saying good-bye, and mentor as a way of life.[3]

These elements of effective mentoring have been found to benefit the mentor, the protégé, and the organization in various ways.[4]

A Christian Perspective on Mentoring

While the secular literature on mentoring is voluminous,[5] there are also many publications on Christian approaches to mentoring.[6] Paul Stanley and Robert Clinton, in their classic book *Connecting*, offered this expanded definition of mentoring from a Christian perspective: "Mentoring is a relational process between mentor, who knows or has experienced something and transfers that something (resources of wisdom, information, experience, confidence, insight, relationships, status, etc.) to a mentoree, at an appropriate time and manner, so that it facilitates development or empowerment."[7] This is their shorter definition of mentoring: "Mentoring is a relational experience in which one person empowers another by sharing God-given resources."[8] It should be noted that mentees, mentorees, and protégés are synonymous in the literature, referring to those who are being mentored.

People who have influenced others and therefore served as effective mentors share these characteristics:

- They quickly see potential in another person.
- They tolerate brashness, abrasiveness, mistakes, etc. to continue to develop the potential in that person.
- They are flexible in dealing with people and circumstances.
- They are patient, realizing that experience and time are needed for another person's growth.
- They have perspective, with the capacity to clearly see the future and guide the mentoree as needed.
- They have appropriate gifts and abilities needed to encourage and build up others.[9]

More specifically, Stanley and Clinton have explained how mentors help mentorees:

- They give to mentorees timely advice, literature such as books and articles that help provide perspective, finances, and freedom to develop as a leader even beyond where the mentor is.
- They are willing to risk their reputation to sponsor a mentoree.
- They model different aspects of leadership functions to help mentorees develop in these functions.
- They guide mentorees to resources they need to further develop.
- They minister together with mentorees to help them grow in confidence, status, and credibility.[10]

James Houston has emphasized that true, biblical mentoring is not about developing ourselves and our abilities so we can excel and perform better with greater productivity in our lives and professions, as secular mentoring aims to do, essentially making the individual better. Christian mentoring is instead a form of Christian discipleship in which individuals are mentored to humbly seek and follow Christ, who alone, by the power of the Spirit, can transform us to whole personhood. The truly mentored life in Christ therefore moves us from individualism to authentic personhood, as God created us to be in his image.[11]

True, biblical mentoring also involves a deep degree of humility so that both mentor and mentoree eventually learn from each other as they follow Christ together and learn from him. A unique aspect of such humble, reciprocal learning and mentoring is the occurrence of reverse mentoring. Earl Creps, in *Reverse Mentoring*, described it as teaching up, when a younger person teaches or mentors an older person or someone more junior teaches someone more senior.[12] His friend Ken described reverse mentors as "young guys who help the older guys learn young stuff."[13] Creps pointed out that reverse mentoring may be more difficult to practice in churches or Christian circles because of the more traditional older-to-younger (teaching down) approach to mentoring that we are most familiar with, thinking it may be the only biblical model. However, we need to be humble enough to learn from younger people and let them be our teachers at times.[14]

Types of Mentoring

There are different types of mentoring depending on the level of involvement and the degree of intensity in the mentoring relationship. According to Stanley and Clinton, they can be divided into three major categories on a continuum. The first is the intensive, more deliberate type of mentoring, in which the mentor functions as a discipler, spiritual guide, and coach to the mentoree. The second category is occasional mentoring, in which the mentor functions more like a counselor, teacher, and sponsor with intermediate involvement and intensity. The third category at the other end of the continuum is passive mentoring, which is much less deliberate, and the mentor may be a contemporary model or a historical (hero) model from the past.[15] We can learn much from models from church history. For example, Edward Smither, in *Augustine as Mentor*, challenged us as mentors to follow Augustine's example to first be disciples ourselves. We need to continue to follow Jesus and learn from him because this is most inspiring and attractive to our mentorees. He concluded by emphasizing the Augustinian value of friendship and community in mentoring others and that this should be prioritized over all other work.[16]

Mentoring can also be done more informally in the context of intentional disciplemaking in which pastors meet one-on-one or with a small group of people to disciple them to follow Christ more deeply and become more like him.[17] In addition to *Discipleship Essentials*, a helpful tool for intentional disciplemaking groups, Greg Ogden has authored or coauthored other useful materials such as *The Essential Commandment*, for further growth in Christ through loving God and others, and *Leadership Essentials*, for deeper development of church leaders. Both can be used when mentoring others.[18]

Although mentoring usually involves a one-on-one relationship between a mentor and a mentoree, mentoring can go beyond such an individual-based focus. There is also small-group mentoring, in which a mentor meets with several mentorees in a small group on a regular basis; peer group mentoring and accountability, in which peers meet to help guide and mentor one another; and master-apprenticeship group mentoring, in which one peer with special expertise or experience in a particular area mentors a group of peers in that area. There is also distance mentoring in which the mentor is geographically at a significant distance from the mentoree, but they can still regularly connect by telephone[19] (and now by texting, Skype, or email). Phil Newton, in *The Mentoring Church*, emphasized the need to go beyond one-on-one mentoring and provided helpful suggestions for how pastors and congregations can cultivate leaders through group mentoring done by a number of people from the church or Christian community and not just by the pastor alone.[20]

The Process of Mentoring

Carson Pue has provided helpful material on how to mentor leaders, with wisdom for developing their character, calling, and competency. He described five phases of the mentoring process, with detailed suggestions for engaging in effective mentoring in each of them. Phase 1 is awareness, focusing on growing in self-awareness and awareness of God. Phase 2 is freeing up, focusing on satisfying needs. Phase 3 is visioneering, focusing on discovering purpose. Phase 4 is implementing, focusing on being purposeful. Phase 5 is sustaining, focusing on realizing purpose.[21]

Mentoring is an essential part of developing the next generation of church leaders,[22] including young leaders and teens.[23] We need to be especially careful when mentoring younger leaders in their teens, making sure we obtain parental permission and keep proper boundaries—for example, mentoring persons of the same gender and meeting only at church or in public places such as restaurants.

Edmund Chan, in *Mentoring Paradigms*, described four essential steps in mentoring others, especially in the context of disciplemaking: (1) discover God's truth for ourselves; (2) apply it to our own lives first; (3) reap the benefits and blessings of obedience and transformation as a result; and then (4) pass it on in real-life and authentic ways to those we are mentoring.[24]

According to Stanley and Clinton, these are ten key principles for effective mentoring:

1. Establish the mentoring.
2. Jointly agree on the purpose of the relationship.
3. Determine the regularity of interaction.
4. Determine the type of accountability.
5. Set up communication mechanisms.
6. Clarify the level of confidentiality.
7. Set the life cycle of the relationship.
8. Evaluate the relationship from time to time.
9. Modify expectations to fit the real-life mentoring situation.
10. Bring closure to the mentoring relationship.[25]

Mentoring of Church Staff

One of the roles of the pastor is serving as a mentor to church staff. Every church is unique, and there are different needs and challenges depending on the kind and size of the church and the number of pastoral or church staff. A solo pastor of a relatively small church may still need to supervise a small staff of lay volunteer coworkers who are helping to run the church and its various ministries. We will examine the topic of mentoring lay volunteer coworkers later in this chapter. For now, we will assume the more common situation in which there is a lead or senior pastor and several pastoral staff serving together under the leadership of the senior pastor.

In my church of several hundred people, we have eleven paid pastoral staff, partly because we have three congregations divided by language: English, Mandarin, and Cantonese. We also have children's ministries and a youth congregation, and we minister every Sunday to three homes for the elderly near our church. In addition to myself, serving as the senior pastor as well as the English pastor, we have an English administrative pastor, English young adults pastor, English youth minister, minister of children's ministries, minister of family life ministries, discipleship and missions minister, worship minister, Mandarin pastor, Mandarin assistant minister, and Cantonese pastor. In the Chinese church context, a pastor refers to an ordained pastor and a minister refers to a nonordained clergyperson. We have a weekly pastoral staff meeting at which we all meet together with our volunteer church administrator and our office administrative assistant, who takes minutes of the meeting. We also have other meetings just for our English staff and just for our Mandarin staff. At our staff meetings, informal mentoring occurs as we share and pray together, cast vision and make strategic plans together, and lead devotionals based on Scripture. At times, I also do some teaching and training, or another staff member does it.

I also schedule time with each of the pastoral staff every six weeks or so to meet with me one-on-one, usually over breakfast or lunch, for a time of sharing and prayer and also for me to mentor them individually. During these times, I review their work and offer some instruction to help them grow in their areas of ministry at the church. I focus especially on being a good shepherd of the people of God and therefore encourage each one to faithfully visit with parishioners on a regular basis. We discuss effective time management and priority setting with good weekly scheduling of pastoral responsibilities, including time for pastoral visitation and pastoral care of parishioners and newcomers. We also share how we are doing in our personal, family, and spiritual lives and pray for each other. I offer much support and encouragement to each pastoral staff member I am meeting with. However, as good mentoring should, my mentoring also includes gentle confrontation and correction of mistakes when needed, even though doing so can be painful. I challenge them to mentor others in the church so that the church becomes a mentoring and disciplemaking church, reproducing disciples and servants as well as leaders for Christ and his church. I do not use a specific curriculum when I meet individually with each of the pastoral staff. I share with them from Scripture or books I have read that may be helpful or relevant for a given time or situation. I also provide guidance and counsel, so some informal spiritual direction and pastoral care are being done in my mentoring of them.

I meet periodically with the other church or office staff (e.g., administrative and secretarial staff) for supervision and informal mentoring, but not as regularly as with the pastoral staff. We have a volunteer children's ministries administrator and I meet with him individually, usually over breakfast, for informal mentoring and supervision sessions.

Mentoring of church staff is a very important part of the pastor's role and ministry in the church. It helps to develop pastors and church leaders. It also facilitates the development of a loving and harmonious team of pastoral and church staff, which is essential for the smooth functioning of a church as a whole and for faithful and fruitful ministries in the church. Stephen Macchia has provided this description of a healthy Christian ministry team: "A Christian ministry team is a manageable group of diversely gifted people who hold one another accountable to serve joyfully together for the glory of God by: sharing a common mission, embodying the loving message of Christ, accomplishing a meaningful ministry, and anticipating transformative results."[26] Healthy teams have TEAMS: they trust, empower, assimilate, manage, and serve. They build trust through community, celebration, communication, and conflict. They empower through gifts and passions, defined responsibilities, teachability and resourcing, and delegation and accountability. They assimilate through cross-pollination, others-orientation, systemic direction, and ministry multiplication. They manage through strategic plans, SMART (specific, measurable, achievable, results-oriented, time-dated) goals, systematic administration, and result evaluation. They serve through heartfelt prayer, discernment of need, fulfillment of call, and transformation of life.[27]

Mentoring of Lay Volunteer Coworkers

A church cannot and should not function only under the leadership of paid pastoral staff. Doing so is not only too costly but also not a biblical approach to church leadership and church ministries. Lay volunteers who serve alongside the paid pastoral staff are equally important in church leadership and church ministries. The Bible teaches that every Christian belongs to the universal priesthood of believers (1 Pet. 2:5, 9), and we are all called to minister to one another, using whatever spiritual gifts God has given us, so that we can all grow into maturity in Christ (Eph. 4:1–16). The professionalization of the clergy and how dangerous and unbiblical this can be have already been mentioned earlier in this book. Greg Ogden and Paul Stevens, among others, have issued a clarion call to return the ministry to the people of God and not limit ministry just to professional pastors or ordained pastors.[28] Leith Anderson and Jill Fox, in *The Volunteer Church* and *Volunteering*, have similarly emphasized the need to mobilize the congregation for growth and effectiveness.[29] Nelson Searcy has written *Connect*, with Jennifer Dykes Henson, on how to double the number of volunteers in a church.[30]

As pastors, we need to recruit, train, supervise, and mentor our lay volunteer coworkers well. Other pastors in our church help me with this important work. However, I spend some of my time mentoring some key volunteer coworkers in our church, ranging from younger millennials to older church leaders who have served for many years. I usually meet with them for breakfast or lunch or in church every six weeks or so. I express much appreciation and affirmation for them and provide guidance, pastoral care, and some informal spiritual direction. The focus is on growing in Christ and becoming more like him and becoming a more Christlike leader (i.e., spiritual formation). I also learn from them. The younger volunteers, especially the millennials, have much to teach me about the younger generations, especially as I get older and older! We enjoy our mentoring times together, and a certain degree of reverse mentoring often takes place.

One of my deepest joys in mentoring others is to see some of them respond in obedience to God's call in their lives to go into full-time pastoral ministry or missionary work. I spent over a year in a mentoring relationship with a young adult volunteer in the young adults ministry at our church. He was devoted to meeting with me every six to eight weeks. He even read my book *Full Service* and took notes to discuss with me whenever we met. These were wonderful times of mentoring, sharing, and prayer together. He eventually felt called by God to go to seminary to prepare for full-time pastoral ministry, and I rejoiced with him. He is now attending seminary on the East Coast, but we still keep in touch. Another young adult leader in our church's youth ministry met regularly with me for mentoring over a three-year period. He also recently felt a call from God to go to seminary to prepare for full-time pastoral ministry. He gave up a promising career as a chiropractor and is now attending seminary. We still meet regularly for mentoring.

To build healthy and harmonious teams of lay volunteer coworkers in the church, it is important as a senior pastor to delegate responsibilities and ministries to them with adequate support, guidance, accountability, and mentoring. Effective pastoral leadership must include effective delegation.[31]

The Generalized Timeline in the Development of a Leader

To effectively mentor church staff and lay volunteer coworkers, we need to keep in mind what Robert Clinton has helpfully described as the generalized timeline in the development of a leader, with six major phases. In phase 1, sovereign foundations, God is laying down crucial foundations in the emerging leader's life in a sovereign way. The leader needs to be sensitive and open to what God is doing.

In phase 2, inner-life growth, the emerging leader grows into a closer and more intimate relationship with God, knowing and experiencing him more deeply and personally. Praying and listening to God become important aspects of his or her life. The leader will also encounter some tests as he or she gets more involved in ministry. Such tests or challenging experiences can help the leader grow and develop character and integrity.

In phase 3, ministry maturing, the emerging leader begins to use his or her spiritual gifts to serve and reach out to others. Ministry becomes more focused and important, and he or she learns how to relate with others in the body of Christ. Personal inadequacies will also become more apparent. Ministry fruitfulness is not the major focus of phases 1, 2, and 3. During these earlier phases of a leader's development, God is working mainly *in* the leader and not so much *through* the leader. An emerging leader can get easily frustrated at this juncture because he or she is looking at results and productivity. We need to encourage him or her to realize that God's work in a leader is as important as, if not more important than, his work through a leader. Leaders can lead or minister only out of who they are, so their character and inner life are crucial.

In phase 4, life maturing, the leader is now using his or her identified spiritual gifts in a ministry that brings fulfillment, with a resulting mature fruitfulness. The leader learns to lead out of being and not just doing, with a mellowing and a maturing of the leader's character. Isolation, crisis, and conflict will take on new meaning and can be used to deepen the leader's communion with God so that a positive response occurs to the various experiences, positive and negative, that God ordains for him or her. Effective ministry over the long haul can then be the eventual outcome.

In phase 5, convergence, the leader is moved by God into a ministry or role that matches the leader's spiritual gifts and experience, thereby maximizing his or her ministry. Life maturing and ministry maturing reach their peak together at this time. The leader is released from ministry that he or she is not particularly suited or gifted for, and the leader is now free to pursue a ministry that fits well. However, many leaders do not experience this phase of convergence. If they do, they experience maximum effectiveness, but they must learn to trust, rest, and wait upon God to lead them toward a ministry that maximizes all the development of the previous phases.

The final phase is phase 6, afterglow (or celebration), which only very few leaders experience. This is a time when the fruit of a lifetime of ministry and development as a leader is given recognition, and continued indirect influence occurs at many broad levels. Others will seek out the leader and the storehouse of wisdom he or she has accumulated over many years of ministry and growth. They will continue to be blessed by the life and example of such a leader molded and used by God. To God be the glory and honor![32]

Finishing Well

Much has been written about the need for leaders to finish well.[33] Randy Reese and Robert Loane, in *Deep Mentoring*, based on Clinton's work, concluded that being skilled or an expert at strategic thinking is not crucial for flourishing and finishing well as Christian leaders. "God's shaping work is of greatest value. A person's willingness to respond faithfully to the Spirit's work in his or her character—the inner life—is an essential factor."[34]

Reese and Loane summarized the following lessons we can learn from those who finish poorly: (1) They misuse, mismanage, and abuse finances. (2) They struggle with issues of power. (3) They become trapped in their own pride. (4) They struggle with boundaries related to sex or issues of sexuality. (5) They fail to deal with family of origin issues. (6) They simply plateau in their development.[35] They also note the following lessons we can learn from those who finish well: (1) They maintain a learning posture throughout life. (2) They value spiritual authority as a primary power base for leadership. (3) They recognize leadership selection and development as important. (4) They work from a dynamic and focused ministry philosophy. (5) They lead from a growing awareness of a personal sense of destiny. (6) They perceive their ministry from a lifetime perspective. (7) They prioritize mentoring relationships for themselves and in developing others.[36] These are helpful lessons for us and those we mentor.

Some people focus on finishing well to leave behind a legacy regarding how they have impacted lives and the world. As pastors, we should not focus on the legacy we will leave behind. As humble, loving servants of Jesus Christ, who are called to serve as leaders and pastors in his kingdom, we should focus only on Jesus and through him be in union and communion with the Triune God: Father, Son, and Holy Spirit. Bill Bright got it right when he said that the only legacy he wanted to leave behind as his epitaph on his tombstone is that he was a slave or servant of Jesus Christ. He wanted to focus on Jesus and not the great things he did as founder of Campus Crusade for Christ. Bill Bright's tombstone actually reads, "Slave (Servant) of Jesus Christ."[37]

Finishing well does not require a preoccupation with our legacy. It is about the Lord's legacy! Ultimately, finishing well is not about us. It is about God's great faithfulness. He will keep us until the end by his grace. He will help us finish well (Phil. 1:6; 1 Thess. 5:23–24) as we fix our eyes on Jesus, "the pioneer and perfecter of faith" (Heb. 12:2).

RECOMMENDED READINGS

Anderson, Keith R., and Randy D. Reese. *Spiritual Mentoring: A Guide for Seeking and Giving Direction*. Downers Grove, IL: InterVarsity, 1999.

Anderson, Leith, and Jill Fox. *The Volunteer Church: Mobilizing Your Congregation for Growth and Effectiveness*. Grand Rapids: Zondervan, 2015.

Bufford, Bob P. *Finishing Well: The Adventure of Life beyond Halftime*. Grand Rapids: Zondervan, 2011.

Creps, Earl. *Reverse Mentoring: How Young Leaders Can Transform the Church and Why We Should Let Them*. San Francisco: Jossey-Bass, 2008.

Croft, Brian. *Prepare Them to Shepherd: Test, Train, Affirm, and Send the Next Generation of Pastors*. Grand Rapids: Zondervan, 2014.

Forman, Rowland, Jeff Jones, and Bruce Miller. *The Leadership Baton: An Intentional Strategy for Developing Leaders in Your Church*. Grand Rapids: Zondervan, 2004.

Houston, James. *The Mentored Life: From Individualism to Personhood*. Colorado Springs: NavPress, 2002.

Johnson, W. Brad, and Charles R. Ridley. *The Elements of Mentoring*. Rev. ed. New York: Palgrave Macmillan, 2008.

Labin, Jenn. *Mentoring Programs That Work*. Alexandria, VA: ATD Press, 2017.

Macchia, Stephen A. *Becoming a Healthy Team: Five Traits of Vital Leadership*. Grand Rapids: Baker Books, 2005.

Malphurs, Aubrey, and Will Mancini. *Building Leaders: Blueprints for Developing Leadership at Every Level of Your Church*. Grand Rapids: Baker Books, 2004.

Newton, Phil A. *The Mentoring Church: How Pastors and Congregations Cultivate Leaders*. Grand Rapids: Kregel, 2017.

Ogden, Greg. *Unfinished Business: Returning the Ministry to the People of God*. Rev. ed. Grand Rapids: Zondervan, 2003.

Pue, Carson. *Mentoring Leaders: Wisdom for Developing Character, Calling, and Competency*. Grand Rapids: Baker Books, 2005.

Reese, Randy D., and Robert Loane. *Deep Mentoring: Guiding Others on Their Leadership Journey*. Downers Grove, IL: InterVarsity, 2012.

Reid, Alvin, and George G. Robinson. *With: A Practical Guide to Informal Mentoring and Intentional Disciple Making*. Spring Hill, TN: Tainer Publishing, 2016.

Rothwell, William J., and Peter Chee. *Becoming an Effective Mentoring Leader: Proven Strategies for Building Excellence in Your Organization*. New York: McGraw-Hill Education, 2013.

Saccone, Steve, with Chen Saccone. *Protégé: Developing Your Next Generation of Church Leaders*. Downers Grove, IL: InterVarsity, 2012.

Stanley, Paul. D., and J. Robert Clinton. *Connecting: The Mentoring Relationships You Need to Succeed in Life*. Colorado Springs: NavPress, 1992.

Stevens, R. Paul. *Liberating the Laity. Equipping All the Saints for Ministry*. Vancouver: Regent College Publishing, 2002.

Zachery, Lois J. *The Mentor's Guide: Facilitating Effective Learning Relationships*. 2nd ed. San Francisco: Jossey-Bass, 2011.

11

Pastoral Care and Counseling

In shepherding God's people, pastors are called to feed the sheep (e.g., in preaching and teaching) but also to take care of them (e.g., in pastoral care and counseling), as Jesus instructed Peter in John 21:15–17. Pastoral care and counseling is another major area of pastoral ministry,[1] and much has been published in this area as well as in the broader field of Christian counseling,[2] especially in the local church context.[3]

Pastoral care and counseling has been in existence since the founding of the church. It even has precedents in the Old Testament. Pastoral care and counseling is not the same as clinical counseling or therapy, although counseling knowledge and skills can be helpful. Pastoral care and counseling is unique in that it involves caring for people in the manner of Christ,[4] or in a specific Christlike way. Pastoral care is the broader term referring more generally to Christlike caring for God's people. It includes pastoral counseling, which focuses more narrowly on helping God's people with their problems or struggles in life. Howard Clinebell and Bridget Claire McKeever, in their classic book, *Basic Types of Pastoral Care and Counseling* provided descriptions of the major types of pastoral care and counseling.[5]

Christian Soul Care

The care of souls (*cura animarum* in Latin), or Christian soul care, includes ideas of both care and cure, as David Benner has pointed out.[6] Care has to do with helping to support the well-being of people, and cure refers to restoring the well-being that has been lost or damaged. Christian soul care has a long history and a central role in the ministries of the church. William Clebsch and Charles Jaekle, in reviewing the history of pastoral care in the church, described four major components: healing, sustaining, reconciling, and guiding.[7] Healing refers to actions aimed at restoring wholeness and well-being to someone who is impaired or disturbed in some way, including physical, emotional, and spiritual healing. Sustaining has to do with helping someone who is hurting to accept and transcend a difficult condition or circumstance that may not be amenable to recovery or restoration. Reconciling refers to actions aimed at reestablishing broken relationships, emphasizing relational contexts of pastoral care and not just an individualistic focus. Guiding has to do with helping someone make wise decisions based on God's Word and spiritually grow into maturity in Christ.

Pastoral care and counseling, since the twentieth century, have unfortunately become too clinical and therapeutic, with pastors often embracing secular counseling and psychotherapy principles and practices too quickly and naively. The historic care of souls, with deep biblical roots, has largely been lost in contemporary pastoral care and counseling, especially in clinical pastoral education approaches. However, in recent years there has been a renewed interest to make pastoral care and counseling more grounded in the classical traditions of the care of souls from earlier church history, as Thomas Oden[8] and others have done. Furthermore, the biblical counseling movement originally initiated by Jay Adams in the 1970s has seen significant development at the turn of the century after a period of decline.[9] Many more conservative pastors and churches are embracing a biblical counseling model of caring for people that emphasizes Scripture as the foundation of God's changeless and eternal truth for helping people with their problems. Such biblical counseling is described as a Christ-centered and gospel-centered way of helping people, with a strong critique and often rejection of secular counseling and psychotherapy concepts and approaches. Many books are available on biblical counseling written by key leaders in this field, such as Robert Kellemen, Heath Lambert, and David Powlison.[10]

Some may feel that the biblical counseling approach, based on Jay Adams's nouthetic counseling, may be too narrow and may not give enough room or validity to general revelation and common and creation grace. Integration approaches are more open to secular counseling and therapy principles and practices as long as they do not contradict Scripture as God's Word and ultimate guide to all truth, including psycho-theological truth.[11] Eric Johnson has more recently proposed and described a distinctively

Christian psychology approach that takes the Bible and historical, biblical, and systematic theology most seriously and yet also takes secular and scientific psychology and counseling seriously, especially in research areas, but with clear biblical critique.[12] Christian psychology is therefore much closer to biblical counseling than earlier integration approaches, which tended to be weaker in biblical convictions and foundations and sometimes too uncritically and unbiblically open to secular counseling concepts and methods.[13]

As pastors, we should deeply ground our pastoral care and counseling in the classical traditions of the care of souls from church history and especially in God's inspired Word. Hence, the biblical counseling movement can be of much help to us in making our pastoral care and counseling more biblical, in a Christ-centered, Bible-based, and Spirit-filled way, just as all true Christian counseling should be.[14]

It is also helpful for a pastor to have a biblical perspective of human nature as a framework to guide him or her in doing pastoral care and counseling. I have described such a basic biblical view with five assumptions. First, the basic spiritual and psychological needs of a human person include needs for security (love), significance (meaning or impact), and hope (forgiveness). Second, the basic problem of humankind has to do with sin or fallenness, but not all emotional suffering is due to personal sin. It may paradoxically at times involve deep obedience to God's will, just as Jesus experienced painful anguish in the Garden of Gethsemane (Matt. 26:36–39; Mark 14:32–36; Luke 22:40–44) yet never sinned (Heb. 4:15). Third, the ultimate goal of humanity is to know God and enjoy him forever, with spiritual health being primary. Fourth, problem feelings are usually due to problem behavior and, more deeply, problem thinking. However, biological and demonic factors may play a role and should be assessed. Fifth, a holistic view of persons as integrated beings is essential. We all have physical, mental/emotional, social, and spiritual dimensions to our beings and our functioning.[15]

Benner has emphasized the need to define Christian soul care in a way that goes beyond the secular idea of therapeutic counseling or clinical helping. He has described five forms of soul care that should be essential parts of the life and ministry of every Christian church, placed along a continuum from the least specialized and broadest to the most specialized and narrowest (but not in degree of importance): Christian friendship, pastoral ministry, pastoral care, pastoral counseling, and spiritual direction. As pointed out earlier, pastoral counseling has a narrower focus, under the umbrella of pastoral care, which is broader, and both pastoral care and counseling are part of pastoral ministry.[16]

Pastoral Care

Pastoral care includes pastoral visitation of parishioners in our congregations. This needs to be done on a regular basis so that a pastor visits as many people in the church as possible. (In a large church, the responsibility of pastoral visitation may be divided among pastoral staff as well as lay church leaders, including small-group or fellowship leaders.) As pastors, we need to visit parishioners and newcomers in a systematic and regular way by planning such visits into our weekly schedules and setting time limits, without being rushed. We need to be wise and careful about whom we visit, where we visit, and when we visit. For example, we should never visit a member of the opposite sex alone in his or her home or in a private place. Visits can take place in the church office when there is someone else, such as an administrative staff member, present. If the visit is done in a home, we should bring along another pastor or church leader or our spouse if we are married. If the visit takes place at our home, our spouse or someone else should be around. Such visits can also occur in restaurants or coffee shops.

When we visit, we need to do so in a prayerful and intentional way, letting the Holy Spirit use us to minister to God's people and shepherd them. Several goals should be kept in mind: spiritual feeding of parishioners, sharing the whole counsel or will of God, helping each believer to grow mature in Christ, equipping God's people for works of service, and equipping them to be disciples who will reach out to others and make more disciples.[17] Therefore, we should engage in meaningful Christ-centered and gospel-centered conversations in a sensitive way with those we are visiting. Small talk and chitchat, however, are appropriate initially to break the ice and build rapport. Time for prayer, after some deep sharing, is a good way to end a visit if the person being visited is open to it.

Pastors are also often called on to make hospital visits of those who are sick, including the terminally ill and dying, and those who may be having a baby or surgery. Hospital visits should be conducted sensitively and with compassionate care and offers to pray with and for those being visited. They should be brief, especially if the person being visited is ill and weak. Follow-up visits may also be necessary.

Evangelistic visitation of nonbelievers is another privilege of pastors.[18] We need to be prayerfully ready to sensitively and winsomely share the gospel with a nonbeliever who is willing and open to an evangelistic visit. If the person is ready, we can lead him or her in a prayer to receive Christ as Lord and Savior. However, it may take several visits, sometimes over a long period of time (months or years), before a person comes to Christ. Salvation is a sovereign act of God, and conversion is the work of the Holy Spirit. We as pastors or church leaders are simply channels and servants of the Lord. We prayerfully leave the results and timing to him.

The writing of letters or notes,[19] and today emails and texts, as well as phone calls, can extend pastoral care to more parishioners. We as pastors may find it helpful to schedule phone calls and the writing of emails, texts, letters, and cards into our weekly plans. As with visits, we should establish appropriate time limits for phone calls, without being rushed.

Another area of pastoral care is providing tender care for missionaries involved in cross-cultural living and ministry. Pastoral care needs to be sensitively provided by pastors before they go, while they are serving on the field, and when they return.[20] It can be done in various ways, including through email, Skype, telephone calls, and personal visits. Pastors should schedule regular times of contact through these means. I call our missionaries every six weeks or so and visit with them after they return from the field.

Pastoral Counseling

Pastoral counseling involves helping people with their problems or struggles in life. Wayne Oates pointed out years ago that pastors and other church leaders involved in pastoral ministry cannot avoid counseling people with problems. He emphasized, "The choice is not between counseling or not counseling, but between counseling in a disciplined and skilled way and counseling in an undisciplined and unskilled way."[21] There are now many materials and training DVDs to help pastors become more disciplined and skilled pastoral counselors. However, what is more crucial than counseling skills is the ministry of the Holy Spirit, who is the Counselor par excellence. His presence and power, spiritual gifts, fruit of agape love, and truth based on Scripture as God's Word are essential in effective pastoral counseling. He can powerfully help us in several specific ways, as already described in chapter 2 of this book.[22] While training in counseling skills is important, the work of the Holy Spirit in pastoral counseling is indispensable. This is actually true for all pastoral ministry.

A particular approach to pastoral counseling developed by Benner is called strategic pastoral counseling.[23] It is strategic because it is time limited and focused. Most pastoral counseling is short term, because most pastors do not have the time or the clinical training to be involved in long-term counseling with people who have difficult or severe problems or emotional disorders.

Benner's strategic pastoral counseling model has seven characteristics. It is brief and time limited (usually up to five sessions), holistic, structured, involves assigned homework, church based, spiritually focused, and explicitly Christian. It follows four principles that are common to all short-term approaches to counseling. First, the counselor needs to be directive and active. Second, the counseling relationship must involve a partnership between the pastor and the parishioner. Third, the counseling should focus on one major and specific problem. Fourth, time limitation needs to be kept.[24]

There are three stages in strategic pastoral counseling—the encounter stage, the engagement stage, and the disengagement stage—with particular tasks to do in each one. In the encounter stage, the pastor engages in four tasks with the parishioner: establishing rapport and boundary setting; exploring the major concerns or problems and their history; doing a pastoral diagnosis; and coming to a mutually agreed-upon focus for counseling. In the engagement stage, the pastor helps the parishioner explore the emotional, cognitive, and behavioral aspects of the main problem and come up with the resources needed to deal with it. In the disengagement stage, the pastor assesses progress and remaining concerns, makes a referral for the parishioner if necessary, and terminates the counseling.[25]

In regard to the task of making a pastoral diagnosis, Benner adapted questions and material from the religious-status interview first described by Newton Malony in 1988, which focused on these dimensions of pastoral diagnosis: awareness of God, acceptance of God's grace, repentance and responsibility, response to God's leadership, involvement in the church, experience of fellowship, ethics, and openness in faith.[26]

Benner has provided two helpful case illustrations demonstrating how a pastor can help a parishioner using the strategic pastoral counseling model. Ellen is a five-session case illustration,[27] and Bill is a one-session case illustration.[28] John Ortberg and I have provided a five-session case illustration of Jim to show how a pastor can conduct strategic pastoral counseling with a parishioner struggling with depression.[29]

Benner also listed five basic but not comprehensive guidelines for the ethical practice of all pastoral counseling, including strategic pastoral counseling: protect the rights of those being counseled (including obtaining informed consent and keeping confidentiality within legal and ethical limits); avoid dual-role relationships that can adversely affect the counseling; avoid sexual or romantic intimacies in counseling; be aware of one's own limitations; and maintain relationships of personal accountability (e.g., seek consultation or supervision).[30]

William Willimon has similarly advocated for short-term pastoral counseling that focuses on care rather than cure in helping parishioners. He has challenged pastors to recover pastoral counseling as a means of spiritual direction, as it was historically. The pastor serves as a guide in pastoral counseling, which involves leading and giving advice, not simply being a passive listener (although deep, empathic listening is still an important part of pastoral counseling).[31] He stated, "Counseling is a means of the historic pastoral work of spiritual direction and growth, not an attempt to do psychotherapy. Our counseling ought to be short-term, with clear goals; modest modification of behavior, better understanding of a situation, accurate information about the persons in a crisis, decision about intervention, and formation of short-term strategies are more appropriate goals than major changes in personality."[32] He also warned about the dangers of transference, referring to the displacement of reactions and needs related to a person in one's past onto a person in one's present—for example, onto the pastor doing the pastoral counseling. Countertransference can also occur when the pastor displaces reactions and needs related to someone in the past onto the parishioner in the present counseling relationship. These psychological phenomena usually take place unconsciously. Willimon provided suggestions regarding how to constructively handle such experiences.[33]

Basic Principles of Effective Pastoral Counseling from a Biblical Perspective

I have previously described thirteen basic principles of effective pastoral counseling from a biblical perspective and based on good research findings.

1. The Holy Spirit's ministry as Counselor is crucial in counseling; therefore, depend prayerfully on him.
2. The Bible as God's Word is a basic and comprehensive (though not exhaustive) guide for counseling.
3. Prayer (whether quiet, silent prayer or explicit prayer aloud with the counselee) is an integral part of Christian biblical counseling.
4. The ultimate goal of counseling is maturity in Christ and fulfilling the Great Commission.
5. The personal qualities of the counselor, especially spiritual ones, are important. The counselor needs to be spiritually mature and filled with the Spirit and love and be a warm, genuine, and empathic person.
6. The client's motivations, attitudes, and desire for help are important.
7. The counseling relationship between the counselor and the counselee is significant, with good therapeutic rapport, based on empathy and genuine caring on the counselor's part.

8. Effective counseling is a process with three main phases of exploration, understanding, and action, with a focus on changing problem thinking.

9. The style or approach in counseling needs to be flexible but still biblically consistent.

10. The specific techniques or interventions used in counseling should be consistent with Scripture and not contradict the truth of God's Word. Cognitive-behavioral interventions can be helpful for cognitive and behavioral change, but with some cautions.

11. Cross-cultural counseling skills, with empathy and cultural sensitivity to counselees from diverse cultures and ethnic backgrounds, are required.

12. Outreach and prevention skills in the context of a church as a caring community are important.

13. One should know one's limitations and make appropriate referrals when needed. Referrals should always be arranged in an empathic, supportive, and sensitive way.[34]

Eric Scalise and I, in our revised and updated edition of *Lay Counseling*, have added one more principle. The fourteenth principle is that crisis counseling is important.[35]

Some Helpful Counseling Interventions for Pastoral Counseling

There are several helpful counseling interventions that can be used in pastoral counseling to help parishioners and others struggling with depression. Here are some examples from *Coping with Depression*, which I coauthored with John Ortberg: inner healing prayer (with seven steps); learning to be assertive (e.g., learning to say no to unrealistic demands without feeling guilty); relaxation and coping skills, such as slow, deep breathing (take in a slow, deep breath, hold it for a few seconds, and then breathe out slowly), calming self-talk (e.g., saying to yourself, "Just relax, take it easy, let all the tension unwind"), and pleasant imagery (e.g., imagining lying on a beach in Hawaii or seeing a beautiful sunset); listening to soothing and relaxing music; taking care of the body by practicing good nutrition, exercising regularly, and getting sufficient sleep (about eight hours each night); cognitive restructuring of negative, unreasonable, irrational, and unbiblical thinking into more positive, reasonable, realistic, and biblical thinking; prayer with thanksgiving (Phil. 4:6–7); appropriate use of humor (Prov. 15:15; 17:22); self-help reading; and contemplative prayer and meditation on Scripture.[36]

Inner healing prayer is a specific spiritual intervention that can be particularly helpful in counseling parishioners who may have painful, even traumatic,

memories from the past. I have described a seven-step strategy for inner healing prayer that involves helping people relive painful experiences or memories
through imagery and to prayerfully ask Jesus to walk back with them and
gently minister his presence and inner healing, including forgiveness of others,
by the power of the Holy Spirit. First, begin with prayer for protection from
evil and ask for the Holy Spirit to take control of the session with his power
and healing presence. Second, guide the counselee into a relaxed state using
relaxation strategies (such as slow, deep breathing; calming self-talk; pleasant
imagery; prayer; and Bible imagery). Third, guide the counselee to focus on a
painful past memory or traumatic experience, usually through imagery (this
can be done in narrative form if imagery doesn't work), and to feel deeply
whatever hurt, pain, anger, or other emotions that may emerge. Fourth, ask
the Lord in prayer, by the power of the Holy Spirit, to come to the counselee
and minister his comfort, love, and healing grace (even gentle rebuke if necessary) in the painful memory. This may be in the form of Jesus imagery or
some other imagery, music (song/hymn), specific Scripture passage, a sense
of his presence or warmth, or other experience of the Sprit's working. No
specific visualization or imagery is given to the counselee at this point. Inner
healing prayer is not synonymous with guided imagery. It is prayer. Fifth, wait
quietly on the Lord to minister to the counselee with his grace and truth, in
whatever way he knows the counselee needs. As the pastor, guide and speak
only if necessary and led by the Holy Spirit. Otherwise, simply be quiet and
wait, only periodically and gently asking the counselee, "What's happening?
What are you experiencing or feeling now?" in order to follow or track with
the counselee. Sixth, close in prayer after an appropriate amount of time has
passed. Inner healing prayer cannot and should not be rushed, and some extra
time may need to be scheduled for a pastoral counseling session that will
include inner healing prayer (perhaps up to two hours). Seventh, discuss the
inner healing prayer experience just concluded and give as homework inner
healing prayer on his or her own, if appropriate.[37]

Lay Pastoral Care and Counseling

Eventually, as a church grows, the pastor or pastoral staff will not be able
to provide all the pastoral care and counseling needed by parishioners and
others. The pastor should therefore equip and train lay church leaders and
parishioners to do lay pastoral care and counseling. The Bible instructs all believers to love one another (John 13:34–35) and to bear or carry one another's
burdens (Gal. 6:2). Lay pastoral care and counseling is a field that has grown

much in the past two decades or so. It refers to help provided by untrained or minimally trained nonprofessional or paraprofessional counselors who do not have the credentials or formal training of professional counselors. Eric Scalise and I have written a revised edition of *Lay Counseling*, a handbook that can be of significant help to a pastor who wants to expand the ministry of church-based pastoral care and counseling through lay pastoral caregivers or lay counselors. It provides detailed information on the biblical basis for lay pastoral counseling; a biblically based model for effective lay counseling that is also research based; a review of the empirical evidence that largely supports the effectiveness of lay counseling in general, with more limited data supporting the effectiveness of lay Christian counseling in particular; practical guidelines for selecting, training, supervising, and evaluating lay Christian counselors, especially in a local church context; and stress, burnout, and self-care in lay counseling. Ethical and legal guidelines for implementing an effective and ethical lay counseling ministry are also provided, as are sample forms and examples of training and lay counseling programs available.[38]

Robert Kellemen has also written a helpful book on equipping counselors for the church using the 4E ministry training strategy of envisioning, enlisting, equipping, and empowering.[39] Melvin Steinbron has strongly stated that the pastor cannot do pastoral-care ministry alone and needs to train and use lay caregivers in the church.[40] He has developed and described a basic approach to lay pastoral care called Lay Pastors' Ministry, using the PACE framework: P stands for pray for members of five to ten households in the church; A stands for be available to them in times of celebration and need; C stands for contact them on a regular basis, at least once a month; and E stands for be the best example possible as a lay pastor. This PACE model is a simple and basic approach to lay pastoral-care ministry, with the need for only a few hours of basic training. There are other models such as Befriender Ministry, People's Ministries, and Stephen Ministries (which involves fifty hours of training).[41]

The American Association of Christian Counselors (AACC) has also developed helpful DVD training programs for equipping lay caregivers and counselors, especially in the local church context. For example, "Caring for People God's Way" is a five-part curriculum with thirty lessons (www.aacc .net). Tim Clinton, the president of the AACC, has also coauthored a series of practical handbooks, each with forty topics, spiritual insights, and easy-to-use action steps. They can be used by pastors as well as lay pastoral caregivers or counselors in pastoral care and counseling ministries. These guides cover counseling for personal and emotional issues; counseling teenagers; sexuality and relationship counseling; counseling women; counseling on money, finances, and relationships; addictions and recovery counseling; and marriage and family counseling.[42]

Lay pastoral care and counseling can also be provided by the leaders of small groups and larger fellowships in a church. Much lay caring can occur through sharing and prayer in such groups. Small groups and fellowships will be covered in more detail in chapter 14 of this book.

There are at least three possible models for a lay pastoral-care and counseling ministry in the local church.[43] The first is the informal, spontaneous model in which lay helping is already being provided informally and spontaneously in relationships between parishioners and others in the church. Friendship or peer helping is a good example. No formal training or supervision is provided. This is what usually happens in many churches. The second model is the informal, organized model in which lay counselors or key pastoral caregivers are selected, trained, and supervised (on a weekly or monthly basis) in an organized way, but the lay caring and counseling takes place in informal settings, such as in homes, restaurants, hospitals, coffee shops, and other community meeting places. A good example is Stephen Ministries developed by Kenneth Haugk.[44] The third model is the organized, formal model in which lay counselors and caregivers are selected, trained, and supervised in a systematic, organized way, and the lay pastoral care and counseling is provided in formal settings, such as in a church counseling center or in a community counseling agency or clinic.

There are at least five steps to starting a lay pastoral care and counseling ministry in the local church. First, choose an appropriate model for the church, whether it will be an organized, informal model or an organized, formal model, or even a combination of both models, especially for a larger church. Second, obtain full support for the idea and the model from the other pastoral staff and church board. Third, screen and select potential lay caregivers and counselors with appropriate spiritual gifts and characteristics. They should meet as many of the following selection criteria as possible: spiritual maturity; psychological and emotional stability; love for and interest in people (with empathy, genuineness, warmth, or respect); appropriate spiritual gifts such as the gift of encouragement (Rom. 12:8); previous training or experience in people helping (helpful but not necessary); age, gender, and socioeconomic and ethnic or cultural background relevant to the needs of the congregation; availability and teachability; and ability to keep confidentiality. The selection of lay caregivers and counselors can be open (anyone can apply) or closed (by nominations only). Potential lay caregivers and counselors should be interviewed, usually by a small committee or the pastor, before being selected to participate in a training program. They should be chosen to serve only after completing a training program. Fourth, provide an adequate training program for the lay caregivers and counselors. This training program can vary from a very basic weekend training on caring and listening skills that lasts a few hours to a more thorough training program that lasts several months with more in-depth instruction on how to help people with specific problems such as anxiety, depression, stress, spiritual dryness, and mental issues. Fifth, develop and implement programs or ministries in which the trained lay caregivers and counselors can be used with further training and supervision.[45]

If a more organized and formal model of lay pastoral care and counseling is chosen, then setting up a more formal center is necessary. The following are ten guidelines for how to do this:

1. decide on clear objectives for the lay pastoral-care and counseling center;
2. clarify the distinctive character or ethos of the center by giving it an appropriate name;
3. carefully select, train, and supervise the lay caregivers and counselors;
4. arrange for suitable facilities and office space for the center;
5. establish operating hours for the center;
6. set up a governing structure (e.g., a director and board of advisers) for the center;
7. publicize the center and its services;
8. clarify what services the center will provide;
9. plan for the financing of the center by including it in the annual church budget; and
10. determine the center's affiliation with the church.[46]

Pastoral care and counseling, and lay pastoral care and counseling, is a significant part of pastoral ministry. It involves taking care of Christ's sheep. It is loving them and shepherding them, as Christ commanded us to do (John 21:15–17), following him who is the good Shepherd himself (John 10:11, 14).

RECOMMENDED READINGS

Appleby, David W., and George Ohlschlager, eds. *Transformative Encounters: The Intervention of God in Christian Counseling and Pastoral Care.* Downers Grove, IL: IVP Academic, 2013.

Benner, David G. *Strategic Pastoral Counseling: A Short-Term Structured Model.* 2nd ed. Grand Rapids: Baker Books, 2003.

Clebsch, William A., and Charles Jaekle. *Pastoral Care in Historical Perspective.* Englewood Cliffs, NJ: Prentice-Hall, 1964.

Clinebell, Howard, and Bridget Clare McKeever. *Basic Types of Pastoral Care and Counseling: Resources for the Ministry of Healing and Growth.* 3rd ed. Nashville: Abingdon, 2011.

Clinton, Tim, and Ron Hawkins. *The Quick-Reference Guide to Biblical Counseling: Personal and Emotional Issues.* Grand Rapids: Baker Books, 2009.

Collins, Gary R. *Christian Counseling: A Comprehensive Guide.* 3rd ed. Nashville: Thomas Nelson, 2007.

Greggo, Stephen P., and Timothy A. Sisemore, eds. *Counseling and Christianity: Five Approaches.* Downers Grove, IL: IVP Academic, 2012.

Johnson, Eric L. *God and Soul Care: The Therapeutic Resources of the Christian Faith.* Downers Grove, IL: IVP Academic, 2017.

Kellemen, Robert W. *Equipping Counselors for Your Church: The 4E Ministry Training Strategy.* Phillipsburg, NJ: P&R, 2011.

———. *Gospel-Centered Counseling: How Christ Changes Lives.* Grand Rapids: Zondervan, 2014.

———. *Gospel Conversations: How to Care Like Christ.* Grand Rapids: Zondervan, 2015.

Kruis, John G. *Quick Scripture Reference for Counseling.* 4th ed. Grand Rapids: Baker Books, 2013.

Lambert, Heath. *A Theology of Biblical Counseling: The Doctrinal Foundations of Counseling Ministry.* Grand Rapids: Zondervan, 2016.

Moon, Gary W., and David G. Benner, eds. *Spiritual Direction and the Care of Souls.* Downers Grove, IL: InterVarsity, 2004.

Oates, Wayne E. *Pastoral Counseling.* Philadelphia: Westminster, 1974.

Oden, Thomas C. *Care of Souls in the Classic Tradition.* Philadelphia: Fortress, 1984.

Powlison, David. *The Biblical Counseling Movement: History and Context.* Greensboro, NC: New Growth Press, 2010.

Sbanotto, Elisabeth A. Nesbit, Heather Davediuk Gingrich, and Fred C. Gingrich. *Skills for Effective Counseling: A Faith-Based Integration.* Downers Grove, IL: IVP Academic, 2016.

Steinbron, Melvin J. *Can the Pastor Do It Alone?* Ventura, CA: Regal, 1987.

Tan, Siang-Yang. *Counseling and Psychotherapy: A Christian Perspective.* Grand Rapids: Baker Academic, 2011.

Tan, Siang-Yang, and John Ortberg. *Coping with Depression.* Rev. ed. Grand Rapids: Baker Books, 2004.

Tan, Siang-Yang, and Eric T. Scalise. *Lay Counseling: Equipping Christians for a Helping Ministry*. Rev. ed. Grand Rapids: Zondervan, 2016.

Wilson, David J. *Mind the Gaps: Engaging the Church in Missionary Care*. Colorado Springs: Believers Press, 2015.

Wilson, Reagon, and David Kronbach. *Tender Care: Providing Pastoral Care for God's Global Servants*. Rockford, IL: Barnabas Books, 2010.

Worthington, Everett L., Jr., Eric L. Johnson, Joshua N. Hook, and Jamie D. Aten, eds. *Evidence-Based Practices for Christian Counseling and Psychotherapy*. Downers Grove, IL: IVP Academic, 2013.

12

Church Boards, Budgets, and Buildings

Another important area of pastoral ministry is administrative in nature, but pastoral and spiritual oversight is still needed. This area involves overseeing church boards, budgets, and buildings. This aspect of pastoral ministry is not often treasured by most pastors. It is, however, an essential part of pastoral ministry because most churches are led and run by the church boards in conjunction with the senior pastor. How they function together depends on the type of church, whether it is independent, nondenominational, or denominational. Independent, nondenominational churches have more freedom and variety in how their church boards and senior pastors function. Denominational churches often function under denominational structures and leaders such as bishops or superintendents.

Church Boards

Much has been written on how to organize governing boards of nonprofit and other organizations and to help them function more effectively.[1] These ideas can be carefully applied to churches. However, there are also helpful books written more specifically for developing healthy and effective church boards.[2]

The following guidelines and suggestions can be helpful to pastors as they work collaboratively with church boards to lead their churches well in faithful and fruitful service in Christ and for his kingdom. The exact details of how many church boards a particular church should have and how they should run will vary from church to church and pastor to pastor. However, we who are pastors need to select and develop spiritually qualified lay church leaders to serve on our church boards whether as elders or deacons or even trustees so that some of the work of the church can be delegated to them. When this happens, under the guidance of the Holy Spirit, the church can grow in a healthy and holy way, and we can be freed up to lead spiritually in various aspects of pastoral ministry. The work of church boards is essentially a spiritual ministry and should be covered with much prayer and done in dependence on the Holy Spirit's guidance and empowering.

Aubrey Malphurs wrote *Leading Leaders* to empower the church board to function effectively in collaboration with the senior pastor as they lead the church together. After pointing out the various problems that affect many church boards that do not function well, he defined a governing board of a church "as a gathering of two or more wise, spiritually qualified leaders who have been entrusted with authority to use their powers to direct the affairs of the church."[3] Churches may have one main church board of elders or deacons or two or three boards all working together to serve with the senior pastor and the pastoral staff. My church has three church boards: an elders board that provides spiritual and pastoral oversight for the entire church, with a personnel committee that deals with personnel issues and annual evaluations of the senior pastor and pastoral staff; a trustees board that is responsible for the financial and legal matters of the church; and a deacons board that is responsible for administrative tasks, including overseeing buildings, facilities, and parking.

While the Bible does not specify that a church should have a board of elders or a board of deacons or even how many boards it should have, the Bible does support a plurality of church leaders (i.e., a board) in church life and ministry. According to Malphurs, a governing board can include the following constituents: board members, senior pastors, board chairperson, board committees, and others.[4]

Members of a church governing board must first be spiritually qualified, following biblical criteria (e.g., see Acts 6:3–5; 1 Tim. 3:1–10; Titus 1:5–9; 1 Pet. 5:1–3). Malphurs provided the following additional qualifications that a church board member should have to effectively serve on a church governing board: "be reliable and teachable, be in doctrinal agreement, be in alignment with the church's DNA, be an involved member of the church, be reasonably loyal to the pastor, respect other board members, be nontraditional, and have their spouse's support."[5] Training church board members so they can be more effective is also important. The pastor can conduct such training. Malphurs suggested training in four areas: character or being (soul work); knowledge or knowing (head work); skills or doing (hand work); and emotions or feeling (heart work).[6] These qualified people provide leadership by guiding the direction of the church in its mission and vision; giving responsibility to the senior pastor to accomplish the direction of the church; holding the senior pastor responsible; and developing policies for the board, the senior pastor, and their collaborative relationship in leading the church.[7]

When a board is composed of spiritually healthy leaders, the members work well together as a team, with a clearly identified leader or chair who sets the agenda and leads the board to function well; they are able to have courage, especially in making tough decisions; they trust and respect one another; and they deal well with disagreements, being able to agree to disagree.[8] A healthy church board does not micromanage and lets the senior pastor and pastoral staff manage church ministries.

Board Functions

According to Malphurs, the typical church board should have four broad functions. First, the board should be deeply involved in prayer for the pastoral staff, the congregation, and the board members as well as for nonbelievers and the neighborhood and the world as mission fields. Praying should take place at board meetings and outside board meetings, perhaps in smaller groups of board members. Second, the board should be involved in overseeing the church in the following areas: the spiritual condition of the church, the essential biblical doctrine of the church, the ministry direction the church is following, and the leadership of the pastor. Third, the board should be involved in decision-making, including making difficult and major decisions that may have a significant impact on the church. It should also draft policies for church governance so that standard decisions can be made in answer to questions or issues. Personnel and congregational policies should also be included, in addition to policies about board functions in collaboration with the functions of the pastor. Fourth, the board should be involved in advising the pastor and giving godly counsel and feedback when appropriate and needed. Advising, however, is not binding. It is not decision-making. The pastor can accept or reject advice given by board members. A church board decision, however, is binding and final.[9]

The church board may on occasion also be involved in selecting the senior pastor, arbitrating disputes, protecting the senior pastor, and approving the ordination and licensing of qualified staff for ministry.[10]

The Policies Approach to Church Board Governance

Malphurs borrowed heavily from the policies approach to board governance first developed by John Carver in the nonprofit sector in 1990[11] in formulating the policies model for church board governance. Malphurs defined policies as *"the beliefs and values that consistently guide or direct how a church or parachurch governing board makes its decisions."*[12] There are four major areas of policy development that a church board should undertake. First, the board should develop policies for the functioning of the board. Second, it should develop policies for the senior pastor's functions. Third, it should formulate policies for the board–senior pastor relationship. Fourth, it should come up with policies for the church's mission (ministry ends). Two other areas that should be covered are personnel policies for pastoral and church staff and their hiring, wages and salaries, benefits, and firing, and congregational policies related to matters such as church membership, weddings, church discipline, and a grievance process.[13] Malphurs delineated several advantages of using a policies approach to church board governance. They include making consistent decisions over time; following the policies already set in place; dealing with the most important and crucial church issues; having shorter and more efficient board meetings, with little to no attention paid to ministry minutiae; minimizing board interference with the senior pastor or pastoral staff; having clear lines of authority and greater trust between the pastor and the board; and preventing a group or particular person from dominating the process of decision-making.[14]

Marks of an Effective Board

Max De Pree, in *Called to Serve*, has also provided helpful guidelines and suggestions for creating and nurturing an effective volunteer board that can be applied to a church board. He described eleven marks of an effective board:

1. It has a mission statement.
2. It builds strong personal relationships.
3. It keeps in touch with its world, whatever its world is.
4. It engages in very good planning.
5. It has inspirational and competent leadership.
6. It spends much time and energy to seriously attend to the growth needs and potential of the members of the board.
7. It gives wisdom, wealth, work, and witness to the institution (or church) it is serving.

8. It knows its responsibilities well and fulfills them in a competent way.
9. It decides what to measure and measures it.
10. It sets aside time for reflection.
11. It expresses appreciation by saying, "Thanks."[15]

De Pree also described six promises that a member can make to the organization (or church) he or she is serving:

1. To be faithful and committed to the organization and what it stands for
2. To decide what unique contributions he or she can make to the board based on his or her special gifts
3. To establish strong relationships with other board members based on a covenantal basis of beliefs, values, commitments, and promises that are shared in common and with love
4. To be an advocate for the organization
5. To set up compassionate and relevant ways to measure what really counts
6. Not to try to manage the organization, which is the responsibility of the president, or in the case of a church, the senior pastor

The board member should also learn to separate his or her ego from the issue at hand and be involved in giving and raising financial support.[16]

A Board Chairperson's Guide

According to De Pree, a board chairperson can effectively lead a board by following six basic guidelines. First, build community by devotional bonding with the board members, who are all devoted to shared beliefs, principles, values, and goals and serving out of love. A chairperson also builds community by meeting the needs of followers and empowering each board member to make his or her unique contributions. Second, design the agenda in a thoughtful and purposeful way so that substantial issues can be discussed and dealt with; do not simply make a list. Third, after some time for warming up and settling down has passed, deal with the key issues on the agenda. At this juncture of a board meeting, almost all the board members are present, awake, and ready to get down to business. Crucial and difficult issues must not be kept until the end of the board meeting, when members' energy may not be at its highest and some members may have left. Fourth, be a good communicator by keeping in touch with the board members regularly and clearly. This can be done by sending out a well-designed agenda ahead of the board meeting, sharing good as well as bad news, and keeping and sending out well-written minutes of the board meetings. Fifth, practice hospitality by affirming board members and helping them feel worthwhile and needed in an authentic way and by attending to their needs for periodic breaks during board meetings, which should be held in an appropriate setting, with snacks and drinks if needed. Finally, hold the board accountable to do what it is supposed to do, maintain its forms, monitor progress and outcomes, and manage time well. De Pree concluded that these guidelines are more relational than technical.[17]

Living with Tensions

The reality is that there are no perfect boards or perfect board members. Tensions are inevitable, and board members need to learn to live with tensions and handle them in a constructive manner. De Pree mentioned several of these tensions: tradition versus change (the need to live with constraints and realistic limits, exercising reasoned restraint yet being open to the reality of change and the need to change at times); facing a crisis and working on it; the need for a leader to move on to a different position; the occurrence of malfeasance and ineffectiveness, with the need to decisively make changes; evaluating the performance of a board member; handling bad surprises; board members trying to move onto the turf of management; new board members trying to change previous board policy and direction, not knowing the decisions already made by previous board members; and evaluating the value and contribution of the board to the organization it is serving. Board work is difficult work with many potential tensions, but it is also important work that can be deeply satisfying.[18]

What the Church Board Owes the Pastor

De Pree described four categories of things that the board owes the pastor: mandate (a clear statement of who the board intends to be, including a mission statement, a strategy, and a statement of expectations of the pastor); trust (with respect and truth, moral purpose, and promises kept); space (opportunity and space to function as the pastor or leader of the church, with a workable structure and support from the board); and care (such as caring for the pastor and his or her family and their needs, including the pastor's health needs, personal growth and mentoring needs, and financial needs).[19]

Church Budgets

Church boards put together church budgets with input from the senior pastor and pastoral staff in order to service and run church buildings and facilities but, even more important, so that members can be involved in church life and ministries that fulfill God's vision and mission for the church, focused on fulfilling the Great Commission to make disciples of all nations (Matt. 28:18–20). A church usually comes up with an annual budget for an entire calendar year (twelve months, e.g., January to December). The budget is put together earlier in the year, typically to be approved at the annual church membership meeting later in the year. At my church, the annual budget for the next year is put together by July—with input from pastoral staff and three church boards of elders, trustees, and deacons—and approved by all before being presented at the annual membership meeting in October for approval.

Every church will have its own way of putting together an annual budget, with different components or items, but specifying line items for specific ministry expenses is important. Here is a sample annual budget for my church, with six major components and specific line items under each one:

1. Staff cost: salary, pension, payroll tax, medical insurance, disability insurance, and internship
2. Occupancy expense: telephone, utilities, repair and maintenance, and janitorial service
3. Capital expense: equipment and improvement
4. Office expense: insurance and legal, tax and licenses, office supplies, printing and typing, advertising, Bibles and books, and miscellaneous office expense
5. Program: food, kitchen supplies, children's ministries, Christian education (Sunday school), Sunday parking, library, choir, retreat, lay training, family life ministries, honorarium, Sunday worship, outreach, fellowship, staff expense, conference and travel, child care, local church missions, local church social concern, and miscellaneous
6. Contribution to First Evangelical Church Association (FECA) (10 percent of our annual church income)

We also have a separate missions fund (to support missions of FECA), love offering/benevolent fund, and church building fund that are dependent on giving for these funds.

A significant part of a church's annual budget, usually 40 to 60 percent, should be allocated for staff salaries and expenses. About 15 to 25 percent of the budget should be allocated for paying the mortgage and reducing debt, according to guidelines provided by Gary McIntosh and Charles Arn.[20] They emphasized that people will give more to pursue a vision than just to pay bills.[21] Therefore, a pastor needs to lead the church with a clear, God-given vision for what the Lord wants to do in and through the church for his kingdom.

Our church paid off its mortgage for our church buildings years ago, so we do not have a line item for mortgage and debt reduction. Many churches have to make mortgage payments and need to have this line item in their annual budget. In some geographical places and countries that are relatively poor or not as wealthy, congregations meet in homes or in simple structures. The budgets for such churches are much less. It is crucial for us to remember that a church is a living organism consisting of God's people, who make up the body of Christ, with Christ as the Head (1 Cor. 12; Eph. 4:15–16). A church is not a building. It is not an organization. It is first and foremost a spiritual body of believers in Christ (1 Cor. 12).

Church Buildings

McIntosh and Arn have provided several ministry rules regarding church buildings. For example, the worship capacity rule states that for optimal growth, worship attendance should be around 65 to 80 percent of the worship room capacity. The adequate parking rule states that a church will grow only up to the size of its parking capacity, so having adequate parking is crucial, whether this is achieved by adding more parking spaces or renting parking facilities that may be available nearby. The restroom capacity rule emphasizes that there should be enough restrooms in the church so that every church attendee can be accommodated within fifteen minutes. The building stress rule states that pastors are especially at risk for increased stress when there is a church building program in progress. A pastor needs to prayerfully anticipate this stress and handle it well by using time wisely, having a building committee or church board help out, being sensitive and open to feedback from church leaders and members, and bearing in mind the need to integrate new and old things for a sense of continuity. The first building rule states that the shape and size of the first church building planned and completed will define and affect the church's ministry in the future. It is essential to plan well for growth, with enough land and space and a master plan for the entire church property.

The building age rule states that if the interior of the church building is more than fifteen years old, it has probably become an obstacle to further growth of the church. Therefore, remodeling or renovating the church interior to bring it up to date every fifteen years or so is important. The relocation rule states that if the church's ministry is being hindered because of the church's present location, then moving the church to a better location for outreach and ministry should be seriously considered.[22] However, some crucial questions should be asked and answered before undertaking a relocation plan. For example, "Has every other possibility been explored and exhausted? Have we prayed about the matter and determined it to be the will of God? Do the people favor it? Are we prepared to buy an adequate amount of property? Are you moving to an area with high growth potential? Can we afford to pay for the new property? What is the salability of our present property?"[23]

Church Building Programs

Another crucial decision that a church may need to make is whether to embark on building a new and usually bigger church with more facilities to support healthy church growth. This decision must be covered with much prayer and made with clear discernment about whether this is indeed God's will. In many parts of the world, there is limited land and limited financial resources, so building a bigger church on a larger area of land is not an option. However, if it is an option, several key questions need to be asked and answered before a decision is made. This is crucial, McIntosh and Arn have pointed out, because "the number of pastoral failures (mental, physical, moral, spiritual) increases dramatically during, and in the year following, a major church building program. This fact raises the question, Is the benefit of building worth the risk? We think so, but pastors are wise to prepare themselves and the congregation by being aware of the potential problems and implementing preventative measures."[24]

Such a major decision should focus on not only whether it is the right thing to do but also whether it is the right time to do it. John Bisagno, in *Pastor's Handbook*, has suggested asking some crucial questions to help discern whether embarking on a major church building program is the right thing to do and whether it is the right time: "Are we absolutely certain that now is the time to construct the new building? Has every other possibility been explored? Has dual or triple usage of existing buildings been considered? Has serious consideration been given to beginning new missions (or church plants)? Have the people been given adequate information about projected cost, options, and the pros and cons of building and not building?"[25]

Bisagno also emphasized the need to take the pulse of the congregation about the proposed church building program by asking these questions: "Do they truly love the Lord and hunger to see the church grow? Is the church financially able to build? Has it been long enough since the last building campaign and accompanying capital (or fund raising) campaign? What were the problems then, and have they been resolved? Is the church in unity? Do the people truly believe in the program? Do they love and follow their pastor?"[26]

If in answering such key questions the senior pastor, pastoral staff, and church board(s) decide that embarking on a church building program is the right thing to do, several other steps need to be taken. A building committee should be set up consisting of qualified members, usually including board members and the senior pastor and other pastoral staff, with a lay church board leader chairing the committee. The committee should then select a competent architect who can draw up a master plan for the entire church property and a design for the new church building. Details about costs, concepts, dates, and so forth must be discussed and worked out. Input and feedback should be solicited from the pastoral staff and church boards as well as from church members. Clear communication with all of them should be given on a regular basis. Once the final architectural plans are confirmed, bids need to be received from various contractors, with a clear timeline for the start and completion of the church building and clear estimates of the costs involved, and the best (not always the lowest) one chosen.[27] Bisagno wisely concluded, "The entire project *will* cost more than you anticipate, and take longer than you expected."[28]

An important part of undertaking a church building program is fundraising to cover the significant costs. Bisagno has provided some helpful guidelines for such fund-raising in *Successful Church Fundraising*.[29] The pastor also needs to periodically preach on tithing and giving, which goes beyond the 10 percent tithe, and Christian stewardship of not just money or treasures but also time, talents, relationships, and bodies, all of which belong to the Lord.[30]

Legal Liability and Security Issues

Church buildings and facilities should be well managed to support pastoral and church ministries, with a close eye on legal liability and security issues,[31] especially in the American context, where there have been recent incidents of shootings in churches as well as child abuse cases.

A church should have a child protection policy in place that requires all paid and volunteer staff ministering to children and youth under the age of eighteen to undergo a mandatory background security check, with fingerprinting and a history questionnaire. The policy should also include the two-adult rule, which states that youth and children should never be left alone with only one adult.

Security on church grounds is also a crucial area. Some churches have security cameras on the church premises. Others, usually larger churches, employ parking attendants and security guards if they can afford to do so. Church board members can rotate on Sundays as point persons to contact in case of emergencies or security issues, with clear guidelines as to what to do in such situations, including calling the police.

Another area that needs attention to minimize legal liability for a church concerns the termination of paid pastoral staff or church office staff. There must be clear guidelines for doing this that cover adequate documentation and an appropriate grievance process, with the involvement of a personnel committee in the church. The personnel committee in our church consists of lay elders, the deacons board chair, the trustees board chair, and the senior pastor. It is chaired by a lay elder.

Church boards, budgets, and buildings are all part of pastoral ministry. A pastor needs to provide leadership and spiritual oversight in these areas while delegating some of the work, especially regarding budgets and buildings, to appropriate church boards and committees. However, the pastor is still ultimately responsible for the effective functioning of the church boards. As the senior pastor, I attend all church board meetings and provide pastoral and spiritual oversight and mentoring to the church boards. Although a church is not a building or an organization per se, it nevertheless has organizational aspects that require effective leadership by the pastor.

RECOMMENDED READINGS

Addington, T. J. *High-Impact Church Boards: How to Develop Healthy, Intentional, and Empowered Church Leaders*. Colorado Springs: NavPress, 2010.

Bisagno, John. *Successful Church Fundraising*. Nashville: B&H, 2002.

Carver, John. *Boards That Make a Difference: A New Design for Leadership in Non-profit and Public Organizations*. 3rd ed. San Francisco: Jossey-Bass, 2006.

Carver, John, and Miriam Carver. *Reinventing Your Board: A Step-by-Step Guide to Implementing Policy Governance*. Rev. ed. San Francisco: Jossey-Bass, 2006.

Coleman, David L. *Board Essentials: 12 Best Practices of Nonprofit Boards*. Lakewood, WA: Andrew/Wallace Books, 2014.

De Pree, Max. *Called to Serve: Creating and Nurturing the Effective Volunteer Board*. Grand Rapids: Eerdmans, 2001.

Hall, Eddy, Ray Bowman, and J. Skip Machmer. *The More with Less Church: Maximize Your Money, Space, Time, and People to Multiply Ministry Impact*. Grand Rapids: Baker Books, 2014.

Malphurs, Aubrey. *Leading Leaders: Empowering Church Boards for Ministry Excellence*. Grand Rapids: Baker Books. 2005.

13

Weddings and Funerals

The pastor is sometimes called on to conduct a number of special services for parishioners—for example, baptisms, child dedications, ordination services, weddings, vow renewals, and funerals or memorial services—in addition to regular worship services. This chapter focuses on the pastor's role in conducting weddings and funerals, which is another important aspect of pastoral ministry in the church.

Weddings are usually joyous occasions, whereas funerals or memorial services are typically sad events involving the loss of a loved one, although they can also include a celebration of the life of the person who has passed away. A pastor needs grace and wisdom from the Lord and the help of the Holy Spirit to sensitively minister to parishioners experiencing a range of emotions, from joy to grief and sadness, even with hope and some celebration.

Weddings

Weddings are joyous occasions in which the pastor officiates at the marriage of a man and a woman who are joined together in the ordinance or sacrament of holy matrimony. A wedding can be conducted in a church or in another setting such as a community center, a hotel, an outside wedding location, a beach, a home, an estate, and so forth. Being united in Christ in holy matrimony by a pastor is one of the most sacred and meaningful experiences for a believing bride and groom. At a Christian wedding, a couple makes a commitment to Christ and to life together in union and communion with him.

Marriage was originally instituted by God as a sacred covenant. In Genesis 2:24 we read, "That is why a man leaves his father and mother and is united to his wife, and they become one flesh." Jesus himself said in Matthew 19:4–6, "Haven't you read . . . that at the beginning the Creator 'made them male and female,' and said, 'For this reason a man will leave his father and mother and be united to his wife, and the two shall become one flesh'? So they are no longer two, but one flesh. Therefore what God has joined together, let no one separate." In this day and age when marriage is no longer held in high esteem and divorce is so rampant, it is all the more imperative that a biblical, Christian perspective on marriage is clearly taught and affirmed. A Christian wedding conducted by a pastor is a crucial and sacred means of doing so, to the glory of God, who instituted marriage in the first place. Marriage should therefore be honored by all and kept pure (Heb. 13:4), while singleness is also equally valued in Scripture (1 Cor. 7:8).

The Bible contains many references to marriage (forty-two) and weddings (nineteen).[1] However, it does not give specific instructions regarding how to conduct a wedding ceremony. There is freedom to creatively plan and carry out wedding ceremonies that are meaningful and incorporate personal preferences and yet are sensitive to cultural, familial, and community customs. There is a wide variety of practices around the world concerning how Christian weddings are planned and conducted. Even within the North American context, wedding ceremonies are diverse, including Christian weddings. Some differences are due to the denominational background of the couple and the church in which they are getting married. Wedding handbooks or manuals can be helpful, for both the pastor and the couple involved, in providing specific options and details for conducting a wedding ceremony.[2]

The Baker Wedding Handbook, by Paul Engle, is a helpful resource for pastors to use in conducting weddings. It provides details on how to conduct a Christian wedding for ten traditions (nine denominational and one nondenominational): Baptist (American Baptist and Southern Baptist); Christian and Missionary Alliance; Christian Church; Episcopal; Evangelical (Evangelical Covenant Church and Evangelical Free Church of America); Lutheran; Methodist (the Free Methodist Church of North America and the Wesleyan Church); nondenominational; Presbyterian (Presbyterian Church in America); and Reformed (Christian Reformed Church and Reformed Church in America).[3] It also covers six alternate wedding ceremonies: a contemporary wedding (with two options); a service of recognition of a civil marriage; a brief wedding ceremony; a ceremony for individuals with children from previous relationships; an ecumenical ceremony from the Consultations on Common Texts; and a service of renewal of wedding vows.[4]

More resources for wedding ceremonies are also provided in the final section of *The Baker Wedding Handbook*. They include wedding meditations; lighting of a unity candle; unity sand ceremony; the Lord's Supper (or Holy Communion) at a wedding; alternate wedding vows; suggested Scripture readings for weddings; wedding prayers; wedding music; and planning charts (request for a wedding, minister's wedding ceremony planning sheet, and processional and recessional diagram).[5]

The church's policy about marrying a Christian and a non-Christian should be clear and clarified with a couple before any commitment to marrying the couple is made by the pastor. Most evangelical churches, including my church, have a policy of conducting weddings only for two believers, not a believer and a nonbeliever. Some churches will conduct a wedding for two nonbelievers, and even for a believer and a nonbeliever. The church's policy must be clear from the start to avoid unnecessary misunderstandings and emotional pain and upset later on.

When two believers are involved, conducting a wedding ceremony is indeed a sacred and joyful privilege for a pastor. It should be done with prayer for God's richest blessings, as well as his protection, to be upon the couple.

Major Elements of a Wedding Ceremony

Based on my pastoral experience over many years, a typical Christian wedding ceremony usually includes the following items:

- prelude
- candle lighting
- seating of parents
- processional
- welcome and opening prayer
- declaration of intent (to marry)
- giving of the bride
- worship
- Scripture reading
- message
- exchange of vows and rings
- lighting of unity candle
- vocal solo
- prayer of blessing

- appreciation of parents
- pronouncement of marriage
- benediction
- presentation of bride and groom
- recessional
- announcements

Usually, a wedding rehearsal takes place a day or two before the wedding to go over these steps in the wedding ceremony with the couple and their wedding party.

Premarital Preparation: Preparing Couples for Marriage

Premarital preparation, or premarital counseling sessions, for couples engaged to be married are usually provided by the pastor officiating at the wedding or another pastor or a lay church leader trained and experienced in providing premarital counseling. This is a wonderful opportunity for a pastor to offer pastoral care and guidance, as well as discipleship training and mentoring, to help the couple have a Christ-centered marriage. There are various premarital preparation programs available for pastors to use. They usually vary from four to six sessions, and sometimes these sessions are conducted in a small group with a few couples. Gary Collins has provided a helpful review of premarital counseling in the third edition of *Christian Counseling*.[6]

A key question is whether premarital preparation is effective in improving marriages, preventing divorce, and reducing the disintegration of the family. Collins pointed out the difficulties that researchers in this area face in trying to determine the effectiveness of premarital counseling, especially in the long run over years, since many other factors may affect the marital functioning of a couple apart from whether they received premarital counseling. Nevertheless, Collins highlighted two important studies that found some support, at least in the short run, for the effectiveness of premarital preparation programs.[7] In 2003, Jason Carroll and William Doherty conducted a statistical meta-analysis of research in this area and found that the average person who took part in a premarital preparation program was significantly better off than 79 percent of those who did not participate. They concluded that such programs are generally effective, resulting in immediate and short-term improvements in overall relationship quality and interpersonal skills. Marriage quality was also found to be significantly better for those who participated in preparation programs than for couples who did not. However, these were all short-term effects; long-term effects of such programs are more difficult to assess.[8] However, Elizabeth Schilling and her colleagues reported in 2003 that there is some evidence for more long-term effects, specifically for men who are taught better communication skills.[9] There is general agreement among researchers that premarital preparation is more effective with couples who have relatively good adjustment skills and are interested in learning from the programs in which they participate.

Scott Stanley has advocated for premarital preparation because it can be helpful in various ways. First, it can help couples slow down and think through things more deliberately. Second, it emphasizes that marriage matters. Third, it helps couples know where to get help if they need it later in their marriage. Fourth, it provides training in crucial skills, such as communication, that can help lower the risks for marital distress or divorce later on.[10] According to Collins, premarital counseling serves the following purposes: teaching about marriage, assessing marital readiness, exploring possible problem areas, and planning the wedding.[11]

A number of useful inventories can be used for premarital counseling that require a pastor to undergo some basic training in how to use and interpret them. Two widely used inventories are the Taylor-Johnson Temperamental Analysis, or TJTA (www.tjta.com), and the Prepare-Enrich assessment (www .prepare-enrich.com).[12] Another well-known assessment tool is the SYMBIS (www.symbis.com), developed by Les and Leslie Parrott based on their best-selling book, *Saving Your Marriage Before It Starts*.[13]

Collins has described a basic six-session premarital counseling program that pastors can follow, emphasizing that pastors can use flexibility and vary the actual number of sessions.[14] Les and Leslie Parrott have offered seven crucial questions that couples need to ask before and after they marry: (1) Have you faced the myths of marriage with honesty? (2) Can you identify your love style? (3) Have you developed the habit of happiness? (4) Can you say what you mean and understand what you hear? (5) Have you bridged the gender gap? (6) Do you know how to fight a good fight? (7) Are you and your partner soul mates?[15] These key questions can be covered in premarital counseling sessions based on their book, which should be assigned to the couple for homework reading. If appropriate, the SYMBIS assessment can also be used to help the couple understand their own personality dynamics and how they affect each other. There are eight major personality types:

1. Achieving spouse: fact-based, efficient, and logical
2. Pioneering spouse: results-oriented, bold, and innovative

3. Energizing spouse: persuasive, outgoing, and enthusiastic

4. Affirming spouse: optimistic, encouraging, and verbal

5. Cooperating spouse: service oriented, peacekeeper, and patient

6. Unwavering spouse: loyal, sincere, and diligent

7. Deliberating spouse: devoted, accurate, and disciplined

8. Analyzing spouse: orderly, conscientious, and careful[16]

Cameron Lee and James Furrow have written a specific resource for premarital counseling, *Preparing Couples for Love and Marriage*, in which they point out that although the overall divorce rate in the United States has gone down from its peak in the 1980s, the bad news is that almost half of those who stay married are not happy with their marriages.[17] They described five basic listening and communication skills a pastor needs in the context of premarital preparation of couples. First, pay attention to process and not just the content of what the couple may bring up. Second, engage in attentive listening. Third, learn to be comfortable with silence. Fourth, keep focused on the task at hand and do not get distracted or sidetracked. Finally, consider whether a couple needs a referral for more professional help, and if so, make the referral in a sensitive and appropriate way. According to the authors, premarital preparation helps couples learn new skills.[18] Such skills need to be used and applied in real-life situations, and working with one couple at a time may be better than working with groups.[19]

Lee and Furrow also described a flexible four-session premarital preparation program based on a tool they developed called the Conversation Jumpstarter, or CJ, which is available as a reproducible copy in appendix A of their book. The CJ is to be completed by the man and woman independently to help them individually reflect on their past experiences and values in regard to six major areas of potential conflict that are common to couples: (1) roles and responsibilities, (2) love and affection, (3) money, (4) parenting, (5) inlaws and extended family relationships, and (6) spirituality and devotion.[20] Before starting the program, the couple meets with the pastor to receive a copy of the CJ, which they both complete and the pastor reads before the first session. The first session focuses on the couple's story and teaching them basic communication skills. The second session involves helping the couple practice constructive communication. The third session includes continuing to practice communication skills and discussing ways to be proactive about conflict and how to make decisions when facing conflicting needs. The fourth and usually final session involves putting it all together and debriefing with the couple.[21]

There is no one best or right method for conducting premarital preparation with a couple. A pastor can adopt various methods based on what is most appropriate and helpful for a specific couple. I have personally used a flexible three- to four-session framework, normally with two-hour sessions because our church is a commuter church and couples may have a long drive to meet with me. I use the Prepare-Enrich assessment as a guide to discuss several areas that reflect their relationship strengths and growth areas: communication; conflict resolution; partner style and habits; financial management; leisure activities; sexual expectations; family and friends; relationship roles; spiritual beliefs; marriage expectations; parenting expectations; and health and wellness. The Prepare-Enrich assessment also provides information on couple typology, overall satisfaction, idealistic distortion, relationship dynamics, personal stress profiling, couple and family mapping, and the SCOPE (with social, change, organized, pleasing, and emotionally steady dimensions) personality scales. A pastor needs to have special training to use the Prepare-Enrich assessment. At the final session, I pull everything together and finalize the wedding ceremony with the couple. I schedule the wedding rehearsal for a day or two before the wedding and a postmarital follow-up session for three months or so after the wedding. I also suggest that they read *Sacred Marriage* (and *Sacred Parenting*) by Gary Thomas and *The Marriage Builder* by Larry Crabb. In the area of physical intimacy in marriage, Cliff and Joyce Penner's *The Gift of Sex* is recommended.[22]

Funerals

Another important part of pastoral ministry is conducting funerals. During this sad and often difficult time when parishioners are grieving the loss of a loved one, a pastor has a unique and sacred opportunity to provide comfort, support, prayer, and hope in Christ for the family, relatives, and friends of the loved one who has died. A pastor can also provide comfort by visiting and caring for the person before death and ministering to the aging and the elderly.[23]

Dan Lloyd has written *Leading Today's Funerals* as a pastoral guide for improving bereavement ministry. He emphasized the need for pastors to first understand the purposes of a funeral. Funerals help us grieve, express sympathy, accept loss, remember positive times, make memory investments, find hope, express respect, and prepare for death.[24]

Therefore, conducting a meaningful Christ-centered funeral, typically in a funeral home or church, is a crucial part of pastoral care for the bereaved. A funeral service is usually conducted with the embalmed body or cremated remains present at the service. A memorial service is usually performed in the absence of a body. However, it is common today to use the terms funeral service and memorial service interchangeably. Sometimes the preferred term is celebration service, which honors and celebrates the life of the deceased person. For simplicity, the following discussion uses the term funeral or funeral service.

Funeral handbooks or manuals, which describe options for conducting a funeral service, can be helpful for pastors.[25] Paul Engle has edited a revised and updated version of *The Baker Funeral Handbook* as a resource for pastors. He emphasized that the comforting presence of pastors is particularly needed by grieving parishioners and their families as they face the death of a loved one. Pastors also need to care for the dying in hospitals and homes and then conduct or participate in the funeral afterward. Funerals serve several functions: allow family and friends to remember and honor the departed one and allow the Christian community to express sympathy and support for the bereaved; affirm one's faith in Christ and heaven for believers; and respectfully lay to rest the body or ashes of the deceased in a graveside committal service in light of future resurrection.[26]

The *Baker Funeral Handbook* provides details for conducting funeral services for eleven denominational traditions: Baptist, Christian Church, Christian Reformed Church, Church of the Nazarene, Episcopal, Evangelical Covenant Church, Evangelical Free Church of America, Free Methodist, Lutheran, Presbyterian, and Reformed Church in America.[27] It also covers special funerals, such as for stillborns, miscarriages, and infant deaths; for a child; for a suicide or other tragic circumstance; for an accident victim; for an unbeliever;[28] and graveside and committal services, including interment and scattering of ashes.[29] Resources are provided for ministry to the dying; Scripture readings and confession of faith; hymns for funeral and memorial services; quotations, illustrations, and last words; creating a eulogy or remembrance; and a template for a funeral or memorial service.[30] Finally, appendixes cover funeral message preparation, a funeral planning guide, a pastor's funeral record, and a preplanning funeral form.[31]

Major Elements of a Funeral Service

According to Lloyd, the four major elements of a funeral service are Scripture reading, the obituary, the eulogy, and prayer. The pastor should arrive prayerfully prepared to set an appropriate tone for the service, conduct the funeral service, and minister to the bereaved, with a good knowledge of the audience present. The pastor needs to be honest, accurate, relevant, brief, and gospel centered, presenting the gospel in some way as he or she speaks or preaches at the service.[32] Lloyd has provided guidelines for presenting the gospel in a sensitive and clear way and also for conducting a funeral service for a non-Christian.[33]

Based on my pastoral experience over many years, a typical funeral service usually includes the following items:

- prelude
- welcome and invocation (opening prayer)
- hymn
- Scripture reading
- eulogy
- words of remembrance (or slide or video presentation)
- message (words of comfort)
- closing hymn
- words of appreciation
- benediction
- postlude

The service is usually followed by a briefer graveside committal service to lay to rest the body or ashes of the departed person.

Difficult Funeral Services

Funeral services can be difficult to conduct for some groups of deceased people: stillborn infants, infants, children and young adults, suicide victims, accident victims, murderers, and so-called wicked people.[34] Pastors need to officiate at such funeral services with love, respect, and sensitivity to the bereaved facing these painful and difficult situations. Prayerful dependence on the Holy Spirit, the great Comforter, is essential in pastoral ministry to the bereaved, especially in these challenging circumstances.

After the Funeral: Caring for the Bereaved

Those who have lost a loved one need time to grieve; and support, understanding, and prayers are needed during the grieving process. Mourning or grieving, even with hope to be reunited with the loved one if the deceased was a fellow believer (1 Thess. 4:13–18; see also Phil. 3:20–21; Rev. 21:3–5), is a necessary human process. It enables the bereaved to express sorrow, show the depth of love for the deceased person, and move on toward healing and wholeness. In *Death and Grief: A Guide for Clergy*, Alan Wolfelt referred to bereavement as a state due to loss, such as death, whereas grief refers to emotional suffering caused by death or some other form of bereavement. Mourning refers to the outward or public expression of grief and bereavement.[35]

Lloyd has offered some practical suggestions for follow-up pastoral care for the bereaved after the funeral:

- Make brief visits to the home (provided the visit is not done alone with a bereaved person of the opposite gender).
- Call the bereaved by phone in a caring and supportive way, with prayer if appropriate, at least about a week and then a month after the funeral and periodically afterward if needed.
- Send brief notes with Scripture promises through the mail or by email or text.
- Visit the gravesite with the bereaved family if needed.
- Invite the bereaved to church if they do not have a church to attend, or refer them to a more appropriate or closer church.
- Make referrals to professional counselors or grief support groups if necessary, in a supportive and sensitive way.
- Equip laypeople in the church to serve as lay pastoral caregivers or lay counselors to minister to the bereaved (individually or in grief support groups).[36]

GriefShare is a helpful program to use in Christ-centered grief support groups (www.griefshare.org), especially in churches. It provides group participants who have lost a loved one helpful ways of recovering and healing from grief, video interviews with Christian grief recovery professionals, video testimonies from people who have healed from grief, small-group discussions, and a program of comforting daily Bible study. Robert Kellemen has written a helpful resource, *God's Healing for Life's Losses*, presented by Grief-Share. There are also other books available to guide and support the bereaved through their mourning and grief.[37]

A pastor may be called on to officiate at weddings and funerals, to participate in a part of the service, such as saying a prayer or pronouncing the benediction, or to simply be present at weddings and funerals conducted by other pastors. Pastoral ministry in these areas, whether as officiant, participant, or attendee, is a crucial part of a pastor's role. A pastor may also be called on to conduct other kinds of special services, such as for anniversaries, dedications, ordinations, and other occasions. Samuel Hutton has written a helpful updated and expanded resource, *Minister's Service Manual*, which covers all these special services and occasions, in addition to weddings and funerals. A pastor's role in weddings, funerals, and other special services is ultimately to serve parishioners and shepherd God's people in all of life's varied experiences and emotions, in times of sorrow as well as joy, grief as well as celebration. This is not easy for a pastor to do and can be quite challenging. However, it is a deep comfort for both pastors and parishioners to know and experience that God's grace is always sufficient, especially in our weakness, in which his power is made perfect (2 Cor. 12:9–10; see also 2 Cor. 9:8).

RECOMMENDED READINGS

Croft, Brian. *Visit the Sick: Ministering God's Grace in Times of Illness*. Rev. ed. Grand Rapids: Zondervan, 2014.

Croft, Brian, and Phil Newton. *Conduct Gospel-Centered Funerals: Applying the Gospel at the Unique Challenges of Death*. Rev. ed. Grand Rapids: Zondervan, 2014.

Engle, Paul E., ed. *The Baker Funeral Handbook*. Rev. ed. Grand Rapids: Baker Books, 2017.

———. *The Baker Wedding Handbook*. Rev. ed. Grand Rapids: Baker Books, 2017.

Hart, Archibald D., and Sharon Hart Morris. *Safe Haven Marriage: A Marriage You Can Come Home To*. Nashville: W Publishing, 2003.

Hutton, Samuel Ward. *Minister's Service Manual*. Rev. ed. Grand Rapids: Baker Books, 2003.

Jacobs, Martha. *A Clergy Guide to End-of-Life Issues*. Cleveland: Pilgrim Press, 2010.

Kellemen, Robert W. *God's Healing for Life's Losses: How to Find Hope When You're Hurting*. Winona Lake, IN: BMH Books, 2010.

Lee, Cameron, and James L. Furrow. *Preparing Couples for Love and Marriage: A Pastor's Resource*. Nashville: Abingdon, 2013.

Parrott, Les, and Leslie Parrott. *Saving Your Marriage Before It Starts: Seven Questions to Ask Before—and After—You Marry*. Rev. ed. Grand Rapids: Zondervan, 2015.

Tautges, Paul. *Comfort the Grieving: Ministering God's Grace in Times of Loss*. Rev. ed. Grand Rapids: Zondervan, 2014.

Thomas, Gary. *A Lifelong Love: What If Marriage Is about More Than Just Staying Together?* Colorado Springs: David C. Cook, 2014.

Wolfelt, Alan D. *Death and Grief: A Guide for Clergy*. New York: Routledge, 1988.

Wright, H. Norman. *Experiencing Grief*. Nashville: Broadman & Holman, 2004.

14

Small Groups and Fellowships

Small groups (usually with a few people or up to about fifteen or so) and fellowships (usually larger than small groups but smaller than congregations) are the bedrock of Christian community in the church. The Triune God (Father, Son, and Holy Spirit) has called us in Christ to enter into union and communion with him in the community of the Trinity, the with-God life. He has also called us into Christian community, or deep fellowship (*koinonia* in Greek), with one another as members of the body of Christ. We read in 1 John 1:3, "We proclaim to you what we have seen and heard, so that you also may have fellowship with us. And our fellowship is with the Father and with his Son, Jesus Christ." We also share in "fellowship with the Spirit" (Phil. 2:1 HCSB). Hebrews 10:24–25 gives us this exhortation: "And let us consider how we may spur one another on toward love and good deeds, not giving up meeting together, as some are in the habit of doing, but encouraging one another—and all the more as you see the Day approaching." Deep fellowship with one another in Christ, meeting together in loving spiritual community, enables us, in the power of the Spirit, to become more like Jesus, for the sake of others and not just for ourselves. Much has been written on the importance of Christian community and the role of small groups and fellowships in enhancing such community.[1] The website SmallGroups.com, launched by *Christianity Today*, contains helpful material available by subscription for small-group ministry concerning the following aspects: build the ministry (cast vision, build a team, organize, and grow the ministry), train leaders (recruit, develop, and strengthen leaders), lead the group (plan meetings, build trust, and nurture growth), explore new ideas, and choose Bible studies (with over one thousand quality Bible studies). Bill Search has succinctly summarized much of this material in *The Essential Guide for Small Group Leaders*,[2] which is of benefit to pastors and small-group leaders.

Biblical Foundations for Community

God created us to be relational human beings who need others, and the importance of community is emphasized throughout Scripture. Search has listed principles of community life found in the Old Testament, in Jesus's teaching, in Paul's letters, and in other parts of the New Testament.[3]

In the Old Testament, biblical principles of community life included the following: we are created in the image of a Triune God who is relational and therefore with a basic need for others (Gen. 1–2); Moses was encouraged by Jethro, his father-in-law, to recruit and appoint leaders from the community to create a small-group-like system to help him deal with the issues and problems of the Israelites (Exod. 18); Moses was supported by a small group consisting of Aaron and Joshua as he led the people of Israel (Exodus); David had the help and support of dozens of mighty men (2 Sam. 23:8–39); and God sent Elisha to Elijah when he experienced discouragement, to be his partner, encourager, and supporter (1 Kings 19).[4]

We see the following biblical principles of community life in the teachings of Jesus: he chose the twelve disciples to be with him and learn from him (Mark 3:14); he showed and taught the importance of outreach to others (Matt. 9:37–38); he taught how to have healthy community by engaging in godly confrontation and avoiding gossip in conflict situations (Matt. 18); he demonstrated true, selfless servanthood and challenged his disciples to do likewise in service to one another (John 13); and in restoring Peter, Jesus taught that love for him is expressed in caring for and nurturing other disciples (John 21).[5]

Paul expressed biblical principles of community life in his letters: show devotion to one another in love (Rom. 12:10); in community with one another, seek harmony (Rom. 12:16); do not pass judgment on another (Rom. 14:13); show interest in one another (1 Cor. 12:25); serve one another humbly in love (Gal. 5:13); confront and restore one another with gentleness (Gal. 6:1); support one another by carrying one another's burdens in tangible and emotional ways (Gal. 6:2); build one another up by using spiritual means (Eph. 5:19); be willing to submit to one another (Eph. 5:21); God, who began the work in his community, will complete it (Phil. 1:6); bear with one another and forgive one another, as the Lord forgave us (Col. 3:13); teach and admonish one another with all wisdom (Col. 3:16); encourage one another (1 Thess. 5:11); and build one another up (1 Thess. 5:11).[6]

In other New Testament literature—especially Hebrews, James, 1 Peter, 1 John, Jude, and Revelation—biblical principles of community life include these: look for opportunities to encourage others on a daily basis (Heb. 3:13); spur one another on toward love and good deeds (Heb. 10:24); do not gossip or slander others (James 4:11); do not complain about or grumble against one another (James 5:9); confess sins to one another in community (James 5:16); pray for one another (James 5:16); genuinely and deeply love one another (1 Pet. 3:8; 4:8); pursue unity in being like-minded (1 Pet. 3:8); practice hospitality by opening up your house and sharing meals without complaining (1 Pet. 4:9); serve others by using the spiritual gifts God has graciously given you (1 Pet. 4:10); be humble and put others' needs before your own (1 Pet. 5:5); truly and genuinely love one another (1 John 4:7–21); be merciful and patiently journey with those who struggle with doubt (Jude 22); and show love and mercy to others without embracing their sin (Jude 23). Jesus also sent messages to seven churches to encourage, admonish, and even rebuke or correct them to continue to be faithful to God and to be in right relationships with one another (Rev. 1–3).[7]

Christian Community: Fellowship with One Another through the Spirit

Fellowship with one another in deep Christian community is a key spiritual discipline empowered and used by the Holy Spirit (Phil. 2:1–2) to help us grow and become more like Jesus together.[8] Fellowship has been defined by J. I. Packer as "a seeking to share in what God has made known of himself to others, as a means to finding strength, refreshment, and instruction for one's soul."[9] In such Christian fellowship, the Holy Spirit enables us to facilitate one another's growth in Christ as we learn to surrender to God's will and engage in loving service to others.

The power of the Holy Spirit works in Christian fellowship in at least four major ways: transforming power to make us more like Jesus; evangelizing power that enables us to lovingly reach out to nonbelievers with the good news of Jesus Christ and invite them to join us in our meeting together; unifying power that pulls us together in one accord so we can become one mind and heart in Christ, pray for one another, and share everything in common with one another, as the early Christians did; and purifying power that helps us become the kind of people God wants us to be in Christlike love and right relationship with one another.[10] There are three crucial ingredients needed to develop such Christian community in a healthy way: support, challenge, and a common mission and purpose.[11]

Jesus himself had a small community with the twelve disciples in which they shared their lives with one another. He taught them, loved and cared for them, guided them, ministered to them and with them as he sent them out to minister to others, corrected them, and prayed for them. He eventually died and rose from the dead and will come back for them and for others who also believe in him and trust him as their Lord and Savior. This fellowship in Christ and with the Spirit is available to all Christians, who can now enter into deep fellowship with one another because of their union with Christ and fellowship with the Triune God (1 John 1:3; Phil. 2:1)

Pastors need to shepherd God's people in the church to be deeply connected with one another in such fellowship, usually through the ministry of small groups and larger fellowships. Douglas Gregg and I have emphasized, "We need others with whom we can share our weaknesses and strengths, who will support us, correct us, and partner with us in mission and service. In the spiritual discipline of fellowship, we help one another to grow out of pride, jealousy, envy, competitiveness, and preoccupation with self. To be in community is a practical concrete way to depend on the Holy Spirit and grow in faith."[12]

Christian community involving deeply connected and loving spiritual relationships can be expressed and experienced in various ways: Christian fellowship, the family, spiritual friendships, and spiritual mentoring or direction.[13]

Christian fellowship is a large part of spiritual community for Christians. It includes fellowship in the larger church or congregational context, such as at worship services and other church meetings and events. It especially occurs in smaller and more personal and intimate contexts, such as in small groups or fellowship groups in which God's people get together to worship God, care and pray for one another, study the Bible (or some other spiritual reading or Christian book) together, and reach out to the world with Christ's love. This chapter focuses mainly on small groups.

Small Groups

There are many types of small groups with varying characteristics. Much helpful material is available on creating an effective small-group ministry, including recruiting and training small-group leaders.[14] A small-group ministry is a key priority in church life and ministry, and the pastor needs to oversee it or delegate responsibility for it to a church leader or another pastoral staff person.

In *The Essential Guide for Small Group Leaders*, Search has provided clear guidelines to help small-group leaders run effective small groups:

- Section 1 covers material on starting a new group, including topics such as how to find and recruit people to the small group; five things to tell potential group members; how to conduct a great first meeting; easy icebreakers for new groups; simple solutions for child care; basic ground rules for new groups; how to create a group covenant that is exceptional; ways to ruin a new group; how to deal with inconsistent attendance; how to keep spiritual batteries charged; and how to find a coach.

- Section 2 focuses on how to develop meaningful relationships in a group, covering topics such as why a group should be open or closed; when a group is too small or too big; how to split a group without causing division; ways to care for group members; how to build relationships during meetings and outside of meetings; dealing with group conflict in healthy ways; six group killers to avoid; dealing with challenging people; how to engage in appropriate confrontation; how to ask a member to leave a group; how to energize a worn-out group; and when and how to end a group.

- Section 3 focuses on growth and transformation, including topics such as how to help people grow in group meetings; how to lead great discussions and ask great questions; how to develop active listening skills and help group members share openly; how to give a testimony; how to make a group a safe place for members to confess sin; things that should not be shared in a group; principles for Bible study; how to use curriculum well and five kinds of curriculum to avoid; how to set personal spiritual goals; how to conduct a great prayer time and creative ways to improve prayer time; how to help members grow outside of group meetings; and how to find and develop future leaders.

- Section 4 focuses on cultivating a heart for others, including topics such as questions to help evaluate a heart for others; how to develop a missional group without leaving the family room; how to be missional outside of group meetings; and how to organize an excellent opportunity for a group to serve together.

- Section 5 covers the biblical foundations for small groups, which were summarized earlier in this chapter.[15]

Two common suggestions made by many and summarized by Search are that a small-group leader needs to invite at least twenty people when trying to fill twelve spaces in a new small group and that the leader should have a coleader. A small-group leader also needs to be clear about how often the group will meet (weekly or biweekly), the length of each meeting (usually about two hours), the duration or life of the small group (start with a ten- to twelve-week commitment that is renewable so it can go longer), and the purpose of the small group (whether it is a deep, disciplemaking group, a support group, or a seeker group that is more outreach oriented to prebelievers).[16]

The Activate Mind-Set for Small Groups

Nelson Searcy and Kerrick Thomas have described a new approach to small groups in *Activate*.[17] Section 1, on rethinking small-group methodology, covers three big ideas. Big idea 1 is to think from the inside out, not from the outside in. Instead of promoting taking care of people on the inside first, they advocate reaching out to others because small groups that focus on serving their own members first tend to stagnate as they become inwardly focused. Big idea 2 is to think larger, not smaller. Instead of promoting the conventional wisdom that smaller groups lead to deeper intimacy, relationships, and spiritual growth, they point out that groups with seven members or fewer have a higher likelihood of failing and are harder to lead, whereas groups of twelve to fifteen people are more effective in producing deeper relationships and spiritual growth. Therefore, small-group leaders should strive for larger, not smaller, groups. (However, in intentional discipleship training groups, smaller groups are more typical, even with only three or four members, as I pointed out earlier in chapter 7 on intentional disciplemaking and spiritual formation.) Big idea 3 is to think friends, not intimacy. Instead of thinking that small groups are a place for forming intimate, close relationships, they see small groups as a place for forming new friendships.

Section 2 of the book covers more big ideas. Big idea 4 is to think short term, not long term. Instead of promoting the conventional wisdom that small groups should last from eighteen months to forever, Searcy and Thomas believe the ideal length for a small group is ten to twelve weeks. Big idea 5 is to think promotion months, not ongoing sign-ups for small groups. Instead of following the traditional thinking that sign-ups for small groups should be ongoing so people can join a small group anytime, they advocate for a focused, shorter sign-up period ("promotion month") that increases participation in and excitement for small groups. Big idea 6 is to think church *of* small groups, not *with* small groups. Traditionally, small groups are seen as just one of many programs available in a church for its attenders, but Searcy and Thomas see small groups as central and crucial in a church, not just one program having to compete with many other church programs. With this view, small groups can be exponentially more effective.

Section 3 covers three more big ideas. Big idea 7 is to think easy, not hard. Conventional wisdom states that people are willing to go through a process with multiple steps in order to join a small group. Searcy and Thomas advocate for one-step sign-ups that make joining a small group easier, faster, and less intimidating and therefore will significantly increase the number of people joining a small group. Big idea 8 is to think ahead, not behind. Most people assume that a month is plenty of time to plan and prepare for a small group. They advocate instead planning and preparing for small groups three to four months ahead of their start date for groups to be successful. Big idea 9 is to think full staff participation, not staff specialist. Conventional wisdom states that a small-group specialist on staff should run the small-group ministry to free up others from having to worry about it. They advocate instead that every staff person should lead or be in a small group, especially the senior or lead pastor. Pastoral staff participation in a small-group ministry is crucial for its effectiveness.

Section 4 of the book covers three final ideas. Big idea 10 is to think apprentice, not expert. Traditional wisdom states that small-group leaders should be longtime Christians who are biblically knowledgeable and have extensive training in how to effectively lead a group. Searcy and Thomas advocate instead that serving as an apprentice or coordinator in a group is sufficient to prepare potential leaders to lead a small group by themselves, no matter how long they have been a Christian or how much expertise or training they have had in leading small groups. Small-group leaders serve as facilitators, not as experts. Big idea 11 is to think decentralization, not staff control. Traditionally, people have assumed that paid staff are needed and should be in control for small groups to be successful. The authors advocate instead that groups are healthier and multiply more quickly when church leaders trust God with volunteer leaders and use them to serve the people. Big idea 12 is to think leader multiplication, not group multiplication. Conventional wisdom states that splitting or dividing existing groups is the best way to grow the number of small groups. They advocate instead that multiplying leaders, through the use of apprenticing, will cause groups to multiply naturally.[18] The book provides detailed guidelines for implementing the activate system for small groups using four Fs: focus, form, fill, and facilitate groups.[19]

Types of Curriculum for Small Groups

With regard to curriculum, there is great variety and flexibility concerning the tools used to guide discussions in a small group. A group can study a book of the Bible, study a spiritual classic or contemporary Christian book, watch a video, answer questions on a printout, or have sermon-based discussions. Bill Search recommended curriculum that requires little to no homework, because of how busy people are today, and is practical, relational, accessible, inclusive, and focused.[20]

SERMON-BASED SMALL GROUPS

Larry Osborne, in *Sticky Church*, strongly advocated using sermon-based small groups in churches, testifying how they make the preacher and the church better.[21] He described what happens during a sermon-based small group in his church: refreshments at the beginning of the group meeting when people first arrive (ten to fifteen minutes); prayer requests and updating each other (fifteen to thirty minutes); study and discussion of the previous week's sermon (around forty-five minutes) with three kinds of questions focusing on getting to know about me and my past, into the Bible, and application; a time of prayer (fifteen to thirty minutes); dessert and time of socializing before heading home. Small-group leaders have the freedom to digress if needed, such as due to a crisis in a group member's life. Worship time in singing is an option. However, groups are required to plan and carry out a service or ministry project once or twice a year and have one social per quarter.[22]

Osborne stated that dividing such groups is not a good idea. People need to stay in the same small group for a long enough time to develop deep relationships and loving, genuine fellowship in Christ. Therefore, splitting or dividing groups every ten to twelve weeks is not advised. He recommended two other strategies for starting new small groups: starting completely new groups with new people and having someone from an existing group lead a new group.[23]

RENOVARÉ SMALL GROUPS FOR SPIRITUAL FORMATION

The purpose of a Renovaré small group is the spiritual formation of its members into deeper Christlikeness. Renovaré (Latin for "to renew") is an organization founded by Richard Foster committed to the renewal of the church of Jesus Christ in all its multifaceted expressions. Renovaré is Christian in commitment, international in scope, and ecumenical in breadth. James Bryan Smith, with Lynda Graybeal, has written *A Spiritual Formation Workbook*,[24] a Renovaré resource that leaders of Renovaré small groups can use to help group members grow in their spiritual formation into Christlikeness. A Renovaré small group usually consists of two to eight members[25] and meets weekly or biweekly. Groups have built-in support and accountability structures that are crucial for spiritual growth into deeper Christlikeness. Whenever the small group meets, members read the following covenant aloud: "In utter dependence upon Jesus Christ as my ever living Savior, Teacher, Lord, and Friend, I will seek continual renewal through spiritual exercises, spiritual gifts, acts of service."[26]

Members in a Renovaré small group take turns reading aloud the common disciplines, following the Christian faith's six great traditions:

- *Contemplative Tradition*: By God's grace, I will set aside time regularly for prayer, meditation, and spiritual reading and will seek to practice the presence of God.
- *Holiness Tradition*: By God's grace, I will strive mightily against sin and will do deeds of love and mercy.
- *Charismatic Tradition*: By God's grace, I will welcome the Holy Spirit, exercising the gifts and nurturing the fruit while living in the joy and power of the Spirit.
- *Social Justice Tradition*: By God's grace, I will endeavor to serve others everywhere I can and will work for justice in all human relationships and social structures.
- *Evangelical Tradition*: By God's grace, I will share my faith with others as God leads and will study the Scriptures regularly.
- *Incarnational Tradition*: By God's grace, I will joyfully seek to show forth the presence of God in all that I am, in all that I do, in all that I say.[27]

Each Renovaré small-group member then has an opportunity to share his or her own experience since the last small-group meeting by responding to questions related to the six traditions of the Christian faith (only the first question for each tradition is used as an example):

- In what ways has God made his presence known to you since our last meeting?
- What temptations have you faced since our last meeting?
- Have you sensed any influence or work of the Holy Spirit since our last meeting?
- What opportunities has God given you to serve others since our last meeting?

- Has God provided an opportunity for you to share your faith with someone since our last meeting?
- In what ways have you been able to manifest the presence of God through your daily work since our last meeting?[28]

The Renovaré small group ends its meeting with some time for sharing and prayer together.

Foster has written *Streams of Living Water*, a comprehensive book describing in more depth the six major traditions of the Christian faith,[29] which can be used for study, discussion, reflection, and application individually or with others in a Renovaré small group.

Ministry Rules for Small Groups

Gary McIntosh and Charles Arn have described six ministry rules for small groups. First, the great diversity rule states that more people will get involved if a church has more kinds of groups. Second, the number of groups rule states that for every one hundred church participants, the church should have seven small groups. Third, the newcomer bonding rule states that the new members will always feel closer to other new members. Fourth, the new groups rule stipulates that one out of every five groups needs to be less than two years old. Fifth, the participation levels rule states that churches that emphasize small groups are likely to have 70 to 80 percent of their total participants involved in small groups. Finally, the group life cycle rule states that every church group has a life cycle, including a natural ending.[30]

Challenges to Christian Community

Christian community, usually in a small-group or a larger fellowship-group context, is not easy or smooth going. It involves open and transparent sharing, including both support and accountability, with people who have their own struggles and strengths, needs and weaknesses, and sinful tendencies and sanctified desires. Genuine Christian community is therefore messy,[31] especially if it involves people from different generations and cultural backgrounds.[32] These challenges may make people feel uncomfortable, but this can be good and necessary.[33] It takes much love and patience to grow together as a family of brothers and sisters in Christ, to cultivate deep spiritual community "in the patient way of Jesus," as Christopher Smith and John Pattison have put it. They have advocated for "slow church" in this day and age of fast and immediate things.[34] While there are helpful guidelines and methods for facilitating growth and healing through different types of small groups in Christian community,[35] we as pastors and church leaders and members all need the presence and the power of the Holy Spirit to enable us to deeply care for and love one another, for Christlike love is the fruit of the Spirit (Gal. 5:22–23) and the result of union and communion with Christ (John 15:5).

I have been involved in leading a small group or a fellowship group (our size varies from twelve to twenty people) together with my wife, Angela, at our home since 2001. We meet biweekly for a couple of hours and have done various things, including studying a book of the Bible, study and discussion of a spiritual classic or a contemporary Christian book, and reflection and sharing using *A Spiritual Formation Workbook*. We have time for deep sharing and prayer as well as for fellowship and eating together before the meeting and dessert and socializing afterward. Group members take turns leading the study and discussion. Much intentional discipleship training and spiritual formation, spiritual direction, pastoral care, and mentoring have happened at our meetings that have touched and transformed many lives over the years. It is an open group, so many new people have joined us, but some have stayed with us for a long time. We have not divided the group. We have been involved in service projects, such as going on short-term mission trips to Mexico, packing gifts for orphans in India, and feeding the homeless. This small-group ministry is a crucial part of my life and pastoral work. Small groups and fellowships are a significant part of pastoral ministry in the church, and every pastor and church leader needs to be involved in a small group.

RECOMMENDED READINGS

Bolsinger, Tod E. *It Takes a Church to Raise a Christian: How the Community of God Transforms Lives*. Grand Rapids: Brazos Press, 2004.

Cloud, Henry, and John Townsend. *Making Small Groups Work: What Every Small Group Leader Needs to Know*. Grand Rapids: Zondervan, 2003.

Donahue, Bill. *Leading Life-Changing Small Groups*. 3rd ed. Grand Rapids: Zondervan, 2012.

Gorman, Julie A. *Community That Is Christian*. 2nd ed. Grand Rapids: Baker Books, 2002.

Greggo, Stephen P. *Trekking toward Wholeness: A Resource for Core Group Leaders*. Downers Grove, IL: IVP Academic, 2008.

Hook, Jan Paul, Joshua N. Hook, and Don E. Davis. *Helping Groups Heal: Leading Small Groups in the Process of Transformation*. West Conshohocken, PA: Templeton Press, 2017.

Icenogle, Gareth Weldon. *Biblical Foundations for Small Group Ministry: An Integrational Approach*. Downers Grove, IL: InterVarsity, 1994.

McCracken, Brett. *Uncomfortable: The Awkward and Essential Challenge of Christian Community*. Wheaton: Crossway, 2017.

Osborne, Larry. *Sticky Church*. Grand Rapids: Zondervan, 2008.

Search, Bill. *The Essential Guide for Small Group Leaders*. Carol Stream, IL: Christianity Today, 2017.

Searcy, Nelson, and Kerrick Thomas. *Activate: An Entirely New Approach to Small Groups*. Rev. ed. Grand Rapids: Baker Books, 2018.

Smith, James Bryan, with Lynda Graybeal. *A Spiritual Formation Workbook: Small Group Resources for Nurturing Christian Growth*. Rev. ed. San Francisco: HarperSanFrancisco, 1999.

Zempel, Heather. *Community Is Messy: The Perils and Promise of Small Group Ministry*. Downers Grove, IL: InterVarsity, 2012.

15

Integrity and Ethics

Jerry Johnson, in *The New Guidebook for Pastors*, asserted that the chapter on the pastor and ethics may be the most important chapter in the book.[1] Although competency in preaching and teaching is essential for a pastor (1 Tim. 3:2), it is even more crucial for a pastor to have integrity and ethics that are aboveboard, to be a moral and spiritual example to the church and before the world even though he or she is not perfect. First Timothy 3:2–7 lists fifteen requirements for a pastor, overseer, elder, or bishop, and they all focus on moral character:

> Now the overseer is to be above reproach, faithful to his wife, temperate, self-controlled, respectable, hospitable, able to teach, not given to drunkenness, not violent but gentle, not quarrelsome, not a lover of money. He must manage his own family well and see that his children obey him, and he must do so in a manner worthy of full respect. (If anyone does not know how to manage his own family, how can he take care of God's church?) He must not be a recent convert, or he may become conceited and fall under the same judgment as the devil. He must also have a good reputation with outsiders, so that he will not fall into disgrace and into the devil's trap.

A pastor's integrity and ethics are crucial for sustaining pastoral ministry in a faithful and fruitful way over the long run. Much has been written about ethics, both personal and professional, for pastors, who have been called to a sacred but stressful and challenging ministry.[2] Spectacular moral sins such as child abuse, marital infidelities, sexual sin, sexual harassment, and financial fraud committed by pastors have received much attention in recent years and resulted in dishonor to the Lord and damage to the church and his people. However, as William Willimon has pointed out, there are more mundane and less dramatic lapses in a pastor's integrity and ethics that still deeply harm millions of parishioners and the church, such as poor sermons, bad administration, and careless pastoral care. They result not so much from a great inclination to sin on the part of pastors but from character weakness and a lack of perseverance to keep on being faithful in pastoral ministry when its challenges and demands are particularly hard.[3]

Therefore, a pastor needs to engage in spiritual disciplines and practices that enable him or her to abide in union and communion with Christ (John 15:5), by the power of the Holy Spirit (see chaps. 3 and 4 of this book), to become a faithful and fruitful servant of Jesus Christ and show perseverance in ministry as a disciplined Christian.[4] Such practices include the inherent tasks of pastoral ministry, such as preaching, and weekly scheduled time for study, prayer, Scripture reading, reflection, and self-examination. These practices help keep pastors focused and on track,[5] as does keeping the Sabbath.[6] Willimon also emphasized that poor time management, in particular, wears down many pastors, and therefore wise time management is important, including maintaining proper boundaries and saying no to what is not essential.[7]

Ultimately, however, we pastors are enabled by God himself, by his grace and the Spirit's power, to persevere, not by trying harder in self-effort to do so but by simply joining God in what he is already doing. Willimon put it well: "The ordained life would be too great a burden for anyone were it not that God has called us to join in work God is already doing. Our ministry is subsequent and derivative of God's. It is God's work, not our own, that sustains. . . . God calls us to do nothing alone."[8]

Michael Wilson and Brad Hoffman, in *Preventing Ministry Failure*, have provided practical and biblically based guidelines and strategies for helping pastors have an effective long-term ministry. They described seven foundation stones to prevent ministry failure. The first foundation stone has to do with intimacy or connecting to the heart of successful pastoring. It includes developing and experiencing intimacy with God, through close friendships, and with a spouse (and what to do if one is single). Practical steps are also provided for growing deeper in human relationships, including a few healthy same-gender friendships. The second foundation stone has to do with calling or the power for ministry effectiveness. It covers understanding one's call to ministry, being sure of the calling, and dealing with called versus not called and staying versus leaving. The third foundation stone relates to stress management or avoiding ineffectiveness and burnout. It covers the energy to accomplish one's calling and the energy drain of the mismanagement of stress. The fourth foundation stone has to do with boundaries or protecting what matters most. It covers personal boundaries and boundaries in the ministry setting, with intimate relationships, with oneself, and with God. The fifth foundation stone relates to recreation or the fuel to reenergize ministry. It covers dealing with being slaves to a schedule, common excuses for not recreating, the three Rs of recreation (rest, recess, and renewal), and coming up with a personal recreation plan. The sixth foundation stone has to do with people skills or managing one's most valuable resource. It covers personality and personality theory, active listening, reflective listening, and useful assertiveness techniques for pastors. Finally, the seventh foundation stone has to do with leadership skills or setting pastors apart from the rest of the people of God. It covers leadership that is transformative, how to deal with change in ministry, and leadership styles and other elements for effective leadership.[9]

Integrity and ethics in regard to pastors can be divided into two categories: personal ethics and professional ethics, although they are closely related to each other.[10]

Personal Ethics

Personal ethics has to do with the integrity of a pastor and how biblically moral and ethical he or she is, especially in his or her personal and family life. Two major areas of personal ethics involve sex and money.[11] Sexual sin, including adultery and child sexual abuse, has been described by James Bryant and Mac Brunson as the most serious sin that a pastor can commit, and all steps should be taken to avoid it.[12]

Bryant and Brunson have taken a very conservative and cautious approach, recommending that a pastor not meet or drive alone with a member of the opposite gender and not counsel a member of the opposite gender unless his or her spouse is present.[13] This recommendation, though well meaning, cannot be followed in certain situations—for example, when a pastor is not married. What is necessary, then, is for a pastor to counsel in an office that has a window, with other staff members around so the meeting is not isolated and private. The authors also mentioned the example Billy Graham set in his long ministry as an evangelist. He never rode in a car alone with a woman and never had a meal with his female secretary alone. Graham also was never totally alone with a woman, was careful in environments that were questionable, was cautious about friendships that could be inappropriate, was mindful of the danger of emotional bonding, and avoided being in situations in which moral compromise was possible.[14]

Bryant and Brunson also addressed what they consider the second most vulnerable ethical area personally for a pastor: dealing with money. They recommended that a pastor never serve as a cosigner of checks in the church and avoid directly handling church funds as far as possible. A pastor should also not use a church's corporate credit card. He or she should use a personal credit card for church expenses to be reimbursed later. Ethically, a pastor should also not live extravagantly and not accept an exorbitant salary from a church.[15] Some of these suggestions may not work in certain church situations. A pastor can serve as a cosigner of certain checks, such as love offering or benevolent fund checks that may be needed immediately in a crisis of need situation. The board of trustees and the church accountant will see these checks, which still require another church trustee to cosign, as is the case in my church. A church's corporate credit card can similarly be used by a pastor for official church purposes and expenses because these charges are regularly checked and monitored by the church accountant and the board of trustees.[16]

Personal accountability is an important part of personal ethics for a pastor. A pastor should have a confidant who serves as an accountability and prayer partner. This accountability partner will ask the hard questions about the pastor's personal life—for example, what TV shows and movies are being watched and how the internet is being used. This person could even monitor websites visited to help a pastor avoid the temptation of pornography, which has become a widespread addiction, even among pastors.[17]

Personal ethics for a pastor is ultimately an issue of Christlike character (Rom. 8:29) and love for God and others (Mark 12:30–31). It is being "above reproach" (1 Tim. 3:2) by abiding in Christ, in union and communion with him (John 15:5) through the power and fruit of the Spirit (Gal. 5:22–23). However, a pastor should also have a personal code of ethics without being legalistic. Joe Trull and Robert Creech have provided a helpful sample code of ethics for a pastor to use, with guidelines for these areas: self, family, the congregation, colleagues, the community, and the denomination. They also have provided a pastoral counselor code.[18]

Professional Ethics

Bryant and Brunson give guidelines regarding professional ethics that a pastor needs to follow. First, a pastor needs to be honest and allow only one church at a time to seriously consider him or her for a pastoral position. Second, a pastor should stay at a church as long as the church wants him or her, unless the Lord calls the pastor to leave and move to another church or another ministry. On average, a pastor today stays at a church for only three years. This may not be long enough to be involved in faithful and fruitful pastoral ministry, which usually takes years. Third, if a pastor leaves a church, this should be done with grace and love instead of bitterness and hatred, even if the pastor leaves feeling rejected (John 1:11). Sometimes a pastor can grow in the fellowship of Christ's sufferings, including rejection (Phil. 3:10), when asked to leave a church. Finally, a pastor must not unethically use the pulpit to attack or lash out at parishioners who do not agree with him or her or who have strongly criticized the pastor.[19] A pastor also must be careful not to engage in gossip and slander of those who have gossiped about and slandered him or her.

Joe Trull and James Carter, in *Ministerial Ethics*, delineated several ethical obligations that a pastor should fulfill as part of his or her professional, ministerial ethics. First, regarding education or competency, if possible, a pastor should go to seminary to receive the theological and pastoral training needed to serve a church well in pastoral ministry. Second, regarding autonomy, a pastor must not allow others to control him or her in decision-making when there should be pastoral autonomy and authority. Third, regarding service, a pastor needs to follow Jesus's example of servanthood (John 13:1–16) and be a faithful and fruitful servant. A pastor should humbly and lovingly lead the church with appropriate biblical sacrificial service. Fourth, regarding dedication, a pastor should surrender and dedicate his or her life to pastoral ministry to God's people in the church and beyond and faithfully preach and teach the gospel, which is the power of God for salvation to everyone who believes (Rom. 1:16). Finally, regarding ethics, a pastor is held to a higher standard of character and is a moral and spiritual example. A pastor needs to humbly, with God's grace and the power of the Spirit, meet the sixteen qualifications listed in 1 Timothy 3:1–7, starting with being "above reproach" (1 Tim. 3:2).[20]

Willimon has emphasized appropriate humor as an essential virtue in our lives and ministries as pastors so that we do not take ourselves too seriously and learn to relax and rely more on God and his grace. Also, in our preaching, we can effectively use satire, irony, and other examples of linguistic subversion, as Jesus did in his use of parables, to more deeply impact people with the gospel and God's truth. Our confidence is ultimately in what God has done and will continue to do in Christ, for us and through us and even despite us.[21]

Willimon also underscored that pastors should never use their pastoral authority for their personal sexual gratification. It is very clear that sex with parishioners is unethical, wrong, and sinful. Citing Rebekah Miles, he pointed out that it is always the pastor's responsibility to keep proper boundaries physically with parishioners and know that it is never right or appropriate to have any sexual contact with them. Even when giving hugs or a handshake, a pastor needs to be careful and sensitive to what a particular parishioner is comfortable or uncomfortable with, especially in private settings where greater caution is warranted.[22]

Ethics for Christian Ministry

In a more recent book, *Ethics for Christian Ministry*, Trull and Creech offered substantial reflections and guidelines for ethics for Christian ministry.[23] They argued that it is important to view pastoral ministry as a profession (besides a calling and a vocation) and pastors as professionals who should be held to high ethical standards and integrity in their lives and ministries. They substantially covered additional topics: being good and doing good in moral formation for ministry; looking in the mirror with integrity in one's personal life; looking at the church with integrity in one's ministry; looking at fellow ministers with integrity with one's colleagues; promoting peace and justice with integrity in the community; facing and dealing with clergy sexual abuse as the cost of lost integrity; and developing a personal code of ethics as a plan for integrity in ministry. They provided four helpful appendixes: appendix A: "A Procedure for Responding to Charges of Clergy Sexual Abuse"; appendix B: "Early Denominational Codes of Ethics"; appendix C: "Contemporary Denominational Codes of Ethics"; and appendix D: "Sample Codes of Ethics." They also included a simple worksheet for a ministerial code of ethics, focusing on personal and family relationships, congregational relationships, collegial relationships, and community relationships.[24]

A Model for Ethical Decision-Making

A helpful nine-step model for ethical decision-making that can be applied to pastors has been described by Randolph Sanders:

1. Assess a situation for its ethical dimensions.
2. Try to define the problem or issue using codes and principles.
3. Understand and process your emotional reaction to the problem or issue.
4. Seek consultation as needed, and this should be done at any point in the process of decision-making.
5. Decide whom you should be considering (e.g., the counselor or family or others) and why in making an ethical decision.

6. Find out if there is precedent in other similar cases that would help you in your decision-making.

7. Explore all the options you could take.

8. Consider the possible consequences of every option.

9. Make a decision and be ready to assume appropriate responsibility for the consequences of the action you decided to take.[25]

Sanders especially emphasized the need for ethical therapists (or pastors) to develop relationships with God and with other professionals for consultation, support, and accountability. An ethical professional will not work too long by himself or herself in isolation from peers. He or she will consult other professionals whenever needed and periodically to overcome blind spots and vulnerabilities that can make one liable to ethical lapses.[26]

The Minister as Moral Theologian

Sondra Wheeler has written two books to help pastors develop integrity and ethics for ministry. The first is *The Minister as Moral Theologian*, on the ethical dimensions of pastoral leadership.[27] Wheeler emphasized that rules of conduct and administrative processes for dealing with offenses after they happen, while necessary, are not enough. She asserted:

> It is vastly more helpful to understand how those who begin with an intention to serve end up doing harm, to identify the factors that contribute to or reduce that risk, and thus help to prevent misconduct before the harm is done . . . to explore what puts ministers as human beings at risk, to help them acknowledge and understand the vulnerabilities that all human beings share, and to help them address these vulnerabilities in safe and appropriate ways. Ultimately, recognizing the profound link between moral performance and spiritual practice will help ministers to develop patterns of life and sustain virtues that will protect them and those they serve.[28]

In describing the minister as moral theologian and the ethical dimensions of pastoral leadership, Wheeler affirmed the role of the minister or pastor as ethicist and the church as a moral community. She provided details on the ethics of duty, the ethics of consequences, and the ethics of virtue. While a pastor has to provide ethical and moral guidance to the congregation, there are some complex ethical issues that may not have clear-cut or easy answers, even with biblical help, and this needs to be honestly acknowledged in a humble and gracious way.[29] There are three major aspects of pastoral ministry in which a pastor can provide ethical and moral guidance and leadership to a congregation: preaching, teaching, and providing moral counsel.

In the area of preaching, a pastor needs to be aware of the dangers of preaching about ethics and especially preaching on morally difficult texts and occasions, although this cannot be avoided. Wheeler provided helpful guidelines for preaching in the face of disaster, preaching the high demands of the kingdom, preaching on troubling texts, and preaching on morally controversial topics or texts, which requires humility, prayer, and tentative conclusions. Wheeler suggested the following conclusion to such a sermon: "And you can say, 'This is my best wisdom on the matter. But God help me, I could be wrong.' Therefore, begin and end all declarations about deeply contested matters with prayer, including the acknowledgment that even our most passionately held views are subject to limitation and error, and pray for God's wisdom and mercy on all."[30]

In the area of teaching about moral issues, Wheeler emphasized the close connection between being good and thinking well. She provided helpful guidelines for using four accepted sources of Christian ethics in a responsible and balanced way: Scripture, tradition, reason, and experience. A pastor should not do all the moral teaching himself or herself, but rather delegate some of it to other church leaders and groups, thereby creating safe places for people to grapple with difficult moral issues without compromising biblical teaching where it is clear and the commitment to faithful discipleship.[31]

In the area of providing moral counsel, a pastor is in a unique position to provide moral guidance in the context of pastoral care and counseling of parishioners and others. Wheeler covered several aspects of moral guidance: listening and inquiry, affirmation and support, a tradition of discernment, challenge and admonition, repentance and forgiveness, fidelity and confidentiality. She also described the following strategies for moral guidance: asking questions, engaging the imagination, raising the long-term view, asking for a letter (to be written but not sent), and establishing a strong foundation of trust.[32]

Wheeler concluded by focusing on the pastor as a moral example[33] and being under the watchful eye or scrutiny of parishioners, whether the pastor likes it or not. Pastors are not perfect, but they can use 1 Corinthians as a guide and love as a practical norm to follow in serving humbly as a moral example, fully dependent on the power and presence of the Holy Spirit, whose fruit is agape love (Gal. 5:22–23). Wheeler elaborated on the characteristics of agape love: it is patient and kind; is not envious; is not boastful, arrogant, or rude; does not insist on its own way; is not irritable or resentful; does not rejoice in wrongdoing but rejoices in the truth; and bears, believes, hopes, endures all things, and never fails. She emphasized that the greatest risk of pastoral ministry is not burnout or even moral failure. What is at the bottom of much pastoral misconduct and exhaustion is cynicism: "loss of faith in the meaningfulness and efficacy of the work that ministers do. It is borne of frustration and despair."[34] This is the greatest danger because it cuts pastors off from the basic trust that God's goodness will ultimately triumph despite all the limitations and losses. She also provided several practical guidelines to help pastors persevere and stay on the path: take your bearings from your deepest sense of call; maintain honesty with yourself; have your own counselors, supervisors, or mentors; keep appropriate transparency; and take time out from the fishbowl. The call to holiness and growth into deeper Christlikeness in character transformation is ultimately the work of the Holy Spirit and God's grace. Life is an ongoing journey, with ups and downs and periods of struggle, including temptation, confusion, doubt, and even despair. But there is always grace for repentance, which can also be translated as "homecoming."[35]

Foundations and Practices for Serving Faithfully

Wheeler has also written *Sustaining Ministry*, which provides foundations and practices to help pastors serve faithfully and avoid ministerial misconduct.[36] She focused on the underlying dynamics responsible for making pastoral ministry potentially dangerous for pastors as well as for those they serve. She covered the subtle distortions in the work of pastoral ministry that point to something that has gone awry before any financial or sexual scandals occur, such as unwillingness to share authority or delegate; reluctance to develop other leaders in the church; tendency to focus the church's worship and life on the pastor as the center of attention; and carelessness about the symbolic power attached to the pastoral office and special obligations of pastors entrusted with the personal confidences of parishioners. Common patterns of life among pastors can also lead to corrosion of pastoral identity; ordinary disciplines of the Christian life, especially the discipline of rest, can help to protect and strengthen that identity.[37]

In regard to laying deeper ethical foundations, Wheeler addressed the needs that make us human, such as relationality (having deep connection with other human companions), embodiment (taking good care of our bodies and physical needs), the dangers of denying basic needs, and the need to practice unselfish self-care.[38]

In regard to protecting space for ministry, Wheeler focused on the need to maintain clear and proper boundaries regarding socializing, emotional support and care, personal disclosure, and one-on-one relationships.[39]

When addressing how pastors can get into trouble, especially sexual misconduct, Wheeler emphasized the need for pastors to be mindful of their own vulnerability to temptation and confusion. The conditions that can lead to greater risk require careful monitoring: fatigue, loneliness, frustration, conflict, marital difficulties, loss, and professional setbacks. Pastors must also be alert to the following danger signs that they may already be in trouble in relationships with parishioners or colleagues: paying special attention to one's appearance; becoming mentally preoccupied with a particular person; changing, extending, or increasing the frequency of meeting times; seeking one-on-one interaction; providing inappropriate personal disclosures; preferring the company of a particular person; changing the kind or frequency of physical touch; hiding contact with a particular person from view; deceiving one's partner or spiritual mentor; engaging in sexual fantasy; and becoming physically aroused.[40]

Pastors need to know how to respond when they realize they are on the edge and when they are over the line and have committed wrongdoing or misconduct. When a pastor is on the edge, four steps must be taken immediately: tell someone; back up; resist the temptation to talk to the particular person involved about personal feelings or struggles; and uncover and deal with the underlying issues, usually with the help of a professional therapist, spiritual director, or pastoral counselor. In situations in which the emotional attachment to the particular person involved is intense and the romantic bonding is high, a pastor may have to leave in order to save his or her ministry.[41]

When a pastor is over the line and has committed wrongdoing or misconduct, the following steps should be taken to work out a way forward: stop the unethical behavior or relationship immediately; find a trustworthy counselor to walk with through the process of repentance—making whatever amends are possible—recovery, and healing; part from the victim of the misconduct in an appropriate way, taking full responsibility for the wrongdoing; get long-term skilled care and spiritual direction to help in understanding and dealing with the personal weaknesses and issues that resulted in the misconduct; be as honest and transparent as possible; and adopt and submit to the community's disciplines or church discipline for ultimate restoration.[42]

Finally, Wheeler emphasized the need for pastors to embrace the spiritual practices that sustain faithfulness and ethical practice in ministry. She described two spiritual practices or spiritual disciplines: prayer and accountability with a prayer partner, mentor, or spiritual director.[43]

Pastoral Care and Counseling

In the more specific area of providing pastoral care and counseling, it is important for pastors to exercise wise time management, maintain proper boundaries, and conduct only short-term counseling, as Bill Blackburn has emphasized[44] and as noted in chapter 11 of this book.

Blackburn has provided six ethical guidelines for pastors who do pastoral counseling with parishioners. First, maintain confidentiality, except for mandatory reporting laws in certain states that apply not only to therapists but also to pastors who counsel. For example, child abuse, elder abuse, danger to self (suicidal risk), and danger to others in many states in the United States require mandatory reporting or crisis intervention that involves breaking confidentiality. Second, avoid manipulating or exploiting the counselee or parishioner. Third, do not make decisions for the parishioner, although the pastor can provide directive counseling and biblical guidance. The final decision is still up to the parishioner, except in emergency situations such as high suicidal risk in which the pastor may have to decide on hospitalization or at least bringing the counselee to the emergency section of a hospital for further assessment and safe care. Fourth, refrain from inappropriately carrying messages to others, such as family members or a spouse, respecting the confidentiality of the parishioner (unless the spouse and family are also involved in the pastoral counseling and it is clear that information or messages can be shared). Fifth, avoid being a voyeur. Do not ask for sexually titillating information that is not relevant to the issue being dealt with in pastoral counseling. Finally, never be sexually or romantically involved with a parishioner being seen in pastoral counseling. Blackburn recommended counseling an opposite-gender person only when someone else is around to reduce the risk of unethical and sinful sexual contact with a parishioner.[45]

Henry Cloud and John Townsend's updated and expanded edition of *Boundaries*, which now includes boundaries for the digital age, is helpful with regard to the specific area of maintaining proper boundaries, including learning when to say yes and how to say no so that pastors take some control of their lives and manage their time well.[46]

Integrity and ethics are important parts of pastoral ministry. A pastor is held to a high ethical standard, both personally and professionally. Because we as pastors are imperfect human beings and models made of clay, we need to prayerfully depend on the Holy Spirit to empower us in Christ to be Christlike in character, to be people who will glorify God and bless rather than harm others. We need to regularly engage in the spiritual disciplines, especially prayer, including solitude and silence, and accountability, which will help sustain us in ministry and help us avoid ministerial misconduct. Ultimately, it is the Holy Spirit who will make us into holy men and women of God who are "above reproach" (1 Tim. 3:2).

RECOMMENDED READINGS

Dimos, Rollie. *Integrity at Stake: Safeguarding Your Church from Financial Fraud.* Grand Rapids: Zondervan, 2016.

Fortune, Marie. *Is Nothing Sacred? When Sex Invades the Pastoral Relationship.* San Francisco: Harper, 1989.

Grenz, Stanley J., and Roy D. Bell. *Betrayal of Trust: Confronting and Preventing Clergy Sexual Misconduct.* 2nd ed. Grand Rapids: Baker Books, 2001.

Proeschold-Bell, Rae Jean, and Jason Byassee. *Faithful and Fractured: Responding to the Clergy Health Crisis.* Grand Rapids: Baker Academic, 2018.

Sanders, Randolph K., ed. *Christian Counseling Ethics: A Handbook for Psychologists, Therapists and Pastors.* 2nd ed. Downers Grove, IL: IVP Academic, 2013.

Trull, Joe E., and James E. Carter. *Ministerial Ethics: Moral Formation for Church Leaders.* Grand Rapids: Baker Academic, 2004.

Trull, Joe E., and R. Robert Creech. *Ethics for Christian Ministry: Moral Formation for 21st Century Leaders.* Grand Rapids: Baker Academic, 2017.

Wheeler, Sondra. *The Minister as Moral Theologian: Ethical Dimensions of Pastoral Leadership.* Grand Rapids: Baker Academic, 2017.

———. *Sustaining Ministry: Foundations and Practices for Serving Faithfully.* Grand Rapids: Baker Academic, 2017.

Wilson, Michael Todd, and Brad Hoffmann. *Preventing Ministry Failure: A ShepherdCare Guide for Pastors, Ministers and Other Caregivers.* Downers Grove, IL: InterVarsity, 2007.

16

Leaving and Retiring

Another aspect of pastoral ministry has to do with leaving a pastoral position for a number of reasons, positive or negative, and the eventual retiring of a pastor from a local church position.[1] Pastoral succession is inevitable in a church, just as CEO succession is inevitable in a corporation. Much has been written recently on both pastoral succession[2] and CEO succession.[3]

Pastoral Succession

In *Next*, a practical and helpful book on pastoral succession that works, William Vanderbloemen and Warren Bird made this assertion: "Every pastor is an interim pastor. Few ministers consider that truth. Few are eager to admit that their time with their present church will one day end. But ultimately, all pastors are 'interim' because the day when a successor takes over will come for everyone in ministry. Planning for that day of succession may be the biggest leadership task a leader and church will ever face. It may also be the most important."[4] Pastoral succession is therefore a significant part of pastoral ministry and a key responsibility for every pastor to prayerfully consider.

Pastoral succession has been defined by Dave Travis, CEO of Leadership Network, as "*the intentional process of the transfer of leadership, power, and authority from one directional leader to another.*"[5] Every organization and every church will eventually need a new leader. Succession refers to when a leader hands over leadership to another, usually younger, leader. Succession planning has to do with coming up with a plan to effectively and efficiently implement the succession.

Why Pastors Leave

James Bryant and Mac Brunson, after pointing out that most pastors today do not stay at one church for a long time, provided seven reasons why pastors leave their pastoral positions in local churches. The first three reasons have to do with family: special care needs of the pastor's children and family, sexual misconduct on the part of the pastor, and divorce or other marital difficulties. The other four reasons are deciding to move to another ministry other than in a local church (such as a parachurch ministry, missions abroad, seminary teaching, or denominational work), conflict with the congregation, conflict with the denomination, or becoming discouraged and burned out or clinically depressed.[6] Many of these reasons for leaving are negative, and even tragic in some situations. A good reason to leave is when a pastor is doing well at a church but senses a call from God to move to a different kind of ministry, and sometimes even to a different kind of church. Even if the congregation supports the decision, with full blessing for the pastor to leave and move on, a pastoral succession plan is still needed.

Some pastors do not get to decide whether to leave a position. Bryant and Brunson pointed out that one out of every four pastors in America will either be forced to resign or be fired during a lifetime of pastoral ministry, with horrible effects for the pastor, his or her family, and the church. It is crucial in such painful situations for the pastor to avoid bitterness and seek the Lord for grace, healing, and ultimate restoration.[7] Support from others and special help from ministries or organizations that provide resources, such as counseling and retreats, for such pastors can also be accessed.[8]

Making the Decision to Leave

If a pastor is not asked to leave or is not fired for reasons such as sexual misconduct or some other unethical offense, he or she needs to carefully and prayerfully discern whether it is God's will for him or her to leave by choice. Gordon MacDonald has suggested several hints or signals that it may be time for a pastor to consider leaving and moving on to another ministry or church:

- incompatibility between the pastor's leadership style and gifts and what the congregation needs so that there is a mismatch;

- immobility of the congregation;
- organizational transition of the church to a different stage or level that the pastor is not suited to lead;
- stagnancy and lack of growth and development on the part of the pastor;
- fatigue and lack of renewal opportunities for the pastor;
- low morale among the pastor's spouse and children, who are being harmed by unrealistic expectations of the church;
- closings and openings and time for a change, including having a new pastor;
- and age, when a pastor is getting older and approaching retirement age.[9]

Vanderbloemen and Bird have listed ten indicators God may use to show a pastor it is time to move.

1. God guides clearly to move (e.g., through Scripture, vision, dream, circumstances).
2. The pastor's spiritual leadership speaks clearly to move (e.g., a bishop, denominational superintendent, or church board).
3. The pastor's part of the mission or ministry is complete.
4. The pastor loses heart, and the fire and passion for ministry at the church are gone.
5. Confirmation for moving comes from other trusted advisers and close friends.
6. The pastor receives a new call from another ministry or church.
7. There is a mismatch between the church's current needs and the pastor's ability to meet them.
8. Collaboration between the church and the pastor and his or her family creates more conflict.
9. The church shows a lack of confidence in the pastor's vision and leadership.
10. The pastor reaches his or her physical and emotional limits and no longer has the energy, strength, and mental capacity to do the work needed.[10]

Bryant and Brunson concluded, "Pastor, stay at your church if you can. Leave if you must. Follow the Word of God and the will of God for your life and for the church. Remember that the call is for a lifetime, but the assignment may change. Most pastors should probably stay a longer time rather than a shorter time at a particular church."[11]

Succession Planning

Vanderbloemen and Bird have cited statistics showing that the average tenure of a senior pastor at a church is eight years, with an average pastoral career for a senior pastor being eighteen years. Therefore, a typical senior pastor may go through pastoral succession two or more times. The practice of staying at one church and pastoring it for a lifetime is no longer the standard. The average senior pastor also plans to retire from full-time pastoral ministry at age sixty-five. The clear message from these statistics is that pastoral succession is inevitable and now is the time to start praying and planning for such succession.[12]

The Bible contains many succession stories, such as Moses succeeded by Joshua (Num. 27:16–17); Aaron succeeded by Eleazar (Num. 20:25–19); Saul succeeded by David (1 Sam. 23:16–17); Elijah succeeded by Elisha (2 Kings 2:9); and Jesus handing over his mission to his disciples (John 21). True success in ministry requires having successors; there is no success without successors. However, there is no one-size-fits-all model or plan for succession. Each situation is unique, and succession can take place in different ways. Preparing successors and future pastors to take over is key,[13] and the time for talking about and praying, planning, and preparing for pastoral succession is never too early.[14]

Vanderbloemen and Bird have provided ten key guidelines for preparing for succession that pastors and church boards would be wise to follow. First, read their book with others, especially with the church board, and discuss it together. Second, establish a healthy pace for the long run by making sure pastors have sabbaticals (e.g., a paid three-month break every seven years) and take regular vacations. Third, prepare an emergency succession plan in case of an accident that could incapacitate the pastor for an extended period of time or a sudden death. Fourth, have a plan for a nonemergency but unforeseen departure by the pastor. Fifth, pastors should anticipate their (eventual) retirement and have a succession plan that is related to retirement, including adequate financial support. Some pastors hang on for too long and do not retire because of lack of financial support for retirement. Sixth, annually evaluate the succession plan and see if modifications and improvements are needed. Seventh, create a broad churchwide culture of leadership development, especially for the next generation or two. Eighth, share the teaching and preaching responsibilities to develop more preachers and teachers. Ninth, share the leading or leadership roles and responsibilities, delegating them to appropriate senior pastoral staff and other church leaders. Tenth, look beyond the passing of the baton to the successor to one's own next meaningful area of ministry after leaving or retiring.[15]

Knowing that there is no success without succession,[16] a pastor should prayerfully think long term and engage in pastoral succession planning with the church board or leadership. If outside consultation is needed, these organizations can help: Vanderbloemen Search Group (info@vanderbloemen .com) and the Leadership Network (dave.travis@leadnet.org or client.care@ leadnet.org).[17]

In an article in *Christianity Today*, Bird summarized some of what was written in *Next* about successful pastoral successions and reviewed four major models: (1) family plan (in which pastoral succession is handed down to a family member or spiritual son or daughter), (2) denominational plan (in which pastoral succession is planned by both the local church and the bishop or denominational superintendent), (3) process-only plan (in which the pastor who is outgoing helps to create and implement a pastoral succession plan and then leaves), and (4) intentional overlap plan (in which the outgoing pastor intentionally overlaps with the successor for a limited time before fully handing the ministry over to the successor).[18] He concluded, "From the Moses-Joshua handoff to Jesus' training of the Twelve, succession planning is both biblical and essential, but there is no cookie-cutter template. The only thing that's certain? It's an inevitable need in every church. And we hope to move it from taboo to normal."[19] He also listed five major reasons why pastoral successions fail. First, pastors do not let go. Second, pastors wait too long. Third, multiple candidates fight it out. Fourth, change comes too quickly. Fifth, pastors hit hidden landmines as successors in a particular church.[20]

Types of Pastoral Succession

According to VanderBloemen and Bird, there are two types of pastoral succession: unexpected and expected. Unexpected pastoral successions can be divided into three categories:

- *Emergency.* This category refers to unanticipated, sudden, and often crisis-based successions, including death and other tragic events. It can be short term, involving a temporary, unplanned absence, usually lasting three or fewer months; long term, usually lasting more than three months; or permanent, in which case the pastor will not be coming back to the pastoral position.

- *Disqualified*. This category refers to situations in which a pastor is disqualified from serving in a pastoral position for various possible reasons. They include moral failure (most frequently involving some abuse of sex, money, and/or power or some major illegal activity), doctrinal heresy or deviation from the church's biblical standards, and loss of physical core competencies (such as health problems or a loss of energy, vision, or preaching ability).
- *Forced*. This category refers to a situation in which a pastor is fired or forced to leave.[21]

When a pastor needs to leave but doesn't want to, a forced farewell may be necessary. Vanderbloemen and Bird have offered several suggestions to help with a forced departure. First, appropriate and intense prayer for the pastor and even with the pastor for God's guidance and blessings on the pastor and the church may lead the pastor to resign. Second, the church board sets clear expectations early enough when the pastor is first hired. Third, the board encourages the pastor to find a new identity or ministry and move toward it. Fourth, the board hires a search firm to guide the pastor to find a new ministry identity. Fifth, the board pays for the pastor to become a certified interim pastor as part of a graceful exit plan. Sixth, the board informs the pastor that a forced retirement or termination may happen. Seventh, the board votes to release the pastor but negotiates quietly with the pastor behind closed doors to maintain confidentiality and respect for the pastor. Eighth, denominational leadership decides to let the pastor go. Ninth, the congregation votes to release the pastor. Tenth, an annual review includes discussion of potential succession.[22]

Expected pastoral successions are the ones that can be best planned far ahead of time. This category includes ministry transition, referring to the pastor embarking on a new and different ministry with partnerships or support from the church (such as church planter, seminary professor, chaplain, interim pastor at other churches, mentor to other pastors, missionary, or author); church rotation, referring to a new assignment to another church by a bishop or denominational leader or the pastor accepting a call from another church; and retirement of the pastor, which can be full retirement or partial retirement, in which the pastor moves into a less senior or part-time pastoral position.[23]

Retirement

It is important that a pastor who is retiring prepare for life and ministry beyond retirement. Dealing with financial issues or the need to have enough financial support, including a good pension and retirement plan from the church, is particularly important for a pastor so that he or she does not stay too long at a church because of a lack of financial support. We as pastors may retire from a specific pastoral position or ministry assignment at a church, but we do not retire from the Christian life or Christian ministry in general. God will call us to different ministries, to continue to faithfully and fruitfully serve him and others, as long as our health and energy allow us to serve. We may no longer serve in a full-time capacity, but we can still serve on a part-time or voluntary basis.

My Personal Experience as a Senior Pastor

I have served as the senior pastor of my church for over twenty years. The previous senior pastor served for thirty years before he retired due to poor health and selected me to be his successor with the full support of the church boards and leadership. I am now in my sixties, and I have been prayerfully discussing with our church boards and leaders a pastoral succession in the coming years. There is no clear candidate yet to eventually take over as senior pastor from me. The plan is to (1) help groom or develop one of the younger pastors on our pastoral staff to do so; (2) look outside the staff but within the church; or (3) look outside the church to cast the net wider to find an appropriate successor. I have been mentoring our pastoral staff and church leaders, both younger and older, over the years, believing in leadership development and intentional disciplemaking churchwide, especially through personal mentoring. I have also delegated pastoral and leadership responsibilities to various pastoral staff and church leaders over the years, including sharing my pulpit preaching and teaching ministry. Although I still do most of the preaching in the English worship service, I have begun to decrease the frequency of my preaching to about twenty-five times a year, giving more opportunities for younger pastors to preach and teach from the pulpit at our English Sunday worship service.

We have a couple of other pastoral staff who are in their mid- to late sixties who are also preparing for pastoral succession or retirement. As a senior pastor, I am responsible for working with our church boards and leaders to have pastoral succession plans for our pastoral staff. Writing this chapter on leaving and retiring has helped me to think more clearly about pastoral succession plans for our church. It has also challenged me to pray more specifically for God to provide successors, as well as to continue mentoring and developing church leaders and pastoral staff. Ultimately, my trust is in God and his sovereignty, in all of life and pastoral ministry, including pastoral succession. He is faithful who has called us in the first place to be his servants in pastoral and church ministry, and he will provide for his church the right kind of Christ-centered and Spirit-filled pastoral successors. However, as pastors we still need to prayerfully put into place pastoral succession plans in our churches, together with our church boards and leaders.

RECOMMENDED READINGS

Bower, Joseph L. *The CEO Within: Why Inside Outsiders Are the Key to Succession.* Boston: Business Review Press, 2007.

Donnelly, Abby. *Straight Talk about Planning Your Succession: A Primer for CEOs.* Greensboro, NC: Strategic Choices Inc., 2017.

Goldsmith, Marshall. *Succession: How to Prepare Yourself, and Your Successor, for the Transition.* Boston: Harvard Business School Press, 2009.

Harper, Steve. *Stepping Aside, Moving Ahead: Spiritual and Practical Wisdom for Clergy Retirement.* Nashville: Abingdon, 2016.

MacDonald, Gordon. *Building Below the Waterline: Strengthening the Life of a Leader.* Peabody, MA: Hendrickson, 2011.

Mullins, Tom. *Passing the Leadership Baton: A Winning Transition Plan for Your Ministry.* Nashville: Thomas Nelson, 2015

Ozier, Jim, and Jim Griffith. *The Changeover Zone: Successful Pastoral Transitions.* Nashville: Abingdon, 2016.

Roberts, Daniel A., and Michael P. Friedman. *Clergy Retirement: Every Ending a New Beginning for Clergy, Their Family, and the Congregation.* New York: Routledge, 2016.

Saporito, Thomas J., and Paul Winum. *Inside CEO Succession: The Essential Guide to Leadership Transition.* San Francisco: Jossey-Bass, 2012.

Vanderbloemen, William, and Warren Bird. *Next: Pastoral Succession That Works.* Grand Rapids: Baker Books, 2014.

Weese, Carolyn, and J. Russell Crabtree. *The Elephant in the Boardroom: Speaking the Unspoken about Pastoral Transitions.* San Francisco: Jossey-Bass, 2004.

Yandian, Bob, with Robb Yandian. *What If the Best Is Yet to Come? A Practical Guide to Pastoral Retirement and Replacement.* Tulsa: Harrison House, 2013.

Epilogue

This book has covered a lot of ground regarding shepherding God's people in faithful and fruitful pastoral ministry. Part 1 focused on biblical and theological foundations of pastoral ministry, including a biblical perspective on pastoral and church ministry; the person and work of the Holy Spirit as crucial and essential for pastoral ministry; the spiritual life of the pastor (e.g., prayer, Scripture, and the spiritual disciplines); and the personal and family life of the pastor. Part 2 focused on these major areas of pastoral ministry: preaching and teaching; corporate worship; intentional disciple-making and spiritual formation; evangelism, missions, and social concern; leadership; mentoring of church staff and lay volunteer coworkers; pastoral care and counseling; church boards, budgets, and buildings; weddings and funerals; small groups and fellowships; integrity and ethics; and leaving and retiring (pastoral succession).

One other major area of pastoral ministry for pastors serving in local churches that are dying is the ministry of church revitalization, or church renewal and revival, to help a church come alive again. There is helpful material available for pastors who need to be involved in church revitalization,[1] although this area of pastoral ministry was not covered in detail in this book. However, many of the areas of pastoral ministry that were covered will also help in church revitalization. It is estimated that around 70 to 80 percent of American churches and denominations are plateauing or in serious decline, and therefore the majority of American churches today are in need of some church revitalization to turn them around.[2] This is not true of many churches in other parts of the world that are growing and thriving, as pointed out earlier in this book.

The challenges of pastoral ministry are many and can be overwhelming to pastors called to shepherd God's people in the various areas of pastoral ministry. The frequent call to excellence rather than mediocrity in pastoral ministry, though well-intentioned,[3] can be potentially dangerous and possibly harmful to many pastors who are already doing their best, with the Holy Spirit's help, in churches that are difficult to pastor, with much spiritual warfare. Such calls to excellence in ministry can become confused with perfectionism and an overemphasis on performance based on self-effort and giftedness that can lead to pride or self-sufficiency, which is sinful. We need to be biblically cautious about such an emphasis on excellence, remembering always that the excellency is of God, and not of us (2 Cor. 3:5–6; 4:7). We simply do our best (Col. 3:23) in the power of the Holy Spirit (Zech. 4:6), serving God, who alone is excellent and perfect. We thus serve, as imperfect and vulnerable pastors[4] and imperfect disciples,[5] fully aware of our limitations, imperfections, and weaknesses but deeply and humbly thankful that God's strength is made perfect in our weakness (2 Cor. 12:9–10). We are also fallen human beings who fail from time to time and yet find hope and grace from God in the midst of ministry failure and disappointments, which afflict all pastors at some time.[6] Talk about excellence can be discouraging, adding more burdens to hurting pastors who are having painful ministry experiences. It is God's call to faithfulness, and not success or excellence, that is more biblical and helpful to pastors who humbly and lovingly minister as servants of Jesus Christ, despite struggles and even failures in ministry.

Humility is a central virtue and fruit of the Spirit (Gal. 5:22–23) in the Christian life and in pastoral ministry. Simon Chan wrote in *Spiritual Theology*, "If pride is the cardinal sin, humility is the only way forward. Scripture counsels humility (James 4:6; 1 Pet. 5:5–6) and warns against having too high an estimate of oneself (Rom. 12:3). Calvin underscores the importance of humility: 'If you ask me concerning the precepts of the Christian religion, first, second, third, and always I would answer "Humility."'"[7]

Years ago, Vernon Grounds wrote a short but powerful article in *Christianity Today* about having the faith to face failure that is relevant to humility. His words are even more relevant in light of our current American church and ministry obsession with success and excellence of the wrong kind. He wrote, "In each of us there is a desire for recognition, a desire to be important or influential . . . to be noticeably superior."[8] John calls this the "pride of life" (1 John 2:16). Grounds claimed that evangelical Christians are bowing before the goddess of worldly success, being sinfully preoccupied with statistics and numbers—with the size of our sanctuaries, salaries, and Sunday schools and with statistics about our budgets, buildings, buses, and baptisms. He lamented that worldly success has crept right into the church and Christian ministries. His conclusion is worth repeating to a new generation of Christians, church leaders, and pastors who may be even more seduced today by worldly success:

> Most of us will work without ever becoming well known. Do we have the faith to face failure? Do we really believe that worldly success is wood, hay, and stubble? We need to remember how often the Church will judge us the way the world does. Before anyone decides on a full-time ministry, for example, they must realize that God may be calling him or her to a ministry of tedious mediocrity. Regardless, God's approval is the most important part. It is far more important to follow God's blueprint for your life than to be another Billy Graham . . . or Bill Bright. Each of us needs the faith to cling to biblical principles of success despite possible worldly failure. And each of us must have the faith to keep serving even if unappreciated, unsung, and unapplauded—in short, we need the faith to face failure.[9]

A biblical perspective on true success does not emphasize pulpit eloquence, communication skills, penetrating insight, remarkable gifts, encyclopedic knowledge, or even mountain-moving faith. It emphasizes instead Christlike agape love (John 13:34–35; 1 Cor. 13:1–8); servanthood and humility (Matt. 20:25–27); faithfulness (Matt. 25:21); obedience to God and his Word (Josh. 1:7–9; 1 Sam. 15:22; Matt. 7:24–29); vulnerability and strength in weakness (2 Cor. 12:9–10); doing our best as unto the Lord (Col. 3:23); and becoming more like Jesus (Rom. 8:29). God's ways and standards are often not our human ways and standards. His ways and thoughts are higher and greater than ours (Isa. 55:8–9). God discerns and judges the internal motives of the heart, and whatever is highly valued by the world is actually detestable in God's sight (Luke 16:15).[10]

Alan Fadling, in reflecting on what he learned from Dallas Willard's life and teachings for developing pastors and churches of the kingdom, shared this: "I was always impressed by Dallas' lack of self-referencing or self-promotion. It stood out in a church world where it always seemed leaders were looking for recognition. Dallas had a deep security in Jesus that I have found myself also seeking."[11] Fadling further wrote, "The way Dallas affirmed the power of a changing life was to remind us that what God treasures in someone's life is the person they become more than the work that they do. Dallas reminded us that the deepest ministry we have with others is who we are more than what we say or do. . . . It is the continuing simplicity of living our lives in communion with Jesus by following the way of Jesus that I hope we all will take from our encounters with Dallas, whether in person or in his writings."[12]

God often shows up in the most unexpected places of our lives—in the ordinary, mundane, simple, and routine places, as Chad Bird has pointed out in *Your God Is Too Glorious*.[13]

Pastoral ministry is ultimately about walking with Jesus on a journey, in union and communion with him (John 15:5), by the power and presence of the Holy Spirit (Zech. 4:6; Eph. 5:18), as we obey his calling to shepherd God's people. It is about faithful and fruitful service in Christ and for his kingdom and not about success or even excellence of the wrong kind. It is ultimately about God. And about people. And about love. His love. It is about shepherding God's people with love.

RECOMMENDED READINGS

Bird, Chad. *Your God Is Too Glorious: Finding God in the Most Unexpected Places.* Grand Rapids: Baker Books, 2018.

Briggs, J. R. *Fail: Finding Hope and Grace in the Midst of Ministry Failure.* Downers Grove, IL: InterVarsity, 2014.

Clifton, Mark. *Reclaiming Glory: Revitalizing Dying Churches.* Nashville: B&H, 2016.

Croft, Brian. *Biblical Church Revitalization: Solutions to Dying and Divided Churches.* Ross-shire, UK: Christian Focus Publications, 2016.

Davis, Andrew M. *ReVitalize: Biblical Keys to Helping Your Church Come Alive Again.* Grand Rapids: Baker Books, 2017.

Hunter, Kent R., with Tracee J. Swank. *Who Broke My Church? 7 Proven Strategies for Renewal and Revival.* New York: FaithWords, 2017.

Jethani, Skye. *Immeasurable: Reflections on the Soul of Ministry in the Age of Church, Inc.* Chicago: Moody, 2017.

Johnston, Ray. *Jesus Called—He Wants His Church Back: What Christians and the American Churches Are Missing.* Nashville: W Publishing, 2015.

Malphurs, Aubrey, and Gordon E. Penfold. *Re:Vision: The Key to Transforming Your Church.* Grand Rapids: Baker Books, 2014.

Moon, Gary W. *Becoming Dallas Willard: The Formation of a Philosopher, Teacher, and Christ Follower.* Downers Grove, IL: InterVarsity, 2018.

———, ed. *Eternal Living: Reflections on Dallas Willard's Teachings on Faith and Formation.* Downers Grove, IL: InterVarsity, 2015.

Stetzer, Ed, and Mike Dodson. *Comeback Churches: How 300 Churches Turned Around and Yours Can Too.* Nashville: B&H, 2007.

Notes

Chapter 1 A Biblical Perspective on Pastoral and Church Ministry

1. R. Albert Mohler Jr., foreword to *On Being a Pastor: Understanding Our Calling and Work*, by Derek J. Prime and Alistair Begg (Chicago: Moody, 2004), 9.

2. Cameren Lee and Kurt Fredrickson, *That Their Work Will Be a Joy: Understanding and Coping with the Challenges of Pastoral Ministry* (Eugene, OR: Cascade Books, 2012), 7–9. See also Jackson W. Carroll, *God's Potters: Pastoral Leadership and the Shaping of Congregations* (Grand Rapids: Eerdmans, 2006); L. Gregory Jones and Kevin R. Armstrong, *Resurrecting Excellence: Shaping Faithful Christian Ministry* (Grand Rapids: Eerdmans, 2006); and John W. Stewart, *Envisioning the Congregation, Practicing the Gospel* (Grand Rapids: Eerdmans, 2015).

3. Wayne Cordeiro, foreword to Lee and Fredrickson, *That Their Work Will Be a Joy*, x–xi.

4. See Brian C. Stiller, Todd M. Johnson, Karen Stiller, and Mark Hutchison, eds., *Evangelicals around the World: A Global Handbook for the 21st Century* (Nashville: Thomas Nelson, 2015). See also Brian C. Stiller, *An Insider's Guide to Praying for the World* (Minneapolis: Bethany House, 2016).

5. David Fisher, *The 21st Century Pastor: A Vision Based on the Ministry of Paul* (Grand Rapids: Zondervan, 1996), 70–88.

6. Ed Silvoso, *Ekklesia: Rediscovering God's Instrument for Global Transformation* (Grand Rapids: Chosen, 2017), 24.

7. Silvoso, *Ekklesia*, 27 (emphasis in original).

8. Silvoso, *Ekklesia*, 28.

9. This list is adapted from Silvoso, *Ekklesia*, 36.

10. Fisher, *21st Century Pastor*, 86.

11. Eddie Gibbs, *The Journey of Ministry: Insights from a Life of Practice* (Downers Grove, IL: InterVarsity, 2012), 11.

12. Gregg R. Allison, *Sojourners and Strangers: The Doctrine of the Church* (Wheaton: Crossway, 2012), 30.

13. Gerald Bray, *The Church: A Theological and Historical Account* (Grand Rapids: Baker Academic, 2016), 60.

14. This list is from John MacArthur Jr., ed., *Rediscovering Pastoral Ministry: Shaping Contemporary Ministry with Biblical Mandates* (Dallas: Word, 1995), xiii.

15. Adapted from Ed Hayes, *The Church: The Body of Christ in the World of Today* (Nashville: Word, 1999), 7–15.

16. Derek Tidball, *Ministry by the Book: New Testament Patterns for Pastoral Leadership* (Downers Grove, IL: IVP Academic, 2008). See also Jamin Goggin and Kyle Strobel, *The Way of the Dragon or the Way of the Lamb: Searching for Jesus' Path of Power in a Church That Has Abandoned It* (Nashville: Thomas Nelson, 2017); and Craig C. Hill, *Servant of All: Status, Ambition, and the Way of Jesus* (Grand Rapids: Eerdmans, 2016).

17. See Siang-Yang Tan, *Full Service: Moving from Self-Serve Christianity to Total Servant-hood* (Grand Rapids: Baker Books, 2006), 23–24, 47–63, 137.

18. See Dave Harvey, *Am I Called? The Summons to Pastoral Ministry* (Wheaton: Crossway, 2012); and Gordon T. Smith, *Consider Your Calling: Six Questions for Discerning Your Vocation* (Downers Grove, IL: InterVarsity, 2016). See also Jason K. Allen, *Discerning Your Call to Ministry: How to Know for Sure and What to Do about It* (Chicago: Moody, 2016), which contains ten questions to help discern one's calling to full-time or vocational ministry: (1) Do you desire the ministry? (2) Does your character meet God's expectations? (3) Is your household in order? (4) Has God gifted you to preach and teach his Word? (5) Does your church affirm your calling? (6) Do you love the people of God? (7) Are you passionate about the gospel and the Great Commission? (8) Are you engaged in fruitful ministry? (9) Are you ready to defend the faith? (10) Are you willing to surrender? (contents).

19. Harvey, *Am I Called?*, 9 (contents).

20. Smith, *Consider Your Calling*, 5 (contents).

21. See recommended readings at the end of this chapter.

22. Marva Dawn and Eugene Peterson, *The Unnecessary Pastor: Rediscovering the Call* (Grand Rapids: Eerdmans, 2000).

23. Richard S. Armstrong with Kirk Walker Morledge, *Help! I'm a Pastor: A Guide to Parish Ministry* (Louisville: Westminster John Knox, 2005), 8–9.

24. Simon Chan, *Spiritual Theology: A Systematic Study of the Christian Life* (Downers Grove, IL: InterVarsity, 1998), 225. See also Timothy S. Laniak, *Shepherds after My Own Heart: Pastoral Traditions and Leadership in the Bible* (Downers Grove, IL: IVP Academic, 2006).

25. MacArthur, *Rediscovering Pastoral Ministry*, xiv.

26. MacArthur, *Rediscovering Pastoral Ministry*, xiv.

27. Wes Roberts and Glenn Marshall, *Reclaiming God's Original Intent for the Church* (Colorado Springs: NavPress, 2004), 162.

28. Dawn and Peterson, *Unnecessary Pastor*, 4 (emphasis in original).

29. John Piper, *Brothers, We Are Not Professionals: A Plea to Pastors for Radical Ministry*, rev. ed. (Nashville: B&H, 2013), 1.

30. Piper, *Brothers, We Are Not Professionals*, xi.

Chapter 2 The Person and Work of the Holy Spirit as Crucial and Essential for Pastoral Ministry

1. For example, see Gordon D. Fee, *God's Empowering Presence: The Holy Spirit in the Letters of Paul* (1994; repr. Grand Rapids: Baker Academic, 2009); Michael Horton, *Rediscovering the Holy Spirit: God's Perfecting Presence in Creation, Redemption, and Everyday Life* (Grand Rapids: Zondervan, 2017); John R. Levison, *Filled with the Spirit* (Grand Rapids: Eerdmans, 2009); John R. Levison, *Fresh Air: The Holy Spirit for an Inspired Life* (Brewster, MA: Paraclete Press, 2012); John R. Levison, *Inspired: The Holy Spirit and the Mind of Faith* (Grand Rapids: Eerdmans, 2018); Anthony C. Thiselton, *The Holy Spirit—In Biblical Teaching, through the Centuries, and Today* (Grand Rapids: Eerdmans, 2013); and Amos Yong, *Spirit of Love: A Trinitarian Theology of Grace* (Waco: Baylor University Press, 2012).

2. For example, see John MacArthur (with a negative view of the charismatic movement), *Strange Fire: The Danger of Offending the Holy Spirit with Counterfeit Worship* (Nashville: Thomas Nelson, 2013); and Michael L. Brown (with a charismatic response that is more positive), *Authentic Fire: A Response to John MacArthur's Strange Fire* (Lake Mary, FL: Creation

House, 2015). For biblical but balanced views, see also R. T. Kendall, *Holy Fire: A Balanced, Biblical Look at the Holy Spirit's Work in Our Lives* (Lake Mary, FL: Charisma House, 2014); J. I. Packer, *Keep in Step with the Spirit: Finding Fullness in Our Walk with God*, rev. ed. (Grand Rapids: Baker Books, 2005); and J. Oswald Sanders, *The Holy Spirit and His Gifts* (Grand Rapids: Zondervan, 1970).

3. Graham Buxton, *Dancing in the Dark: The Privilege of Participating in the Ministry of Christ* (Carlisle, UK: Paternoster Press, 2001), 9.

4. This list is from Kendall, *Holy Fire*, 12–32.

5. Kendall, *Holy Fire*, 32. See also J. I. Packer, "Piety on Fire," *Christianity Today*, May 12, 1989, 18–23.

6. Siang-Yang Tan and Douglas H. Gregg, *Disciplines of the Holy Spirit: How to Connect to the Spirit's Power and Presence* (Grand Rapids: Zondervan, 1997).

7. See Gary L. Thomas, *Authentic Faith: The Power of a Fire-Tested Life* (Grand Rapids: Zondervan, 2002).

8. See Levison, *Filled with the Spirit*; Levinson, *Fresh Air*; and Levinson, *Inspired*.

9. Tan and Gregg, *Disciplines of the Holy Spirit*, 21.

10. Adapted from Tan and Gregg, *Disciplines of the Holy Spirit*, 21–24.

11. Siang-Yang Tan, *Full Service: Moving from Self-Serve Christianity to Total Servanthood* (Grand Rapids: Baker Books, 2006), 23–24.

12. See Andrew Purves, *The Crucifixion of Ministry: Surrendering Our Ambitions to the Service of Christ* (Downers Grove, IL: InterVarsity, 2007); Andrew Purves, *The Resurrection of Ministry: Serving in the Hope of the Risen Christ* (Downers Grove, IL: InterVarsity, 2010); and Steve W. Smith, *Dying to Preach: Embracing the Cross in the Pulpit* (Grand Rapids: Kregel, 2009).

13. Thiselton, *Holy Spirit*, 500.

14. Yong, *Spirit of Love*, 160.

15. See Siang-Yang Tan, *Counseling and Psychotherapy: A Christian Perspective* (Grand Rapids: Baker Academic, 2011), 363–67.

16. Sam Storms, *Practicing the Power: Welcoming the Gifts of the Holy Spirit in Your Life* (Grand Rapids: Zondervan, 2017), 15 (emphasis in original).

17. C. Peter Wagner, *Your Spiritual Gifts Can Help Your Church Grow*, rev. ed. (Ventura, CA: Regal, 2005), 5.

18. Neil Cole, *Primal Fire: Reigniting the Church with the Fire Gifts of Jesus* (Carol Stream, IL: Tyndale Momentum, 2014), v.

19. See Kenneth Berding, *What Are Spiritual Gifts? Rethinking the Conventional View* (Grand Rapids: Kregel, 2006); and Kenneth Berding, *Walking in the Spirit* (Wheaton: Crossway, 2011).

20. Tan, *Counseling and Psychotherapy*, 365.

21. Charles R. Swindoll, "Helping and the Holy Spirit," *Christian Counseling Today* 2, no. 1 (1994): 16–19.

22. These points are adapted from Tan, *Counseling and Psychotherapy*, 366–67.

Chapter 3 The Spiritual Life of the Pastor

1. Dallas Willard, *Renovation of the Heart: Putting on the Character of Christ* (Colorado Springs: NavPress, 2002), 235. See also Howard Baker, *The One True Thing: What Is Worthy of Your Lifelong Devotion?* (Colorado Springs: NavPress, 2007); and Arron Chambers, *Devoted: Isn't It Time to Fall More in Love with Jesus?* (Colorado Springs: NavPress, 2014).

2. Jamin Goggin and Kyle Strobel, *Beloved Dust: Drawing Closer to God by Discovering the Truth about Yourself* (Nashville: Thomas Nelson, 2014).

3. See Siang-Yang Tan, *Full Service: Moving from Self-Serve Christianity to Total Servanthood* (Grand Rapids: Baker Books, 2006), 30–39.

4. *Daily Light on the Daily Path*, comp. Jonathan Bagster (Grand Rapids: Zondervan, 1981); and A. J. Russell, ed., *God Calling* (Uhrichsville, OH: Barbour Publishing, 1984).

5. Chris Webb, *The Fire of the Word: Meeting God on Holy Ground* (Downers Grove, IL: InterVarsity, 2011); and Chris Webb, *God-Soaked Life: Discovering a Kingdom Spirituality* (Downers Grove, IL: InterVarsity, 2017)

6. See Kevin DeYoung, *Crazy Busy: A (Mercifully) Short Book about a (Really) Big Problem* (Wheaton: Crossway, 2013). See also Wayne Cordeiro, *Leading on Empty: Refilling Your Tank and Renewing Your Passion* (Minneapolis: Bethany House, 2009).

7. See Alan Fadling, *An Unhurried Life: Following Jesus' Rhythms of Work and Rest* (Downers Grove, IL: InterVarsity, 2013); Alan Fadling, *An Unhurried Leader: The Lasting Fruit of Daily Influence* (Downers Grove, IL: InterVarsity, 2017); John Koessler, *The Radical Pursuit of Rest: Escaping the Productivity Trap* (Downers Grove, IL: InterVarsity, 2016); A. J. Swoboda, *Subversive Sabbath: The Surprising Power of Rest in a Nonstop World* (Grand Rapids: Brazos Press, 2018); and Siang-Yang Tan, *Rest: Experiencing God's Peace in a Restless World* (Vancouver: Regent College Publishing, 2003).

8. Emilie Griffin, *Wilderness Time: A Guide for Spiritual Retreat* (San Francisco: HarperSanFrancisco, 1997).

9. See David Runcorn, *A Center of Quiet: Hearing God When Life Is Noisy* (Downers Grove, IL: InterVarsity, 1990).

10. See Richard J. Foster, *Prayer: Finding the Heart's True Home* (New York: HarperCollins, 1992); Richard J. Foster, *Sanctuary of the Soul: Journey into Meditative Prayer* (Downers Grove, IL: InterVarsity, 2011); Gary Neal Hansen, *Kneeling with Giants: Learning to Pray with History's Best Teachers* (Downers Grove, IL: InterVarsity, 2012); Daniel Henderson with Margaret Saylar, *Fresh Encounters: Experiencing Transformation through United Worship-Based Prayer* (Colorado Springs: NavPress, 2004); Timothy Keller, *Prayer: Experiencing Awe and Intimacy with God* (New York: Dutton, 2014); J. Gary Miller, *Calling on the Name of the Lord: A Biblical Theology of Prayer* (Downers Grove, IL: InterVarsity, 2016); J. I. Packer and Carolyn Nystrom, *Praying: Finding Our Way through Duty to Delight* (Downers Grove, IL: InterVarsity, 2006); C. Peter Wagner, *Prayer Shield: How to Intercede for Pastors and Christian Leaders*, rev. ed. (Bloomington, MN: Chosen, 2014); and Philip Yancey, *Prayer: Does It Make Any Difference?* (Grand Rapids: Zondervan, 2006).

11. Each of these types of prayer is treated in a separate chapter of Foster's book *Prayer*.

12. Siang-Yang Tan and Douglas H. Gregg, *Disciplines of the Holy Spirit: How to Connect to the Spirit's Power and Presence* (Grand Rapids: Zondervan, 1997), 57–60.

13. See Phyllis Tickle, *The Divine Hours, Pocket Edition* (New York: Oxford University Press, 2007).

14. See Wesley Campbell and Stacey Campbell, *Praying the Bible: The Book of Prayers* (Ventura, CA: Regal, 2002); and Donald S. Whitney, *Praying the Bible* (Wheaton: Crossway, 2015).

15. Henderson with Saylar, *Fresh Encounters*.

16. Wagner, *Prayer Shield*.

17. E. M. Bounds, *Power through Prayer* (Grand Rapids: Zondervan, 1962), 12. See also Tan and Gregg, *Disciplines of the Holy Spirit*, 67–68.

18. Foster, *Prayer*, 256.

19. J. I. Packer, *Truth and Power: The Place of Scripture in the Christian Life* (Downers Grove, IL: InterVarsity, 1996).

20. John Piper, *A Peculiar Glory: How the Christian Scriptures Reveal Their Complete Truthfulness* (Wheaton: Crossway, 2016); and John Piper, *Reading the Bible Supernaturally: Seeing and Savoring the Glory of God in Scripture* (Wheaton: Crossway, 2017).

21. Webb, *Fire of the Word*. See also Larry Crabb, *66 Love Letters: A Conversation with God That Invites You into His Story* (Nashville: Thomas Nelson, 2009).

22. Tan and Gregg, *Disciplines of the Holy Spirit*, 80–83.

23. Tan and Gregg, *Disciplines of the Holy Spirit*, 84–91.

24. See Jan Johnson, *Meeting God in Scripture: A Hands-On Guide to Lectio Divina* (Downers Grove, IL: InterVarsity, 2016); and James G. Wilhoit and Evan B. Howard, *Discovering Lectio Divina: Bringing Scripture into Ordinary Life* (Downers Grove, IL: InterVarsity, 2012).

25. See Christopher Catherwood, *Church History: A Crash Course for the Curious* (Wheaton: Crossway, 2007); and Donald Harman, *Church History for Modern Ministry: Why Our Past Matters for Everything We Do* (Bellingham, WA: Lexham Press, 2016). See also Gregg R. Allison, *Historical Theology: An Introduction to Christian Doctrine* (Grand Rapids: Zondervan, 2011); Wayne Grudem, *Systematic Theology: An Introduction to Biblical Doctrine* (Grand Rapids: Zondervan, 1994); and Michael Lawrence, *Biblical Theology in the Life of the Church: A Guide for Ministry* (Wheaton: Crossway, 2010).

26. See John Chryssavgis, *In the Heart of the Desert: The Spirituality of the Desert Fathers and Mothers*, rev. ed. (Bloomington, IN: World Wisdom, 2008); Christopher A. Hall, *Reading Scripture with the Church Fathers* (Downers Grove, IL: InterVarsity, 1998); Christopher A. Hall, *Learning Theology with the Church Fathers* (Downers Grove, IL: InterVarsity, 2002); Christopher A. Hall, *Worshiping with the Church Fathers* (Downers Grove, IL: IVP Academic, 2009); Christopher A. Hall, *Living Wisely with the Church Fathers* (Downers Grove, IL: IVP Academic, 2017); Christine Valters Paintner, *Desert Fathers and Mothers: Early Christian Wisdom Sayings—Annotated and Explained* (Woodstock, VT: Skylight Paths, 2012); Benedicta Ward, *The Sayings of the Desert Fathers: The Alphabetical Collection* (Collegeville, MN: Liturgical Press, 1984); and John Wortley, *The Book of the Elders: Sayings of the Desert Fathers—The Systematic Collection* (Collegeville, MN: Liturgical Press, 2012).

27. See Jamin Goggin and Kyle Strobel, eds., *Reading the Christian Spiritual Classics: A Guide for Evangelicals* (Downers Grove, IL: IVP Academic, 2013); Greg Peters, *The Story of Monasticism: Retrieving an Ancient Tradition for Contemporary Spirituality* (Grand Rapids: Baker Academic, 2015); and Julia L. Roller, ed., *25 Books Every Christian Should Read* (New York: HarperOne, 2011).

28. See Anthony M. Coniaris, *A Beginner's Introduction to the Philokalia* (Minneapolis: Light & Life Publishing, 2004); and Allyne Smith, *Philokalia: The Eastern Christian Spiritual Texts—Selections Annotated and Explained* (Woodstock, VT: Skylight Path, 2006).

29. Richard J. Foster, *Celebration of Discipline: The Path to Spiritual Growth*, special anniversary ed. (New York: HarperOne, 2018); and Dallas Willard, *The Spirit of the Disciplines* (San Francisco: HarperSanFrancisco, 1988). For more recent books on spiritual disciplines and practices, see recommended readings at the end of this chapter.

30. Adele Ahlberg Calhoun, *Spiritual Disciplines Handbook: Practices That Transform Us*, rev. ed. (Downers Grove, IL: InterVarsity, 2015), 7–8 (contents).

31. See Kent Annan, *Slow Kingdom Coming: Practices for Doing Justice, Loving Mercy and Walking Humbly in the World* (Downers Grove, IL: InterVarsity, 2016); Kyle David Bennett, *Practices of Love: Spiritual Disciplines for the Life of the World* (Grand Rapids: Brazos Press, 2017); and Barry D. Jones, *Dwell: Life with God for the World* (Downers Grove, IL: InterVarsity, 2014).

32. See Ken Shigematsu, *God in My Everything: How an Ancient Rhythm Helps Busy People Enjoy God* (Grand Rapids: Zondervan, 2013); and Tish Harrison Warren, *Liturgy of the Ordinary: Sacred Practices in Everyday Life* (Downers Grove, IL: InterVarsity, 2016). See also Chad Bird, *Your God Is Too Glorious: Finding God in the Most Unexpected Places* (Grand Rapids: Baker Books, 2018); and Kenneth Boa, *Life in the Presence of God: Practices for Living in the Light of Eternity* (Downers Grove, IL: InterVarsity, 2017).

33. See Tod E. Bolsinger, *It Takes a Church to Raise a Christian: How the Community of God Transforms Lives* (Grand Rapids: Brazos Press, 2004); and James C. Wilhoit, *Spiritual Formation as if the Church Mattered: Growing in Christ through Community* (Grand Rapids: Baker Academic, 2009).

34. See David Benner, *Sacred Companions: The Gift of Spiritual Friendship and Direction* (Downers Grove, IL: InterVarsity, 2002); Bruce Demarest, *Soulguides: Following Jesus As Spiritual Director* (Colorado Spring: NavPress, 2003); Angela H. Reed, Richard D. Osmer, and Marcus G. Smucker, *Spiritual Companioning: A Guide to Protestant Theology and Practice* (Grand Rapids: Baker Academic, 2015); and Gordon T. Smith, *Spiritual Direction: A Guide to Giving and Receiving Direction* (Downers Grove, IL: InterVarsity, 2014).

35. Larry Crabb, *Connecting: Healing for Ourselves and Our Relationships—A Radical New Vision* (Nashville: Word, 1997); Larry Crabb, *The Safest Place on Earth: Where People Connect and Are Forever Changed* (Nashville: Word, 1999); and Larry Crabb, *Soul Talk: The Language God Longs for Us to Speak* (Brentwood, TN: Integrity Publishers, 2003).

36. Gary L. Thomas, *Authentic Faith: The Power of a Fire-Tested Life* (Grand Rapids: Zondervan, 2002), 19.

37. Thomas, *Authentic Faith*, 18–19.

38. Thomas, *Authentic Faith*, 16.

39. Alan Nelson, *Embracing Brokenness: How God Refines Us through Life's Disappointments* (Colorado Springs: NavPress, 2002), 18, 31. See also Larry Crabb, *Shattered Dreams: God's Unexpected Pathway to Joy* (Colorado Springs: WaterBrook Press, 2001); Larry Crabb, *A Different Kind of Happiness: Discovering the Joy That Comes from Sacrificial Love* (Grand Rapids: Baker Books, 2016); J. I. Packer, *Weakness Is the Way: Life with Christ Our Strength* (Wheaton: Crossway, 2013); and Ann Voskamp, *The Broken Way: A Daring Path into the Abundant Life* (Grand Rapids: Zondervan, 2016).

40. See Kelly Kapic, ed., *Santification: Explorations in Theology and Practice* (Downers Grove, IL: IVP Academic, 2014); Sinclair B. Ferguson, *Devoted to God: Blueprints for Sanctification* (Carlisle, PA: Banner of Truth, 2016); and David Powlison, *How Does Sanctification Work?* (Wheaton: Crossway, 2017).

41. One-time, quick-fix, total sanctification was often erroneously taught at Keswick Conventions in England. See J. I. Packer, *Keep in Step with the Spirit: Finding Fullness in Our Walk with God*, rev. ed. (Grand Rapids: Baker Books, 2005), 120–33; and Andrew David Naselli, *No Quick Fix: Where Higher Life Theology Came From, What It Is and Why It's Harmful* (Bellingham, WA: Lexham Press, 2017).

42. See Randy Alcorn, *If God Is Good: Faith in the Midst of Suffering and Evil* (Colorado Springs: Multnomah, 2009); Timothy Keller, *Walking with God through Pain and Suffering* (New York: Dutton, 2013); Gerald W. Peterman and Andrew J. Schmutzer, *Between Pain and Grace: A Biblical Theology of Suffering* (Chicago: Moody, 2016); John Piper and Justin Taylor, eds., *Suffering and the Sovereignty of God* (Wheaton: Crossway, 2016); David Powlison, *God's Grace in Your Suffering* (Wheaton: Crossway, 2018); and Eleonore Stump, *Wandering in Darkness: Narrative and the Problem of Suffering* (Oxford, UK: Oxford University Press, 2010).

43. Nelson, *Embracing Brokenness*, 104–5, 108–16.

Chapter 4 The Personal and Family Life of the Pastor

1. Jason K. Allen, ed., *Portraits of a Pastor: The 9 Essential Roles of a Church Leader* (Chicago: Moody, 2017).

2. John R. W. Stott, *The Preacher's Portrait: Some New Testament Word Studies* (Grand Rapids: Eerdmans, 1961).

3. William H. Willimon, *Pastor: The Theology and Practice of Ordained Ministry*, rev. ed. (Nashville: Abingdon, 2016), 56–70.

4. Gary L. Harbaugh, *Pastor as Person* (Minneapolis: Augsburg, 1984).

5. Andrew Purves, *Reconstructing Pastoral Theology: A Christological Foundation* (Louisville: Westminster John Knox, 2004).

6. Rankin Wilbourne, *Union with Christ: The Way to Know and Enjoy God* (Colorado Springs: David C. Cook, 2016).

7. John Ortberg, foreword to *Union with Christ*, 13.

8. Wilbourne, *Union with Christ*, 41–58.

9. Wilbourne, *Union with Christ*, 51.

10. Wilbourne, *Union with Christ*, 47.

11. See recommended readings at the end of this chapter.

12. Donald S. Whitney, "Pastor as Man of God," in Allen, *Portraits of a Pastor*, 161–77.

13. Whitney, "Pastor as Man of God," 175, 176 (emphasis in original).

14. Adapted from Cameron Lee and Kurt Fredrickson, *That Their Work Will Be a Joy: Understanding and Coping with the Challenges of Pastoral Ministry* (Eugene, OR: Cascade Books, 2012), 87–198.

15. See Lee and Fredrickson, *That Their Work Will Be a Joy*, 114–15, for the research reviewed.

16. Bob Burns, Tasha D. Chapman, and Donald C. Guthrie, *Resilient Ministry: What Pastors Told Us about Surviving and Thriving* (Downers Grove, IL: InterVarsity, 2013).

17. Recent research regarding a nutritious diet has shown the importance and power of gut microbes or bacteria in healing and protecting the brain: our gut health affects our brain health. Good nutritional practices for gut health include taking probiotics and eating yogurt and kimchi. See David Perlmutter with Kristin Loberg, *Brain Maker: The Power of Gut Microbes to Heal and Protect Your Brain—for Life* (New York: Little, Brown, 2015).

18. Adapted from Burns, Chapman, and Guthrie, *Resilient Ministry*, 18–29.

19. Peter Scazzero, *The Emotionally Healthy Church: A Strategy for Discipleship That Actually Changes Lives*, rev. ed. (Grand Rapids: Zondervan, 2015); Peter Scazzero, *Emotionally Healthy Spirituality: It's Impossible to Be Spiritually Mature, While Remaining Emotionally Immature*, rev. ed. (Grand Rapids: Zondervan, 2017); and Peter Scazzero, *The Emotionally Healthy Leader: How Transforming Your Inner Life Will Deeply Transform Your Church, Team, and the World* (Grand Rapids: Zondervan, 2015).

20. Adapted from Scazzero, *Emotionally Healthy Leader*, 27–33.

21. Adapted from Scazzero, *Emotionally Healthy Leader*, 35–42.

22. Adapted from Scazzero, *Emotionally Healthy Leader*, 173–300.

23. Adapted from Scazzero, *Emotionally Healthy Leader*, 47–172.

24. Siang-Yang Tan, *Rest: Experiencing God's Peace in a Restless World* (Vancouver: Regent College Publishing, 2003). See also Siang-Yang Tan, *Full Service: Moving from Self-Serve Christianity to Total Servanthood* (Grand Rapids: Baker Books, 2006), 105–15.

25. See Siang-Yang Tan, *Counseling and Psychotherapy: A Christian Perspective* (Grand Rapids: Baker Academic, 2011), 19–23. See also Sondra Wheeler, *Sustaining Ministry: Foundations and Practices for Serving Faithfully* (Grand Rapids: Baker Academic, 2017), who used the term "unselfish self-care" (p. 50).

26. Burns, Chapman, and Guthrie, *Resilient Ministry*, 21.

27. See Siang-Yang Tan and Melissa Castillo, "Self-Care and Beyond: A Brief Literature Review from a Christian Perspective," *Journal of Psychology and Christianity* 33 (2014): 90–95.

28. This list is from Michael J. Mahoney, *Constructive Psychotherapy: A Practical Guide* (New York: Guilford Press, 2003), 260–61.

29. Sally S. Canning, "Out of Balance: Why I Hesitate to Practice and Teach 'Self-Care,'" *Journal of Psychology and Christianity* 30 (2011): 70–74.

30. Tan and Castillo, "Self-Care and Beyond," 94.

31. This list is adapted from Burns, Chapman, and Guthrie, *Resilient Ministry*, appendix B, 270–72.

32. For example, see Daniel L. Akin, "Pastor as Husband and Father," in Allen, *Portraits of a Pastor*, 33–56; Burns, Chapman, and Guthrie, *Resilient Ministry*, 169–98; Brian Croft and Cara Croft, *The Pastor's Family: Shepherding Your Family through the Challenges of Pastoral Ministry* (Grand Rapids: Zondervan, 2013); Ajith Fernando, *The Family Life of a Christian Leader* (Wheaton: Crossway, 2016); Lee and Fredrickson, *That Their Work Will Be a Joy*, 170–98;

Barnabas Piper, *The Pastor's Kid: Finding Your Own Faith and Identity* (Colorado Springs: David C. Cook, 2014); and Kay Warren, *Sacred Privilege: Your Life and Ministry as a Pastor's Wife* (Grand Rapids: Revell, 2017).

33. Lee and Fredrickson, *That Their Work Will Be a Joy*, 173–80.

34. Adapted from Akin, "Pastor as Husband and Father," 38–46.

35. Adapted from Akin, "Pastor as Husband and Father," 49–56.

36. Tan, *Full Service*, 151–66.

37. Tan, *Full Service*, 151–61.

38. Gary Thomas, *Sacred Marriage: What If God Designed Marriage to Make Us Holy More Than to Make Us Happy?* (Grand Rapids: Zondervan, 2000), 22, 26, 186–87.

39. R. Paul Stevens, *Marriage Spirituality: Ten Disciplines for Couples Who Love God* (Downers Grove, IL: InterVarsity, 1989), 155.

40. Larry Crabb, *The Marriage Builder* (Grand Rapids: Zondervan, 1982), 60–64.

41. Gary Chapman, *The Five Love Languages: How to Express Heartfelt Commitment to Your Mate* (Chicago: Northfield Publishing, 1992).

42. Scott Stanley, *The Heart of Commitment* (Nashville: Thomas Nelson, 1998), 191.

43. Gary Thomas, *Sacred Parenting: How Raising Children Shapes Our Souls* (Grand Rapids: Zondervan, 2004). See also Tan, *Full Service*, 161–66.

44. R. Paul Stevens, *Seven Days of Faith: Every Day Alive with God* (Colorado Springs: NavPress, 2001), 65, 73 (emphasis in original).

45. See Piper, *Pastor's Kid*, 31–74.

46. Dan B. Allender, *How Children Raise Parents: The Art of Listening to Your Family* (Colorado Springs: WaterBrook Press, 2003), 21, 27.

47. See Tan, *Full Service*, 165–66.

48. Scazzero, *Emotionally Healthy Leader*, 100–111.

49. See Wheeler, *Sustaining Ministry*; and Sondra Wheeler, *The Minister as Moral Theologian: Ethical Dimensions of Pastoral Leadership* (Grand Rapids: Baker Academic, 2017).

50. Tim Chester, *Closing the Window: Steps to Living Porn Free* (Downers Grove, IL: InterVarsity, 2010), 7–10.

51. Carol Archebelle, advertisement in *Christianity Today*, November 2017, 2.

52. See Chester, *Closing the Window*; Tim Clinton and Mark Laaser, *The Fight of Your Life: Manning Up to the Challenge of Sexual Integrity* (Shippensburg, PA: Destiny Image, 2015); and Heath Lambert, *Finally Free: Fighting for Purity with the Power of Grace* (Grand Rapids: Zondervan, 2013).

53. These questions are from H. B. Charles Jr., *On Pastoring: A Short Guide to Living, Leading, and Ministering as a Pastor* (Chicago: Moody, 2016), 30.

Chapter 5 Preaching and Teaching

1. D. Martyn Lloyd-Jones, *Preaching and Preachers* (Grand Rapids: Zondervan, 1971), 9.

2. Lloyd-Jones, *Preaching and Preachers*, 97. See also Peter Lewis, "The Doctor as a Preacher," in *Martyn Lloyd-Jones: Chosen by God*, ed. Christopher Catherwood (Westminster, IL: Crossway, 1986), 76.

3. Lloyd-Jones, *Preaching and Preachers*, 325. See also Tony Sargent, *The Sacred Anointing: The Preaching of Dr. Martyn Lloyd-Jones* (Wheaton: Crossway, 1994).

4. Jason K. Allen, "Pastor as Preacher," in *Portraits of a Pastor: The 9 Essential Roles of a Church Leader*, ed. Jason K. Allen (Chicago: Moody, 2017), 57.

5. James W. Bryant and Mac Brunson, *The New Guidebook for Pastors* (Nashville: B&H, 2007), 40.

6. John Stott, *Between Two Worlds: The Art of Preaching in the Twentieth Century* (Grand Rapids: Eerdmans, 1982), 15.

7. J. I. Packer, *Truth and Power: The Place of Scripture in the Christian Life* (Downers Grove, IL: InterVarsity, 1996), 125, 132. Packer emphasized application of truth to life that sets preaching apart from just teaching.

8. See Owen D. Strachan, "Pastor as Theologian," in Allen, *Portraits of a Pastor*, 71–90. For theological interpretation of the Bible, see Craig G. Bartholomew and Heath A. Thomas, eds., *A Manifesto for Theological Interpretation* (Grand Rapids: Baker Academic, 2016); Joel B. Green, *Practicing Theological Interpretation: Engaging Biblical Texts for Faith and Formation* (Grand Rapids: Baker Academic, 2011); and Kevin J. Vanhoozer, Craig G. Bartholomew, David J. Treier, and N. T. Wright, eds., *Dictionary for Theological Interpretation of the Bible* (Grand Rapids: Baker Academic, 2005).

9. See Gerald Hiestand and Todd Wilson, *The Pastor Theologian: Resurrecting an Ancient Vision* (Grand Rapids: Zondervan, 2015); and Todd Wilson and Gerald Hiestand, eds., *Becoming a Pastor Theologian: New Possibilities for Church Leadership* (Downers Grove, IL: IVP Academic, 2016).

10. See Christian T. George, "Pastor as Church Historian," in Allen, *Portraits of a Pastor*, 91–106. See also Gregg R. Allison, *Historical Theology: An Introduction to Christian Doctrine* (Grand Rapids: Zondervan, 2011); and Donald Hartman, *Church History for Modern Ministry: Why Our Past Matters for Everything We Do* (Bellingham, WA: Lexham Press, 2016).

11. See recommended readings at the end of this chapter.

12. See recommended readings at the end of this chapter.

13. Haddon Robinson, *Biblical Preaching: The Development and Delivery of Expository Messages*, 3rd ed. (Grand Rapids: Baker Academic, 2014), 3.

14. Packer, *Truth and Power*, 123 (emphasis in original).

15. Packer, *Truth and Power*, 123.

16. Abraham Kuruvilla, *A Vision for Preaching: Understanding the Heart of Pastoral Ministry* (Grand Rapids: Baker Academic, 2015), 10.

17. Kuruvilla, *Vision for Preaching*, 10.

18. Jason C. Meyer, *Preaching: A Biblical Theology* (Wheaton: Crossway, 2013), 21 (emphasis in original).

19. Meyer, *Preaching*, 22.

20. Meyer, *Preaching*, 240.

21. Robinson, *Biblical Preaching*, 5.

22. Jerry Vines and Jim Shaddix, *Power in the Pulpit: How to Prepare and Deliver Expository Sermons* (Chicago: Moody, 1999), 27.

23. Jerry Vines and Jim Shaddix, *Power in the Pulpit: How to Prepare and Deliver Expository Sermons*, rev. ed. (Chicago: Moody, 2017), 30.

24. Vines and Shaddix, *Power in the Pulpit* (2017), 47.

25. Lloyd-Jones, *Preaching and Preachers*, 71.

26. Stott, *Between Two Worlds*, 125.

27. R. Albert Mohler Jr., *He Is Not Silent: Preaching in a Postmodern World* (Chicago: Moody, 2008), 50.

28. Allen, "Pastor as Preacher," 61.

29. Allen, "Pastor as Preacher," 62 (emphasis in original).

30. Vines and Shaddix, *Power in the Pulpit*, rev. ed., 45–46.

31. Vines and Shaddix, *Power in the Pulpit*, rev. ed., 46–47.

32. Tony Merida, *The Christ-Centered Expositor: A Field Guide for Word-Driven Disciple Makers* (Nashville: B&H Academic, 2016), 5. See also 5–8 on "What Does the Bible Say about Preaching and Teaching?"

33. See Allen, "Pastor as Preacher," 58–60. See also Vines and Shaddix, *Power in the Pulpit*, rev. ed., 24–29, on the biblical roots of expository preaching; and Robinson, *Biblical Preaching*, 2–3.

34. See David Dunn-Wilson, *A Mirror for the Church: Preaching in the First Five Centuries* (Grand Rapids: Eerdmans, 2005).

35. See Michael Pasquarello III, *Sacred Rhetoric: Preaching as a Theological and Pastoral Practice of the Church* (Grand Rapids: Eerdmans, 2005).

36. Packer, *Truth and Power*, 120.

37. See Bryant and Brunson, *New Guidebook for Pastors*, 37.

38. These steps are from Bryant and Brunson, *New Guidebook for Pastors*, 38–39.

39. Lloyd John Ogilvie, *A Passionate Calling* (Eugene, OR: Harvest House, 2014), 73–104.

40. Phillips Brooks, *Lectures on Preaching* (Grand Rapids: Baker, 1969), 5.

41. See Timothy Keller, *Preaching: Communicating Faith in an Age of Skepticism* (New York: Viking, 2015), 249–51. See also Duane Litfin, "New Testament Challenge to Big Idea Preaching," in *The Big Idea of Biblical Preaching: Connecting the Bible to People*, ed. Keith Wilhite and Scott M. Gibson (Grand Rapids: Baker Books, 1998), 53–66.

42. Ogilvie, *Passionate Calling*, 72–73.

43. Ogilvie, *Passionate Calling*, 155.

44. Ogilvie, *Passionate Calling*, 158–63.

45. Packer, *Truth and Power*, 131.

46. See Charles W. Koller, *How to Preach without Notes* (Grand Rapids: Baker Books, 2007); and Joseph M. Webb, *Preaching without Notes* (Nashville: Abingdon, 2001).

47. Ogilvie, *Passionate Calling*, 67.

48. Ogilvie, *Passionate Calling*, 7.

49. See Keller, *Preaching*, 11–12.

50. Steven W. Smith, *Dying to Preach: Embracing the Cross in the Pulpit* (Grand Rapids: Kregel, 2009).

51. John F. Evans, *A Guide to Biblical Commentaries and Reference Works*, 10th ed. (Grand Rapids: Zondervan, 2016). See also John Glynn and Michael H. Burer, eds., *Best Bible Books: New Testament Resources* (Grand Rapids: Kregel, 2018).

52. Keller, *Preaching*, 296n7.

53. Cornelius Plantinga Jr., *Reading for Preaching: The Preacher in Conversation with Storytellers, Biographers, Poets, and Journalists* (Grand Rapids: Eerdmans, 2013).

54. Eugene H. Peterson, *Take and Read: Spiritual Reading: An Anointed List* (Grand Rapids: Eerdmans, 1996).

55. Eugene H. Peterson, *Five Smooth Stones for Pastoral Work* (Grand Rapids: Eerdmans, 1980); Eugene H. Peterson, *Working the Angles: The Shape of Pastoral Integrity* (Grand Rapids: Eerdmans, 1987); Eugene H. Peterson, *The Contemplative Pastor: Returning to the Art of Spiritual Direction* (Carol Stream, IL: Christianity Today, 1989); and Eugene H. Peterson, *Under the Unpredictable Plant: An Exploration in Vocational Holiness* (Grand Rapids: Eerdmans, 1992).

56. Eugene H. Peterson, *Christ Plays in Ten Thousand Places: A Conversation in Spiritual Theology* (Grand Rapids: Eerdmans, 2005); Eugene H. Peterson, *Eat This Book: A Conversation in the Art of Spiritual Reading* (Grand Rapids: Eerdmans, 2006); Eugene H. Peterson, *The Jesus Way: A Conversation on the Ways that Jesus Is the Way* (Grand Rapids: Eerdmans, 2007); Eugene H. Peterson, *Tell It Slant: A Conversation on the Language of Jesus in His Stories and Prayers* (Grand Rapids: Eerdmans, 2008); Eugene H. Peterson, *Practice Resurrection: A Conversation on Growing Up in Christ* (Grand Rapids: Eerdmans, 2010); and, most recently, Eugene H. Peterson, *As Kingfishers Catch Fire: A Conversation on the Many Ways of God Formed by the Words of God* (Colorado Springs: WaterBrook Press, 2017). See also Jason Byassee and L. Roger Owens, eds., *Pastoral Work: Engagements with the Vision of Eugene Peterson* (Eugene, OR: Cascade Books, 2014).

57. See Roger E. Van Harn, *Preacher, Can You Hear Us Listening?* (Grand Rapids: Eerdmans, 2005).

58. See Matthew D. Kim, *Preaching with Cultural Intelligence: Understanding the People Who Hear Our Sermons* (Grand Rapids: Baker Academic, 2017).

59. Packer, *Truth and Power*, 134–39 (quotation from p. 138). See also Richard Baxter, *A Christian Directory* (Morgan, PA: Soli Deo Gloria, 1996), 473–77.

60. See Joe Thorn, *Note to Self: The Discipline of Preaching to Yourself* (Wheaton: Crossway, 2011).

61. H. B. Charles Jr., *On Preaching: Personal and Pastoral Insights for the Preparation and Practice of Preaching* (Chicago: Moody, 2014), 9–11.

62. Adapted from John Piper, *The Supremacy of God in Preaching*, rev. ed. (Grand Rapids: Baker Books, 2015), 85–107. See also pages 111–20.

63. Piper, *Supremacy of God in Preaching*, 31.

64. Piper, *Supremacy of God in Preaching*, 119 (emphasis in original).

65. Jared E. Alcántara, *Learning from a Legend: What Gardner C. Taylor Can Teach Us about Preaching* (Eugene, OR: Cascade Books, 2016), 132. There are other preachers throughout history we can also learn from—e.g., John Wesley and John Calvin. See Michael Pasquarello III, *John Wesley: A Preaching Life* (Nashville: Abingdon, 2010); and Steven J. Lawson, *The Expository Genius of John Calvin* (Lake Mary, FL: Reformation Trust Publishing, 2007).

66. See Kay Warren, *Sacred Privilege: Your Life and Ministry as a Pastor's Wife* (Grand Rapids: Revell, 2017), 29–31, 88, 103–4, 185–86.

67. Morgan Lee, "The Truth about Suicide," an interview with Al Hsu, *Christianity Today*, November 2017, 52.

68. See Siang-Yang Tan, "Psychology Collaborating with the Church: A Pastor-Psychologist's Perspective and Personal Experience," in *Psychology and the Church*, ed. Mark R. McMinn and Amy W. Dominguez (New York: Nova Science, 2005), 49–55.

69. Tim Clinton and Jared Pingleton, eds., *The Struggle Is Real: How to Care for Mental and Relational Health Needs in the Church* (Bloomington, IN: WestBow Press, 2017); and Gary R. Collins, *Christian Counseling: A Comprehensive Guide*, 3rd ed. (Nashville: Thomas Nelson, 2007). See also Stephen Grcevich, *Mental Health and the Church* (Grand Rapids: Zondervan, 2018); W. Brad Johnson and William L. Johnson, *The Minister's Guide to Psychological Disorders and Treatments*, 2nd ed. (New York: Routledge, 2014); Amy Simpson, *Troubled Minds: Mental Illness and the Church's Mission* (Downers Grove, IL: InterVarsity, 2013); and Matthew S. Stanford, *Grace for the Afflicted: A Clinical and Biblical Perspective on Metal Illness*, rev. ed. (Downers Grove, IL: InterVarsity, 2017). See also Karen Mason, *Preventing Suicide: A Handbook for Pastors, Chaplains and Pastoral Counselors* (Downers Grove, IL: InterVarsity, 2014).

70. Mark R. McMinn, *The Science of Virtue: Why Positive Psychology Matters to the Church* (Grand Rapids: Brazos Press, 2017).

71. Ellen T. Charry, *God and the Art of Happiness* (Grand Rapids: Eerdmans, 2010).

72. Dallas Willard, *Knowing Christ Today: Why We Can Trust Spiritual Knowledge* (New York: HarperOne, 2009), 193–212; and Dallas Willard and Gary Black Jr., *The Divine Conspiracy Continued: Fulfilling God's Kingdom on Earth* (New York: HarperOne, 2014), 269–84.

73. Ralph Douglas West, foreword to Alcántara, *Learning from a Legend*, ix.

74. Lloyd-Jones, *Preaching and Preachers*, 297.

75. Darrell W. Johnson, *The Glory of Preaching: Participating in God's Transformation of the World* (Downers Grove, IL: IVP Academic, 2009), 17.

Chapter 6 Corporate Worship

1. Bob Kauflin, *Worship Matters: Leading Others to Encounter the Greatness of God* (Wheaton: Crossway, 2008), 241.

2. See Keith Getty and Kristyn Getty, *Sing! How Worship Transforms Your Life, Family, and Church* (Nashville: B&H, 2017).

3. This list is from Bryan Chapell, *Christ-Centered Worship: Letting the Gospel Shape Our Practice* (Grand Rapids: Baker Academic, 2009), 145–46.

4. Brian Croft and Jason Adkins, *Gather God's People: Understand, Plan, and Lead Worship in Your Local Church* (Grand Rapids: Zondervan, 2014), 45.

5. See recommended readings at the end of this chapter.

6. John Piper, *Let the Nations Be Glad! The Supremacy of God in Missions*, 3rd ed. (Grand Rapids: Baker Academic, 2010), 15.

7. Piper, *Let the Nations Be Glad!*, 250–51 (emphasis in original).

8. Piper, *Let the Nations Be Glad!*, 251–54.

9. Ralph P. Martin, *The Worship of God: Some Theological, Pastoral, and Practical Reflections* (Grand Rapids: Eerdmans, 1982), 4 (emphasis in original).

10. Daniel I. Block, *For the Glory of God: Recovering a Biblical Theology of Worship* (Grand Rapids: Baker Academic, 2014), 29 (emphasis in original).

11. Gerrit Gustafson, *The Adventure of Worship: Discovering Your Highest Calling* (Grand Rapids: Chosen, 2006), 23.

12. Siang-Yang Tan and Douglas H. Gregg, *Disciplines of the Holy Spirit* (Grand Rapids: Zondervan, 1997), 142.

13. A. W. Tozer, *That Incredible Christian* (Harrisburg, PA: Christian Publications, 1964), 126. See also Sam Hamstra Jr., *What's Love Got to Do with It? How the Heart of God Shapes Worship* (Eugene, OR: Wipf & Stock, 2016); and Arron Chambers, *Devoted: Isn't It Time to Fall More in Love with Jesus?* (Colorado Springs: NavPress, 2014).

14. See Tan and Gregg, *Disciplines of the Holy Spirit*, 151–53.

15. Piper, *Let the Nations Be Glad!*, 255.

16. See recommended readings at the end of this chapter.

17. Croft and Adkins, *Gather God's People*, 19–27.

18. Croft and Adkins, *Gather God's People*, 20.

19. Croft and Adkins, *Gather God's People*, 20–23.

20. Croft and Adkins, *Gather God's People*, 23–25.

21. Croft and Adkins, *Gather God's People*, 25.

22. Kauflin, *Worship Matters*, 55. See also William H. Willimon, *Pastor: The Theology and Practice of Ordained Ministry*, rev. ed. (Nashville: Abingdon, 2016), 75–90, 91–108. For more detailed guidance on planning and conducting specific corporate worship services, see Constance M. Cherry, *The Worship Architect: A Blueprint for Designing Culturally Relevant and Biblically Faithful Services* (Grand Rapids: Baker Academic, 2010); Constance M. Cherry, *The Special Service Worship Architect: Blueprints for Weddings, Funerals, Baptisms, Holy Communion, and Other Occasions* (Grand Rapids: Baker Academic, 2013); Constance M. Cherry, *The Music Architect: Blueprints for Engaging Worshipers in Song* (Grand Rapids: Baker Academic, 2016); and Nelson Searcy and Jason Hatley with Jennifer Dykes Henson, *Engage: A Guide to Creating Life-Transforming Worship Services* (Grand Rapids: Baker Books, 2011).

23. Alexis D. Abernethy, ed., *Worship That Changes Lives: Multidisciplinary and Congregational Perspectives on Spiritual Transformation* (Grand Rapids: Baker Academic, 2008).

24. Adapted from Abernethy, *Worship That Changes Lives*, 273–77.

Chapter 7 Intentional Disciplemaking and Spiritual Formation

1. Dallas Willard, *Renovation of the Heart: Putting on the Character of Christ* (Colorado Springs: NavPress, 2002), 235. For other key books on spiritual formation, see recommended readings at the end of this chapter.

2. John Stott, foreword to *Side by Side: A Handbook: Disciple-Making for a New Century*, ed. Steve and Lois Rabey (Colorado Springs: Cook and NavPress, 2000), 7. For a few earlier classic or well-known books on discipleship and disciplemaking, see Dietrich Bonhoeffer, *The Cost of Discipleship* (1937; repr. New York: Touchstone, 1995); Alexander Balmain Bruce, *The*

Training of the Twelve (Grand Rapids: Kregel, 1972); Robert E. Coleman, *The Master Plan of Discipleship* (Grand Rapids: Revell, 1987); and LeRoy Eims, *The Lost Art of Disciple Making* (Grand Rapids: Zondervan, 1978).

3. For other key books on discipleship and disciplemaking, see recommended readings at the end of this chapter.

4. For example, see Edmund Chan, *Mentoring Paradigms: Reflections on Mentoring, Leadership and Discipleship* (Singapore: Covenant EFC, 2008); Edmund Chan, *Cultivating Your Inner Life: Reflections on Spiritual Formation in Discipleship Today* (Singapore: Covenant EFC, 2011); Edmund Chan, *A Certain Kind: Intentional Disciplemaking That Redefines Success in Ministry* (Singapore: Covenant EFC, 2013); and Edmund Chan, *Radical Discipleship: Five Defining Questions* (Singapore: Covenant EFC, 2014). See also Edmund Chan with Ann Chan, *Roots and Wings* (Singapore: Covenant EFC, 2009); and Edmund Chan and Lian Seng Tan, *Discipleship Missions: Getting Missional in Your Life* (Singapore: Covenant EFC, 2016).

5. Chan, *Certain Kind*, 29–30; and Chan, *Radical Discipleship*, 149.

6. Chan, *Certain Kind*, 51.

7. Adapted from Chan, *Certain Kind*, 52–53.

8. Adapted from Chan, *Certain Kind*, 55–61.

9. Jim Putman and Bobby Harrington with Robert E. Coleman, *DiscipleShift: Five Steps That Help Your Church to Make Disciples Who Make Disciples* (Grand Rapids: Zondervan, 2013), 51.

10. Greg Ogden, *Discipleship Essentials: A Guide to Building Your Life in Christ*, rev. ed. (Downers Grove, IL: InterVarsity, 2007), 17, 24.

11. Elaine O'Rourke, *A Dallas Willard Dictionary* (San Bernardino, CA: Soul Training Publications, 2013), 257.

12. Putman and Harrington with Coleman, *DiscipleShift*, 233n14.

13. Jack Hayford, "Spirit-Formed in Purity and Power," *Spectrum* 6, no. 2 (Spring 2005): 5–6.

14. Dallas Willard, *The Great Omission: Reclaiming Jesus' Essential Teachings on Discipleship* (New York: HarperOne, 2006), 5–6.

15. Willard, *Great Omission*, xi (emphasis in original).

16. Willard, *Great Omission*, 3.

17. Matthew W. Bates, *Salvation by Allegiance Alone: Rethinking Faith, Works, and the Gospel of Jesus the King* (Grand Rapids: Baker Academic, 2017).

18. Willard, *Renovation of the Heart*, 77–92.

19. Willard, *Renovation of the Heart*, 251. See also Dallas Willard, *The Divine Conspiracy: Rediscovering Our Hidden Life in God* (San Francisco: HarperSanFrancisco, 1998); Dallas Willard, *The Spirit of the Disciplines* (San Francisco: HarperSanFrancisco, 1988); and Dallas Willard and Gary Black Jr., *The Divine Conspiracy Continued: Fulfilling God's Kingdom on Earth* (New York: HarperOne, 2014).

20. James Bryan Smith with Lynda Graybeal, *A Spiritual Formation Workbook: Small-Group Resources for Nurturing Christian Growth*, rev. ed. (San Francisco: HarperSanFrancisco, 1999). See also Richard J. Foster, *Streams of Living Water: Celebrating the Great Traditions of Christian Faith* (San Francisco: HarperSanFrancisco, 1998).

21. Diane J. Chandler, *Christian Spiritual Formation: An Integrated Approach for Personal and Relational Wholeness* (Downers Grove, IL: IVP Academic, 2014), 20–21.

22. Adapted from Kenneth Boa, *Conformed to His Image: Biblical and Practical Approaches to Spiritual Formation* (Grand Rapids: Zondervan, 2001), 11–13.

23. Gordon T. Smith, *Called to Be Saints: An Invitation to Christian Maturity* (Downers Grove, IL: IVP Academic, 2014), 184.

24. G. T. Smith, *Called to Be Saints*, 184–85.

25. G. T. Smith, *Called to Be Saints*, 185–214. With regard to preaching in the church as a teaching-learning community for spiritual formation, see also Kay L. Northcut, *Kindling Desire for God: Preaching as Spiritual Direction* (Minneapolis: Fortress, 2009); and John W.

Wright, *Telling God's Story: Narrative Preaching for Christian Formation* (Downers Grove, IL: IVP Academic, 2007).

26. Bill Hull, *The Disciple-Making Pastor: Leading Others on the Journey of Faith*, rev. ed. (Grand Rapids: Baker Books, 2007), 75.

27. Hull, *Disciple-Making Pastor*, 243–44.

28. Adapted from Glenn W. McDonald, *The Disciple Making Church: From Dry Bones to Spiritual Vitality* (Grand Haven, MI: FaithWalk Publishing, 2004), xi.

29. McDonald, *Disciple Making Church*, xii.

30. Adapted from McDonald, *Disciple Making Church*, 237–51.

31. This list is from Randy Pope with Kitti Murray, *Insourcing: Bringing Discipleship Back to the Local Church* (Grand Rapids: Zondervan, 2013), 15.

32. Adapted from Pope with Murray, *Insourcing*, 30–36.

33. Adapted from Pope with Murray, *Insourcing*, 211.

34. Adapted from Pope with Murray, *Insourcing*, 65.

35. Adapted from Pope with Murray, *Insourcing*, 202–8.

36. Putman and Harrington with Coleman, *DiscipleShift*, 9–10.

37. Adapted from Putman and Harrington with Coleman, *DiscipleShift*, 215–30. See also Jim Putman, *Real-Life Discipleship: Building Churches That Make Disciples* (Colorado Springs: NavPress, 2010); and Avery Willis, Jim Putman, Bill Krause, and Brandon Guindon, *Real-Life Discipleship Training Manual* (Colorado Springs: NavPress, 2010).

38. Adapted from Bobby Harrington and Alex Absalom, *Discipleship That Fits: The Five Kinds of Relationships God Uses to Help Us Grow* (Grand Rapids: Zondervan, 2016), 62.

39. Harrington and Absalom, *Discipleship That Fits*, 29.

40. Harrington and Absalom, *Discipleship That Fits*, 16–17, 153.

41. Bobby Harrington and Josh Patrick, *The Disciple Maker's Handbook: Seven Elements of a Discipleship Lifestyle* (Grand Rapids: Zondervan, 2017), 185.

42. Adapted from Harrington and Patrick, *Disciple Maker's Handbook*, 187.

43. Greg Ogden, *Transforming Discipleship: Making Disciples a Few at a Time* (Downers Grove, IL: InterVarsity, 2003), 153–54.

44. Ogden, *Discipleship Essentials*, 5–6 (contents).

45. Ogden, *Discipleship Essentials*, 14.

46. These questions are from David Platt, *Follow Me: A Call to Die. A Call to Live* (Carol Stream, IL: Tyndale, 2013), 203–33. See also Francis Chan with Mark Beuving, *Multiply: Disciples Making Disciples* (Colorado Springs: David C. Cook, 2012), for material on disciples making disciples based on God's Word, covering topics such as living as a disciplemaker, living as the church, how to study the Bible, and understanding the Old Testament. Material and videos are available free online at www.multiplymovement.com.

47. Adapted from Chan, *Certain Kind*, 158–63.

48. Adapted from Chan, *Certain Kind*, 240–45.

49. Neil Cole, *Cultivating a Life for God: Multiplying Disciples through Life Transformation Groups* (Signal Hill, CA: CMA, 1999).

50. For example, see Kent Carlson and Mike Lueken, *Renovation of the Church: What Happens When a Seeker Church Discovers Spiritual Formation* (Downers Grove, IL: InterVarsity, 2011).

51. Michael Yaconelli, *Messy Spirituality: God's Annoying Love for Imperfect People* (Grand Rapids: Zondervan, 1992).

52. Jared C. Wilson, *The Imperfect Disciple: Grace for People Who Can't Get Their Act Together* (Grand Rapids: Baker Books, 2017).

53. See Zack Eswine, *The Imperfect Pastor: Discovering Joy in Our Limitations through a Daily Apprenticeship with Jesus* (Wheaton: Crossway, 2015). See also Chuck DeGroat,

Wholeheartedness: Busyness, Exhaustion, and Healing the Divided Self (Grand Rapids: Eerdmans, 2016).

54. For example, see Alvin R. Reid and George G. Robinson, *With: A Practical Guide to Informal Mentoring and Intentional Disciple Making* (Spring Hill, TN: Rainer Publishing, 2016); and Chan, *Mentoring Paradigms.*

55. Platt, *Follow Me*, 226.

Chapter 8 Evangelism, Missions, and Social Concern

1. Siang-Yang Tan and Douglas H. Gregg, *Disciplines of the Holy Spirit* (Grand Rapids: Zondervan, 1997), 206. See also J. I. Parker, *Evangelism and the Sovereignty of God* (Downers Grove, IL: InterVarsity, 1979), 37–57.

2. Howard Snyder, *The Community of the King* (Downers Grove, IL: InterVarsity, 1977), 91.

3. Gary L. McIntosh and Charles Arn, *What Every Pastor Should Know: 101 Indispensable Rules of Thumb for Leading Your Church* (Grand Rapids: Baker Books, 2013), 13.

4. Win Arn and Charles Arn, *The Master's Plan for Making Disciples: Every Christian an Effective Witness through an Enabling Church*, 2nd ed. (Grand Rapids: Baker Books, 1998).

5. See John Mark Yeats, "Pastor as Evangelist," in *Portraits of a Pastor: The 9 Essential Roles of a Church Leader*, ed. Jason K. Allen (Chicago: Moody, 2017), 107–24. See also James Bryant and Mac Brunson, *The New Guidebook for Pastors* (Nashville: B&H, 2007), 116–24; and William H. Willimon, *Pastor: The Theology and Practice of Ordained Ministry*, rev. ed. (Nashville: Abingdon, 2016), 215–37.

6. See Jason G. Duesing, "Pastor as Missionary," in Allen, *Portraits of a Pastor*, 125–46. See also Bryant and Brunson, *New Guidebook for Pastors*, 124–28; and Willimon, *Pastor*, 263–79.

7. See recommended readings at the end of this chapter.

8. James Chuong, *True Story: A Christianity Worth Believing In* (Downers Grove, IL: InterVarsity, 2008), 205–18. For other helpful books on evangelism, see recommended readings.

9. See Siang-Yang Tan, *Full Service: Moving from Self-Serve Christianity to Total Servanthood* (Grand Rapids: Baker Books, 2006), 131–32.

10. Adam S. McHugh, *Introverts in the Church: Finding Our Place in an Extroverted Culture*, rev. ed. (Downers Grove, IL: InterVarsity, 2017), 178–93, especially 190–92.

11. Randy Newman, *Questioning Evangelism: Engaging People's Hearts the Way Jesus Did*, 2nd ed. (Grand Rapids: Kregel, 2017).

12. Michael L. Simpson, *Permission Evangelism: When to Talk, When to Walk* (Colorado Springs: NexGen, 2003).

13. Elaine A. Heath, *The Mystic Way of Evangelism: A Contemplative Vision for Christian Outreach*, 2nd ed. (Grand Rapids: Baker Academic, 2017).

14. C. Peter Wagner, *Your Spiritual Gifts Can Help Your Church Grow*, rev. ed. (Ventura, CA: Regal, 2005), 164.

15. Tan and Gregg, *Disciplines of the Holy Spirit*, 213–14.

16. See Tan and Gregg, *Disciplines of the Holy Spirit*, 214–18.

17. See Tan and Gregg, *Disciplines of the Holy Spirit*, 221–22.

18. Steve Sjogren, *Conspiracy of Kindness* (Ann Arbor, MI: Servant Publications, 1993), 22. See also Tan, *Full Service*, chap. 10, 116–33.

19. Steve Sjogren, *Servant Warfare: How Kindness Conquers Spiritual Darkness* (Ann Arbor, MI: Servant Publications, 1996), 82.

20. Sjogren, *Servant Warfare*, 14.

21. Sjogren, *Servant Warfare*, 15.

22. Philip Yancey, *What's So Amazing about Grace?* (Grand Rapids: Zondervan, 1997), 272.

23. Adapted from McIntosh and Arn, *What Every Pastor Should Know*, 13–31.

24. For example, see Josh McDowell and Sean McDowell, *Evidence That Demands a Verdict: Life-Changing Truth for a Skeptical World*, rev. ed. (Nashville: Thomas Nelson, 2017). See also

Joshua D. Chatraw and Mark D. Allen, *Apologetics at the Cross: An Introduction for Christian Witness* (Grand Rapids: Zondervan, 2018).

25. See Dallas Willard, *The Allure of Gentleness: Defending the Faith in the Manner of Jesus* (New York: HarperOne, 2015).

26. Ed Silvoso, *That None Should Perish* (Ventura, CA: Regal, 1994), 57. See also Ed Silvoso, *Prayer Evangelism* (Ventura, CA: Regal 2000).

27. C. Peter Wagner, *Church Planting for a Greater Harvest: A Comprehensive Guide* (Ventura, CA: Regal, 1990), 11 (emphasis in original). See also Aubrey Malphurs, *The Nuts and Bolts of Church Planting: A Guide to Starting Any Kind of Church* (Grand Rapids: Baker Books, 2011).

28. David Garrison, *Church Planting Movements: How God Is Redeeming a Lost World* (Monument, CO: WIGTake Resources, 2004); and Steve Smith with Ying Kai, *T4T: A Discipleship Re-Revolution* (Monument, CO: WIGTake Resources, 2004). See also Craig Ott and Gene Wilson, *Global Church Planting: Biblical Principles and Best Practices for Multiplication* (Grand Rapids: Baker Academic, 2011).

29. FECA Annual Report, 2016, www.feca.org.

30. For example, see George Miley, *Loving the Church . . . Blessing the Nations: Pursuing the Role of Local Churches in Global Mission* (Waynesboro, GA: Gabriel Publishing, 2003); and Paul Sparks, Tim Soerens, and Dwight J. Friesen, *The New Parish: How Neighborhood Churches Are Transforming Mission, Discipleship, and Community* (Downers Grove, IL: InterVarsity, 2014).

31. For example, see A. Scott Moreau, Gary R. Corwin, and Gary B. McGee, *Introducing World Missions: A Biblical, Historical, and Practical Survey*, 2nd ed. (Grand Rapids: Baker Academic, 2015); John Piper, *Let the Nations Be Glad! The Supremacy of God in Missions*, 3rd ed. (Grand Rapids: Baker Academic, 2010); Scott W. Sunquist, *Understanding Christian Mission: Participation in Suffering and Glory* (Grand Rapids: Baker Academic, 2013); Andrew F. Walls and Cathy Ross, eds., *Mission in the Twenty-First Century: Exploring the Five Marks of Global Mission* (Maryknoll, NY: Orbis, 2008); Ralph D. Winter and Steven C. Hawthorne, eds., *Perspectives on the World Christian Movement: A Reader*, 4th ed. (Pasadena, CA: William Carey Library, 2013); Christopher J. H. Wright, *The Mission of God: Unlocking the Bible's Grand Narrative* (Downers Grove, IL: IVP Academic, 2006); and Christopher J. H. Wright, *The Mission of God's People: A Biblical Theology of the Church's Mission* (Grand Rapids: Zondervan, 2010).

32. See Willimon, *Pastor*, 263–79; and Duesing, "Pastor as Missionary," 125–46.

33. This list is from Walls and Ross, eds., *Mission in the Twenty-First Century*, xiv.

34. Piper, *Let the Nations Be Glad!*, 257.

35. Piper, *Let the Nations Be Glad!*, 255, 259.

36. Adapted from Duesing, "Pastor as Missionary," 128–33. See also Philip Jenkins, *The New Christendom: The Coming of Global Christianity*, 3rd ed. (New York: Oxford University Press, 2011); Mark Noll, *The New Shape of World Christianity: How American Experience Reflects Global Faith* (Downers Grove, IL: IVP Academic, 2008); and Piper, *Let the Nations Be Glad!*, 16–32.

37. See Wright, *Mission of God*.

38. Wright, *Mission of God's People*, 286.

39. Sam Metcalf, letter to author, November, 2017.

40. Jason Mandryk, *Operation World: The Definitive Prayer Guide to Every Nation*, 7th ed. (Colorado Springs: Biblica Publishing, 2010); and Brian C. Stiller, *An Insider's Guide to Praying for the World* (Grand Rapids: Bethany House, 2016).

41. Adapted from Wright, *Mission of God*, 533–34.

42. Wright, *Mission of God*, 22–23 (emphasis in original).

43. See Wright, *Mission of God*; and Wright, *Mission of God's People*.

44. For example, see Lance Ford and Brad Brisco, *The Missional Quest: Becoming a Church of the Long Run* (Downers Grove, IL: InterVarsity, 2013); Michael Frost and Alan Hirsch, *The Shaping of Things to Come: Innovation and Mission for the 21st Century Church*, rev. ed. (Grand Rapids: Baker Books, 2013); Kim Hammond and Darren Cronshaw, *Sentness: Six Postures of Missional Christians* (Downers Grove, IL: InterVarsity, 2014); Ross Hastings, *Missional God, Missional Church: Hope for Re-Evangelizing the West* (Downers Grove, IL: IVP Academic, 2012); Alan J. Roxburgh and M. Scott Boren, *Introducing the Missional Church: What It Is, Why It Matters, How to Become One* (Grand Rapids: Baker Books, 2009); J. R. Woodward, *Creating a Missional Culture: Equipping the Church for the Sake of the World* (Downers Grove, IL: InterVarsity, 2012); and J. R. Woodward and Dan White Jr., *The Church as Movement: Starting and Sustaining Missional-Incarnational Communities* (Downers Grove, IL: InterVarsity, 2016).

45. Frost and Hirsch, *Shaping of Things to Come*, 277–78.

46. Frost and Hirsch, *Shaping of Things to Come*, 35–38.

47. Frost and Hirsch, *Shaping of Things to Come*, 25–26, 273 (for definition of APEST). See also Woodward, *Creating a Missional Culture*, 113–67, for more on APEST as the five culture creators, following Jesus as the Archetypical Culture Creator.

48. Roxburgh and Boren, *Introducing the Missional Church*, 27.

49. Roxburgh and Boren, *Introducing the Missional Church*, 45.

50. Ford and Brisco, *Missional Quest*, 23.

51. Ford and Brisco, *Missional Quest*, 27.

52. Hammond and Cronshaw, *Sentness*, 11–12.

53. Hammond and Cronshaw, *Sentness*, 23, see also 44–176.

54. Hastings, *Missional God, Missional Church*, 15 (emphasis in original).

55. Hastings, *Missional God, Missional Church*, 36.

56. See Patrick W. T. Johnson, *The Mission of Preaching: Equipping the Community for Faithful Witness* (Downers Grove, IL: IVP Academic, 2015); and Zack Eswine, *Preaching to a Post-Everything World: Crafting Biblical Sermons That Connect with Our Culture* (Grand Rapids: Baker Books, 2008).

57. See Craig L. Blomberg, *Christians in an Age of Wealth: A Biblical Theology of Stewardship* (Grand Rapids: Zondervan, 2013); Steve Corbett and Brian Fikkert, *When Helping Hurts: How to Alleviate Poverty without Hurting the Poor . . . and Yourself*, rev. ed. (Chicago: Moody, 2012); Gary Haugen, *Just Courage: God's Great Expedition for the Restless Christian* (Downers Grove, IL: InterVarsity, 2008); Bryant L. Myers, *Engaging Globalization: The Poor, Christian Mission, and Our Hyperconnected World* (Grand Rapids: Baker Academic, 2017); and Ronald J. Sider, *Rich Christians in an Age of Hunger: Moving from Affluence to Generosity*, rev. ed (Nashville: Thomas Nelson, 2010).

58. Richard Stearns, *The Hole in Our Gospel* (Nashville: Thomas Nelson, 2010).

59. Mark Labberton, *The Dangerous Act of Worship: Living God's Call to Justice* (Downers Grove, IL: InterVarsity, 2007); and Mark Labberton, *The Dangerous Act of Loving Your Neighbor: Seeing Others through the Eyes of Jesus* (Downers Grove, IL: InterVarsity, 2010).

60. Douglas J. Moo and Jonathan A. Moo, *Creation Care: A Biblical Theology of the Natural World* (Grand Rapids: Zondervan, 2018).

61. Makoto Fujimura, *Culture Care: Reconnecting with Beauty for Our Common Life* (Downers Grove, IL: InterVarsity, 2017).

62. Andy Crouch, *Culture Making: Recovering Our Creative Calling* (Downers Grove, IL: InterVarsity, 2008).

Chapter 9 Leadership

1. See Ronnie W. Floyd, "Pastor as Leader," in *Portraits of a Pastor: The 9 Essential Roles of a Church Leader*, ed. Jason K. Allen (Chicago: Moody, 2017), 147–60; James W. Bryant and Mac Brunson, *The New Guidebook for Pastors* (Nashville: B&H, 2007), 69–82; Derek J. Prime and

Alistair Begg, *On Being a Pastor: Understanding Our Calling and Work* (Chicago: Moody, 2004), 205–23; and William H. Willimon, *Pastor: The Theology and Practice of Ordained Ministry*, rev. ed. (Nashville: Abingdon, 2016), 281–93.

2. See recommended readings at the end of this chapter.

3. Bernice M. Ledbetter, Robert J. Banks, and David C. Greenhalgh, *Reviewing Leadership: A Christian Evaluation of Current Approaches*, 2nd ed. (Grand Rapids: Baker Academic, 2016).

4. Siang-Yang Tan, *Full Service: Moving from Self-Serve Christianity to Total Servanthood* (Grand Rapids: Baker Books, 2006), 47–63, 134–50.

5. Siang-Yang Tan, "The Primacy of Servanthood," in *The Three Tasks of Leadership: Worldly Wisdom for Pastoral Leaders*, ed. Eric O. Jacobsen (Grand Rapids: Eerdmans, 2009), 77–90.

6. For example, see Edward C. Zaragoza, *No Longer Servants, but Friends: A Theology of Ordained Ministry* (Nashville: Abingdon, 1999). Zaragoza is critical not only of servant leadership but also of servanthood. I believe that he has gone too far and is too negative, especially about servanthood, which is a biblical concept based on deep friendship with Jesus and serving our Best Friend (John 15:15–17; see also John 13:14–17). See Tan, *Full Service*, 47–54.

7. Robert K. Greenleaf, *Servant Leadership: A Journey into the Nature of Legitimate Power and Greatness* (New York: Paulist Press, 1977).

8. Steve Hayner, "Playing to an Audience of One," *World Vision Today* (Summer 1998): 5–6.

9. Robert Banks and Bernice M. Ledbetter, *Reviewing Leadership: A Christian Evaluation of Current Approaches* (Grand Rapids: Baker Academic, 2004), 111 (emphasis in original).

10. Zaragoza, *No Longer Servants*, 60

11. Tan, *Full Service*, 190.

12. Barbara Kellerman, *The End of Leadership* (New York: Harper Business, 2012), 200.

13. Matthew Stewart, *The Management Myth: Why the Experts Keep Getting It Wrong* (New York: Norton, 2009), 303.

14. See Christopher A. Beeley, *Leading God's People: Wisdom from the Early Church for Today* (Grand Rapids: Eerdmans, 2012); John A. Berntsen, *Cross-Shaped Leadership: On the Rough and Tumble of Parish Practice* (Herndon, VA: Alban Institute, 2008); Lance Ford, *Unleader: Reimagining Leadership . . . and Why We Must* (Kansas City, KS: Beacon Hill Press, 2012); Taylor Field, *Upside-Down Leadership: Rethinking Influence and Success* (Birmingham, AL: New Hope Publishers, 2012); Bill Hull, *The Christian Leader: Rehabilitating Our Addiction to Secular Leadership* (Grand Rapids: Zondervan, 2016); and Joseph M. Stowell, *Redefining Leadership: Character-Driven Habits of Effective Leaders* (Grand Rapids: Zondervan, 2014).

15. This list is from Eric Yaverbaum, *Leadership Secrets of the World's Most Successful CEOs* (New York: Barnes and Noble, 2006), 257. See also Warren G. Bennis and Robert Thomas, *Geek and Geezers: How Era, Values and Defining Moments Shape Leaders* (Boston: Harvard Business School Press, 2002); and Daniel Goleman, Richard Boyatzis, and Annie McKee, *Primal Leadership: Realizing the Power of Emotional Intelligence* (Boston: Harvard Business School Press, 2002).

16. Jack Welch with Suzy Welch, *Winning* (New York: Harper Business, 2005), 63.

17. Marcus Buckingham, *The One Thing You Need to Know: . . . about Great Managing, Great Leading, and Sustained Individual Success* (New York: Free Press, 2005), 197.

18. James C. Collins, *Good to Great: Why Some Companies Make the Leap—and Others Don't* (New York: Harper Business, 2001).

19. "The Good to Great Pastor: An Interview with Jim Collins," *Leadership* (Spring 2006): 48.

20. Jim Collins, *How the Mighty Fall and Why Some Companies Never Give In* (New York: HarperCollins, 2009), 20–26. See also Jim Collins and Morten T. Hansen, *Great by Choice: Uncertainty, Chaos, and Luck—Why Some Thrive Despite Them All* (New York: Harper Business, 2011).

21. Collins and Hansen, *Great by Choice*, 123.

22. John Maxwell, *The 21 Irrefutable Laws of Leadership: Follow Them and People Will Follow You*, rev. ed. (Nashville: Thomas Nelson, 2007).

23. John Maxwell, *The 21 Indispensable Qualities of a Leader: Becoming the Person Others Will Want to Follow*, international ed. (Nashville: Thomas Nelson, 2012).

24. Walter Wright, *Relational Leadership: A Biblical Model for Leadership Service* (Carlisle, UK: Paternoster, 2000), 2.

25. Wright, *Relational Leadership*, 12.

26. John Stott, *Basic Christian Leadership: Biblical Models of Church, Gospel, and Ministry* (Downers Grove, IL: InterVarsity, 2002), 11.

27. J. Robert Clinton, *The Making of a Leader: Recognizing the Lessons and Stages of Leadership Development*, rev. ed. (Colorado Springs: NavPress, 2012), 10.

28. Eugene Peterson, "Follow the Leader," *Fuller Focus* (Fall 2001): 31.

29. Aubrey Malphurs, *Being Leaders: The Nature of Authentic Christian Leadership* (Grand Rapids: Baker Books, 2003), 10, 14–22.

30. Ford, *Unleader*, 24–41.

31. Ford, *Unleader*, 40.

32. Ford, *Unleader*, 138–61.

33. Ford, *Unleader*, 175.

34. See Tan, *Full Service*; Berntsen, *Cross-Shaped Leadership*; and Neil Cole, *Organic Leadership: Leading Naturally Right Where You Are* (Grand Rapids: Baker Books, 2009).

35. Field, *Upside-Down Leadership*, 7–8.

36. Stott, *Basic Christian Leadership*, 114.

37. Stowell, *Redefining Leadership*, 168.

38. Stowell, *Redefining Leadership*, 175.

39. R. Albert Mohler Jr., *The Conviction to Lead: 25 Principles for Leadership That Matters* (Grand Rapids: Bethany House, 2012).

40. For example, see Aubrey Malphurs, *Advanced Strategic Planning: A 21st Century Model for Church and Ministry Leaders*, 3rd ed. (Grand Rapids: Baker Books, 2013); Aubrey Malphurs, *Developing a Vision for Ministry*, 3rd ed. (Grand Rapids: Baker Books, 2015); Aubrey Malphurs, *Ministry Nuts and Bolts: What They Don't Teach Pastors in Seminary*, 2nd ed. (Grand Rapids: Kregel, 2016); Andy Stanley, *Visioneering: God's Blueprint for Developing and Maintaining Vision* (Sisters, OR: Multnomah, 2005); Andy Stanley, *Making Vision Stick* (Grand Rapids: Zondervan, 2007); Lovett H. Weems Jr. and Tom Berlin, *Bearing Fruit: Ministry with Real Results* (Nashville: Abingdon, 2011), 35–42, 55–77; C. Jeff Woods, *Better Than Success: 8 Principles of Faithful Leadership* (Valley Forge, PA: Judson Press, 2001), 1–28; and C. Jeff Woods, *On the Move: Adding Strength, Speed, and Balance to Your Congregation* (St. Louis: Chalice, 2009), 34–47 on vision and 48–65 on mission.

41. Woods, *On the Move*, 49–50.

42. Zaragoza, *No Longer Servants*, 44.

43. Zaragoza, *No Longer Servants*, 46–49.

44. Ford, *Unleader*, 31.

45. Max De Pree, *Leadership Is an Art* (New York: Currency Books, 2004), 11.

46. See Ruth Haley Barton, *Pursuing God's Will Together: A Discernment Practice for Leadership Groups* (Downers Grove, IL: InterVarsity, 2012); and Ruth Haley Barton, *Strengthening the Soul of Your Leadership: Seeking God in the Crucible of Ministry* (Downers Grove, IL: InterVarsity, 2008).

47. Tan, *Full Service*, 137.

Chapter 10 Mentoring of Church Staff and Lay Volunteer Coworkers

1. For example, see Brian Croft, *Prepare Them to Shepherd: Test, Train, Affirm, and Send the Next Generation of Pastors* (Grand Rapids: Zondervan, 2014); Brian Croft, *The Pastor's*

Ministry: Biblical Priorities for Faithful Shepherds (Grand Rapids: Zondervan, 2015), 159–76; Rowland Forman, Jeff Jones, and Bruce Miller, *The Leadership Baton: An Intentional Strategy for Developing Leaders in Your Church* (Grand Rapids: Zondervan, 2004); and Aubrey Malphurs and Will Mancini, *Building Leaders: Blueprints for Developing Leadership at Every Level of Your Church* (Grand Rapids: Baker Books, 2004).

2. W. Brad Johnson and Charles R. Ridley, *The Elements of Mentoring*, rev. ed (New York: Palgrave Macmillan, 2008), xi.

3. Johnson and Ridley, *Elements of Mentoring*, iii–v, x–xi (contents).

4. Johnson and Ridley, *Elements of Mentoring*, xi–xii.

5. See recommended readings at the end of this chapter.

6. See recommended readings at the end of this chapter.

7. Paul D. Stanley and J. Robert Clinton, *Connecting: The Mentoring Relationships You Need to Succeed in Life* (Colorado Springs: NavPress, 1992), 40.

8. Stanley and Clinton, *Connecting*, 38.

9. This list is from Stanley and Clinton, *Connecting*, 38.

10. This list is from Stanley and Clinton, *Connecting*, 39–40.

11. James Houston, *The Mentored Life: From Individualism to Personhood* (Colorado Springs: NavPress, 2002).

12. Earl Creps, *Reverse Mentoring: How Young Leaders Can Transform the Church and Why We Should Let Them* (San Francisco: Jossey-Bass, 2008), xvii.

13. Creps, *Reverse Mentoring*, xviii.

14. Creps, *Reverse Mentoring*, xx–xxi.

15. Adapted from Stanley and Clinton, *Connecting*, 41–42.

16. Edward L. Smither, *Augustine as Mentor: A Model for Preparing Spiritual Leaders* (Nashville: B&H, 2008), 258–59.

17. See Alvin Reid and George G. Robinson, *With: A Practical Guide to Informal Mentoring and Intentional Disciple Making* (Spring Hill, TN: Tainer Publishing, 2016).

18. Greg Ogden, *The Essential Commandment: A Disciple's Guide to Loving God and Others* (Downers Grove, IL: InterVarsity, 2011); and Greg Ogden and Daniel Meyer, *Leadership Essentials: Shaping Vision, Mulitplying Influence, Defining Character* (Downers Grove, IL: InterVarsity, 2007).

19. Stanley and Clinton, *Connecting*, 208–11.

20. See Phil A. Newton, *The Mentoring Church: How Pastors and Congregations Cultivate Leaders* (Grand Rapids: Kregel, 2017).

21. Adapted from Carson Pue, *Mentoring Leaders: Wisdom for Developing Character, Calling, and Competency* (Grand Rapids: Baker Books, 2005), 19–23.

22. See Steve Saccone with Cheri Saccone, *Protégé: Developing Your Next Generation of Church Leaders* (Downers Grove, IL: InterVarsity, 2012); and Randy D. Reese and Robert Loane, *Deep Mentoring: Guiding Others on Their Leadership Journey* (Downers Grove, IL: InterVarsity, 2012).

23. See Jeff Myers with Paul Gutacker and Paige Gutacker, *Cultivate: Forming the Emerging Generation through Life-on-Life Mentoring* (Dayton, TN: Passing the Baton International, 2010).

24. Edmund Chan, *Mentoring Paradigms: Reflections on Mentoring, Leadership and Discipleship* (Singapore: Covenant EFC, 2008), 57–59.

25. This list is from Stanley and Clinton, *Connecting*, 197–98.

26. Stephen A. Macchia, *Becoming a Healthy Team: Five Traits of Vital Leadership* (Grand Rapids: Baker Books, 2005), 182. See also Larry Osborne, *Sticky Teams: Keeping Your Leadership Team and Staff on the Same Page* (Grand Rapids: Zondervan, 2010).

27. Adapted from Macchia, *Becoming a Healthy Team*, 182–83.

28. Greg Ogden, *Unfinished Business: Returning the Ministry to the People of God*, rev. ed (Grand Rapids: Zondervan, 2003); and R. Paul Stevens, *Liberating the Laity: Equipping All the Saints for Ministry* (Vancouver: Regent College Publishing, 2002).

29. Leith Anderson and Jill Fox, *The Volunteer Church: Mobilizing Your Congregation for Growth and Effectiveness* (Grand Rapids: Zondervan, 2015); and Leith Anderson and Jill Fox, *Volunteering: A Guide to Serving in the Body of Christ* (Grand Rapids: Zondervan, 2015).

30. Nelson Searcy with Jennifer Dykes Henson, *Connect: How to Double Your Number of Volunteers* (Grand Rapids: Baker Books, 2012).

31. See Derek J. Prime and Alistair Begg, *On Being a Pastor: Understanding Our Calling and Work* (Chicago: Moody, 2004), 224–45, on delegation as an essential part of effective pastoral leadership.

32. Adapted from J. Robert Clinton, *The Making of a Leader: Recognizing the Lessons and Stages of Leadership Development*, rev. ed. (Colorado Springs: NavPress, 2012), 37–40.

33. For example, see Bob P. Bufford, *Finishing Well: The Adventure of Life beyond Halftime* (Grand Rapids: Zondervan, 2011); David W. F. Wong, *Finishing Well: Closing Life's Significant Chapters* (Bloomington, IN: WestBow Press, 2015); and David W. F. Wong, *Beyond Finishing Well: Writing Life's Next Chapter* (Bloomington, IN: WestBow Press, 2016).

34. See Reese and Loane, *Deep Mentoring*, 225.

35. Reese and Loane, *Deep Mentoring*, 225–28.

36. Reese and Loane, *Deep Mentoring*, 228–31.

37. Siang-Yang Tan, *Full Service: Moving from Self-Serve Christianity to Total Servanthood* (Grand Rapids: Baker Books, 2006), 66.

Chapter 11 Pastoral Care and Counseling

1. For example, see James W. Bryant and Mac Brunson, *The New Guidebook for Pastors* (Nashville: B&H, 2007), 155–69; Derek J. Prime and Alistair Begg, *On Being a Pastor: Understanding Our Calling and Work* (Chicago: Moody, 2004), 142–61, 162–87; and William H. Willimon, *Pastor: The Theology and Practice of Ordained Ministry*, rev. ed. (Nashville: Abingdon, 2016), 167–81.

2. See recommended readings at the end of this chapter.

3. For more recent books on biblical counseling, especially those written mainly from a nouthetic counseling perspective, originally described by Jay Adams, see Robert W. Kellemen, *Gospel-Centered Counseling: How Christ Changes Lives* (Grand Rapids: Zondervan, 2014); Robert W. Kellemen, *Gospel Conversations: How to Care Like Christ* (Grand Rapids: Zondervan, 2015); Bob Kellemen and Jeff Forrey, eds., *Scripture and Counseling: God's Word for Life in a Broken World* (Grand Rapids: Zondervan, 2014); Heath Lambert, *A Theology of Biblical Counseling: The Doctrinal Foundations of Counseling Ministry* (Grand Rapids: Zondervan 2016); James MacDonald, Bob Kellemen, and Steve Viars, eds., *Christ-Centered Biblical Counseling: Changing Lives with God's Changeless Truth* (Eugene, OR: Harvest House, 2013); and David Powlison, *The Biblical Counseling Movement: History and Context* (Greensboro, NC: New Growth Press, 2010).

4. Willimon, *Pastor*, 168.

5. Howard Clinebell and Bridget Claire McKeever, *Basic Types of Pastoral Care and Counseling: Resources for the Ministry of Healing and Growth*, 3rd ed. (Nashville: Abingdon, 2011).

6. See David G. Benner, *Strategic Pastoral Counseling: A Short-Term Structured Model*, 2nd ed. (Grand Rapids: Baker Books, 2003), 14–29.

7. William A. Clebsch and Charles Jaekle, *Pastoral Care in Historical Perspective* (Englewood Cliffs, NJ: Prentice-Hall, 1964).

8. See Thomas C. Oden, *Care of Souls in the Classic Tradition* (Philadelphia: Fortress, 1984); Thomas C. Oden, *Classical Pastoral Care*, vol. 3, *Pastoral Counseling* (Grand Rapids: Baker

Books, 1994); and Thomas C. Oden, *Classical Pastoral Care*, vol. 4, *Crisis Ministries* (Grand Rapids: Baker Books, 1994). See also Willimon, *Pastor*, 167–81.

9. See Powlison, *The Biblical Counseling Movement*; and Heath Lambert, *The Biblical Counseling Movement after Jay Adams* (Wheaton: Crossway, 2012).

10. See references on biblical counseling in note 3 above.

11. See Eric L. Johnson, ed., *Psychology and Christianity: Five Views* (Downers Grove, IL: IVP Academic, 2010); and Stephen P. Greggo and Timothy A. Sisemore, eds., *Counseling and Christianity: Five Approaches* (Downers Grove, IL: IVP Academic, 2012).

12. Eric L. Johnson, *Foundations of Soul Care: A Christian Psychology Proposal* (Downers Grove, IL: IVP Academic, 2007); and Eric L. Johnson, *God and Soul Care: The Therapeutic Resources of the Christian Faith* (Downers Grove, IL: IVP Academic, 2017).

13. See Siang-Yang Tan, *Counseling and Psychotherapy: A Christian Perspective* (Grand Rapids: Baker Academic, 2011), for a Christian, biblical critique of ten major secular schools of counseling and psychotherapy.

14. Tan, *Counseling and Psychotherapy*, 363. See also Jeremy Pierre and Deepak Reju, *The Pastor and Counseling: The Basics of Shepherding Members in Need* (Wheaton: Crossway, 2015).

15. Adapted from Tan, *Counseling and Psychotherapy*, 329. See also Siang-Yang Tan and Eric T. Scalise, *Lay Counseling: Equipping Christians for a Helping Ministry*, rev. ed. (Grand Rapids: Zondervan, 2016), 40–44; and Lawrence J. Crabb Jr., *Effective Biblical Counseling* (Grand Rapids: Zondervan, 1977).

16. Benner, *Strategic Pastoral Counseling*, 16–29.

17. Prime and Begg, *On Being a Pastor*, 144.

18. Prime and Begg, *On Being a Pastor*, 162–70. For more specific help on ministering to those who are sick, dying, or grieving, see Brian Croft, *Visit the Sick: Ministering God's Grace in Times of Illness*, rev. ed. (Grand Rapids: Zondervan, 2014); Martha Jacobs, *A Clergy Guide to End-of-Life Issues* (Cleveland: Pilgrim Press, 2010); and Paul Tautges, *Comfort the Grieving: Ministering God's Grace in Times of Loss*, rev. ed. (Grand Rapids: Zondervan, 2014).

19. Prime and Begg, *On Being a Pastor*, 170–72.

20. See Reagon Wilson and David Kronbach, *Tender Care: Providing Pastoral Care for God's Global Servants* (Rockford, IL: Barnabas Books, 2010); Kelly O'Donnell, ed., *Doing Member Care Well: Perspectives and Practices from around the World* (Pasadena, CA: William Carey Library, 2013); and David J. Wilson, *Mind the Gaps: Engaging the Church in Missionary Care* (Colorado Springs: Believers Press, 2015).

21. Wayne E. Oates, *An Introduction to Pastoral Counseling* (Nashville: Broadman, 1959), vi.

22. See Tan, *Counseling and Psychotherapy*, 364–67.

23. Benner, *Strategic Pastoral Counseling*.

24. Adapted from Benner, *Strategic Pastoral Counseling*, 47–70.

25. Adapted from Benner, *Strategic Pastoral Counseling*, 73–103.

26. Benner, *Strategic Pastoral Counseling*, 82–83. See also H. Newton Malony, "The Clinical Assessment of Optimal Religious Functioning," *Review of Religious Research* 30 (1988): 2–17.

27. Benner, *Strategic Pastoral Counseling*, 105–34.

28. Benner, *Strategic Pastoral Counseling*, 125–45.

29. See Siang-Yang Tan and John Ortberg, *Coping with Depression*, rev. ed. (Grand Rapids: Baker Books, 2004), 107–13.

30. Adapted from Benner, *Strategic Pastoral Counseling*, 148–49.

31. Willimon, *Pastor*, 174–76, 180–81. See also Rebekah Miles, *The Pastor as Moral Guide* (Minneapolis: Fortress, 1999).

32. Willimon, *Pastor*, 175.

33. Willimon, *Pastor*, 176–78.

34. Adapted from Tan, *Counseling and Psychotherapy*, 333–37.

35. Tan and Scalise, *Lay Counseling*, 46–63.

36. Adapted from Tan and Ortberg, *Coping with Depression*, 64–70, 80–83, 95–97. See also Siang-Yang Tan, *Rest: Experiencing God's Peace in a Restless World* (Vancouver: Regent College Publishing, 2003), 170, for a brief summary.

37. Adapted from Tan, *Counseling and Psychotherapy*, 345–46. See also Tan and Ortberg, *Coping with Depression*, 64–70. Transcripts of hypothetical inner healing prayer sessions are provided in these references.

38. Tan and Scalise, *Lay Counseling*. See also Siang-Yang Tan, "Lay Helping: The Whole Church in Soul-Care Ministry," in *Competent Christian Counseling*, ed. Timothy Clinton and George Ohlschlager, vol. 1, *Foundations and Practice of Compassionate Soul Care* (Colorado Springs: WaterBrook Press, 2002), 424–36, 759–62.

39. Robert W. Kellemen, *Equipping Counselors for Your Church: The 4E Ministry Training Strategy* (Phillipsburg, NJ: P&R, 2011).

40. Melvin J. Steinbron, *Can the Pastor Do It Alone?* (Ventura, CA: Regal, 1987); and Melvin J. Steinbron, *The Lay-Driven Church* (Ventura, CA: Regal, 1997).

41. Steinbron, *Lay-Driven Church*, 169.

42. For example, see Tim Clinton and Ron Hawkins, *The Quick-Reference Guide to Biblical Counseling: Personal and Emotional Issues* (Grand Rapids: Baker Books, 2009). See also Tim Clinton and Chap Clark with Joshua Straub, *The Quick-Reference Guide to Counseling Teenagers* (Grand Rapids: Baker Books, 2010); Tim Clinton and Mark Laaser, *The Quick-Reference Guide to Sexuality and Relationship Counseling* (Grand Rapids: Baker Books, 2010); Tim Clinton and Diane Langberg, *The Quick-Reference Guide to Counseling Women* (Grand Rapids: Baker Books, 2011); Tim Clinton, Bethany Palmer, and Scott Palmer, *The Quick-Reference Guide to Counseling on Money, Finances, and Relationships* (Grand Rapids: Baker Books, 2012); Tim Clinton and Eric Scalise, *The Quick-Reference Guide to Addictions and Recovery Counseling* (Grand Rapids: Baker Books, 2013); and Tim Clinton and John Trent, *The Quick-Reference Guide to Marriage and Family Counseling* (Grand Rapids: Baker Books, 2009). For a helpful book on quick Scripture references for counseling, see John G. Kruis, *Quick Scripture Reference for Counseling*, 4th ed. (Grand Rapids: Baker Books, 2013).

43. Tan and Scalise, *Lay Counseling*, 89–91.

44. See Kenneth Haugk, *Christian Caregiving—A Way of Life* (Minneapolis: Augsburg, 1984). For more information on Stephen Ministries, contact Stephen Ministries, 2045 Innerbelt Business Center Dr., St. Louis, MO 63114 (314-428-2600),) or see www.stephenministries.org.

45. Adapted from Tan and Scalise, *Lay Counseling*, 91–92.

46. Adapted from Tan and Scalise, *Lay Counseling*, 93–100.

Chapter 12 Church Boards, Budgets, and Buildings

1. For example, see John Carver, *Boards That Make a Difference: A New Design for Leadership in Nonprofit and Public Organizations*, 3rd ed. (San Francisco: Jossey-Bass, 2006); John Carver and Miriam Carver, *Reinventing Your Board: A Step-by-Step Guide to Implementing Policy Governance*, rev. ed. (San Francisco: Jossey-Bass, 2006); David L. Coleman, *Board Essentials: 12 Best Practices of Nonprofit Boards* (Lakewood, WA: Andrew/Wallace Books, 2014); Max De Pree, *Called to Serve: Creating and Nurturing the Effective Volunteer Board* (Grand Rapids: Eerdmans, 2001); and Gayle L. Gifford, *How to Make Your Board Dramatically More Effective, Starting Today* (Medfield, MA: Emerson and Church Publishers, 2012).

2. For example, see T. J. Addington, *High-Impact Church Boards: How to Develop Healthy, Intentional, and Empowered Church Leaders* (Colorado Springs: NavPress, 2010); and Aubrey Malphurs, *Leading Leaders: Empowering Church Boards for Ministry Excellence* (Grand Rapids: Baker Books, 2005).

3. Malphurs, *Leading Leaders*, 23–24.

4. Malphurs, *Leading Leaders*, 43–47.

5. Malphurs, *Leading Leaders*, 50.

6. Malphurs, *Leading Leaders*, 117–23.

7. Malphurs, *Leading Leaders*, 43.

8. Malphurs, *Leading Leaders*, 55–59.

9. Adapted from Malphurs, *Leading Leaders*, 66–71.

10. Malphurs, *Leading Leaders*, 71–74.

11. See Carver, *Boards That Make a Difference*; and Carver and Carver, *Reinventing Your Board*.

12. Malphurs, *Leading Leaders*, 82 (emphasis in original).

13. Adapted from Malphurs, *Leading Leaders*, 82–84.

14. Adapted from Malphurs, *Leading Leaders*, 84–85. See also in Malphurs appendix C: "Policies Governing the Board: The Board's Function"; appendix D: "Policies Governing the Senior Pastor: The Senior Pastor's Function"; appendix E: "Policies Governing the Board–Senior Pastor Relationship"; appendix F: "Mission Statement: Ends Policies"; appendix G: "Men's Character Assessment for Leadership"; appendix H: "Women's Character Assessment for Leadership"; appendix I: "Board Member Covenant"; and appendix N: "Elder Board Policy Manual."

15. Adapted from De Pree, *Called to Serve*, 9–22.

16. Adapted from De Pree, *Called to Serve*, 53–60.

17. Adapted from De Pree, *Called to Serve*, 63–71.

18. Adapted from De Pree, *Called to Serve*, 73–79.

19. Adapted from De Pree, *Called to Serve*, 81–88. See also Max De Pree, *Leading without Power: Finding Hope in Serving Community* (San Francisco: Jossey-Bass, 2003).

20. Gary L. McIntosh and Charles Arn, *What Every Pastor Should Know: 101 Indispensable Rules of Thumb for Leading Your Church* (Grand Rapids: Baker Books, 2013), 203–4, 204–6, 210–11, 200–215 (ministry rules for finances).

21. McIntosh and Arn, *What Every Pastor Should Know*, 208–10. See also John Bisagno, *Pastor's Handbook* (Nashville: B&H, 2011), 349–76.

22. Adapted from McIntosh and Arn, *What Every Pastor Should Know*, 177–99 (ministry rules for facilities).

23. Bisagno, *Pastor's Handbook*, 380–81.

24. McIntosh and Arn, *What Every Pastor Should Know*, 159.

25. Bisagno, *Pastor's Handbook*, 362. See also Eddy Hall, Ray Bowman, and J. Skip Machmer, *The More with Less Church: Maximize Your Money, Space, Time, and People to Multiply Ministry Impact* (Grand Rapids: Baker Books, 2014).

26. Bisagno, *Pastor's Handbook*, 362–63.

27. Adapted from Bisagno, *Pastor's Handbook*, 363–64.

28. Bisagno, *Pastor's Handbook*, 364.

29. John Bisagno, *Successful Church Fundraising* (Nashville: B&H, 2002).

30. See Bisagno, *Pastor's Handbook*, 349–53.

31. See Bisagno, *Pastor's Handbook*, 371–73, 390–92.

Chapter 13 Weddings and Funerals

1. Paul E. Engle, ed., *The Baker Wedding Handbook*, rev. ed. (Grand Rapids: Baker Books, 2017), 8.

2. Engle, *Baker Wedding Handbook*. See also Samuel Ward Hutton, *Minister's Service Manual*, rev. ed. (Grand Rapids: Baker Books, 2003).

3. Engle, *Baker Wedding Handbook*, 17–116.

4. Engle, *Baker Wedding Handbook*, 119–54.

5. Engle, *Baker Wedding Handbook*, 157–217.

6. Gary R. Collins, *Christian Counseling: A Comprehensive Guide*, 3rd ed. (Nashville: Thomas Nelson, 2007), 523–43.

7. Collins, *Christian Counseling*, 531.

8. Jason S. Carroll and William Doherty, "Evaluating the Effectiveness of Premarital Prevention Programs: A Meta-Analytic Review of Outcome Research," *Family Relations: Interdisciplinary Journal of Applied Family Studies* 52 (2003): 105–18.

9. Elizabeth A. Schilling et al., "Altering the Course of Marriage: The Effect of PREP Communication Skills Acquisition on Couples' Risk of Becoming Maritally Distressed," *Journal of Family Psychology* 17 (2003): 41–53.

10. Adapted from Scott M. Stanley, "Making a Case for Premarital Education," *Family Relations: Interdisciplinary Journal of Applied Family Studies* 50 (2001): 272–80.

11. Collins, *Christian Counseling*, 533–36.

12. Collins, *Christian Counseling*, 535.

13. Les Parrott and Leslie Parrott, *Saving Your Marriage Before It Starts: Seven Questions to Ask Before—and After—You Marry*, rev. ed. (Grand Rapids: Zondervan, 2015).

14. Collins, *Christian Counseling*, 537–39.

15. Adapted from Parrott and Parrott, *Saving Your Marriage Before It Starts*, 7, see also 19–174.

16. Adapted from Parrott and Parrott, *Saving Your Marriage Before It Starts*, 175–82.

17. Cameron Lee and James L. Furrow, *Preparing Couples for Love and Marriage: A Pastor's Resource* (Nashville: Abingdon, 2013), v.

18. Adapted from Lee and Furrow, *Preparing Couples for Love and Marriage*, 5–12.

19. Lee and Furrow, *Preparing Couples for Love and Marriage*, 21. See also Elizabeth B. Fawcett et al., "Do Premarital Education Programs Really Work? A Meta-Analytic Study," *Family Relations: Interdisciplinary Journal of Applied Family Studies* 59 (2010): 232–39.

20. Lee and Furrow, *Preparing Couples for Love and Marriage*, 112–25 (appendix A).

21. Adapted from Lee and Furrow, *Preparing Couples for Love and Marriage*, 21–31; see also 35–64.

22. Gary Thomas, *Sacred Marriage: What If God Designed Marriage to Make Us Holy More Than to Make Us Happy?* (Grand Rapids: Zondervan, 2000); Gary Thomas, *Sacred Parenting: How Raising Children Shapes Our Souls* (Grand Rapids: Zondervan, 2004); Larry Crabb, *The Marriage Builder* (Grand Rapids: Zondervan, 1982); and Cliff and Joyce Penner, *The Gift of Sex: A Guide to Sexual Fulfillment*, rev. ed. (Nashville: Thomas Nelson, 2003). There are many other books on Christian marriage, but a few of the more helpful ones are Dan B. Allender and Tremper Longman III, *The Intimate Mystery: Creating Strength and Beauty in Your Marriage* (Downers Grove, IL: InterVarsity, 2005); Tim Clinton and Julie Clinton, *The Marriage You've Always Wanted* (Nashville: Word, 2000); Archibald D. Hart and Sharon Hart Morrris, *Safe Haven Marriage: A Marriage You Can Come Home To* (Nashville: W Publishing, 2003); Parrott and Parrott, *Saving Your Marriage Before It Starts*; Les Parrott and Leslie Parrott, *Saving Your Second Marriage Before It Starts: Nine Questions to Ask Before—and After—You Remarry*, rev. ed. (Grand Rapids: Zondervan, 2015); Paul Stevens, *Marriage Spirituality: Ten Disciplines for Couples Who Love God* (Downers Grove, IL: InterVarsity, 1989); Gary Thomas, *A Lifelong Love: What If Marriage Is about More Than Just Staying Together?* (Colorado Springs: David C. Cook, 2014); Gary Thomas, *Cherish: The One Word That Changes Everything for Your Marriage* (Grand Rapids: Zondervan, 2017); and H. Norman Wright, *The Marriage Checkup* (Ventura, CA: Regal, 2002).

23. For example, see Brian Croft, *Visit the Sick: Ministering God's Grace in Times of Illness*, rev. ed. (Grand Rapids: Zondervan, 2014); Brian Croft, *The Pastor's Ministry: Biblical Priorities for Faithful Shepherds* (Grand Rapids: Zondervan, 2015), 81–128; Martha Jacobs, *A Clergy Guide to End-of-Life Issues* (Cleveland: Pilgrim Press, 2010); Robert W. Kellemen, *God's Healing for Life's Losses: How to Find Hope When You're Hurting* (Winona Lake, IN: BMH Books, 2010); Paul Tautges, *Comfort the Grieving: Ministering God's Grace in Times of Loss*, rev. ed. (Grand Rapids: Zondervan, 2014); Alan D. Wolfelt, *Death and Grief: A Guide for Clergy* (New York: Routledge, 1988); H. Norman Wright, *Experiencing Grief* (Nashville: Broadman &

Holman, 2004); Susan J. Zonnebelt-Smeenge and Robert C. De Vries, *Getting to the Other Side of Grief: Overcoming the Loss of a Spouse* (Grand Rapids: Baker Books, 1998); Susan J. Zonnebelt-Smeenge and Robert C. De Vries, *Living Fully in the Shadow of Death: Assurance and Guidance to Finish Well* (Grand Rapids: Baker Books, 2004); and Susan J. Zonnebelt-Smeenge and Robert C. De Vries, *Traveling Through Grief: Learning to Live Again after the Death of a Loved One* (Grand Rapids: Baker Books, 2006). For helpful books on ministry to the aging and elderly in our congregations and churches, see James M. Houston and Michael Parker, *A Vision for the Aging Church: Renewing Ministry for and by Seniors* (Downers Grove, IL: IVP Academic, 2011); and R. Paul Stevens, *Aging Matters: Finding Your Calling for the Rest of Your Life* (Grand Rapids: Eerdmans, 2016).

24. Dan S. Lloyd, *Leading Today's Funerals: A Pastoral Guide for Improving Bereavement Ministry* (Grand Rapids: Baker Books, 1997), 15–23.

25. For example, see Engle, *Baker Funeral Handbook*; Lloyd, *Leading Today's Funerals*; and Hutton, *Minister's Service Manual*. See also John Bisagno, *Pastor's Handbook* (Nashville: B&H, 2011), 117–27; James W. Bryant and Mac Brunson, *The New Guidebook for Pastors* (Nashville: B&H, 2007), 139–54; and Brian Croft and Phil Newton, *Conduct Gospel-Centered Funerals: Applying the Gospel at the Unique Challenges of Death*, rev. ed. (Grand Rapids: Zondervan, 2014).

26. Adapted from Engle, *Baker Funeral Handbook*, 11–12.

27. Engle, *Baker Funeral Handbook*, 19–116.

28. Engle, *Baker Funeral Handbook*, 117–40.

29. Engle, *Baker Funeral Handbook*, 141–53.

30. Engle, *Baker Funeral Handbook*, 155–89.

31. Engle, *Baker Funeral Handbook*, 191–206.

32. Adapted from Lloyd, *Leading Today's Funerals*, 41–52.

33. Lloyd, *Leading Today's Funerals*, 59–73.

34. This list is from Lloyd, *Leading Today's Funerals*, 75–87.

35. See Wolfelt, *Death and Grief*, 1.

36. Adapted from Lloyd, *Leading Today's Funerals*, 89–98.

37. For example, see Wright, *Experiencing Grief*; Zonnebelt-Smeenge and DeVries, *Getting to the Other Side of Grief*; Zonnebelt-Smeenge and DeVries, *Living Fully in the Shadow of Death*; and Zonnebelt-Smeenge and DeVries, *Traveling Through Grief*.

Chapter 14 Small Groups and Fellowships

1. See recommended readings. See also Siang-Yang Tan, *Rest: Experiencing God's Peace in a Restless World* (Vancouver: Regent College Publishing, 2003), 125–45 (chap. 9 on spiritual community); and Siang-Yang Tan and Douglas H. Gregg, *Disciplines of the Holy Spirit* (Grand Rapids: Zondervan, 1997), 159–74 (chap. 11 on fellowship).

2. Bill Search, *The Essential Guide for Small Group Leaders* (Carol Stream, IL: Christianity Today, 2017).

3. Search, *Essential Guide for Small Group Leaders*, 143–53.

4. Adapted from Search, *Essential Guide for Small Group Leaders*, 147.

5. Adapted from Search, *Essential Guide for Small Group Leaders*, 149.

6. Adapted from Search, *Essential Guide for Small Group Leaders*, 151.

7. Adapted from Search, *Essential Guide for Small Group Leaders*, 153. For more on biblical foundations for community and small-group ministry, see also Gareth Weldon Icenogle, *Biblical Foundations for Small Group Ministry: An Integrational Approach* (Downers Grove, IL: InterVarsity, 1994); and Julie A. Gorman, *Community That Is Christian*, 2nd ed. (Grand Rapids: Baker Books, 2002).

8. See Tan and Gregg, *Disciplines of the Holy Spirit*, 159–74 (chap. 11 on fellowship).

9. J. I. Packer, *God's Words: Studies of Key Bible Themes* (Downers Grove, IL: InterVarsity, 1981), 195.

10. Tan and Gregg, *Disciplines of the Holy Spirit*, 143–53.

11. Tan and Gregg, *Disciplines of the Holy Spirit*, 19–22.

12. Tan and Gregg, *Disciplines of the Holy Spirit*, 161.

13. Tan, *Rest*, 128.

14. See recommended readings at the end of this chapter.

15. Search, *Essential Guide for Small Group Leaders*, 7–8 (contents).

16. Adapted from Search, *Essential Guide for Small Group Leaders*, 19–22.

17. Nelson Searcy and Kerrick Thomas, *Activate: An Entirely New Approach to Small Groups*, rev. ed. (Grand Rapids: Baker Books, 2018).

18. Adapted from Searcy and Thomas, *Activate*, 7–8 (contents).

19. Searcy and Thomas, *Activate*, 8–9 (contents).

20. Search, *Essential Guide for Small Group Leaders*, 109–10, 113–14.

21. Larry Osborne, *Sticky Church* (Grand Rapids: Zondervan, 2008), 59–71, 73–158.

22. Adapted from Osborne, *Sticky Church*, 82–90.

23. Osborne, *Sticky Church*, 121, 115–22.

24. James Bryan Smith with Lynda Graybeal, *A Spiritual Formation Workbook: Small Group Resources for Nurturing Christian Growth*, rev. ed. (San Francisco: HarperSanFrancisco, 1999).

25. Material in this section on Renovaré small groups is adapted from Tan, *Rest*, 134–36.

26. Smith with Graybeal, *Spiritual Formation Workbook*, 99.

27. Adapted from Smith with Graybeal, *Spiritual Formation Workbook*, 100.

28. This list of questions is from Smith with Graybeal, *Spiritual Formation Workbook*, 100.

29. Richard J. Foster, *Streams of Living Water: Celebrating the Great Traditions of Christian Faith* (San Francisco: HarperSanFrancisco, 1998).

30. Adapted from Gary L. McIntosh and Charles Arn, *What Every Pastor Should Know: 101 Indispensable Rules of Thumb for Leading Your Church* (Grand Rapids: Baker Books, 2013), 92–107.

31. Heather Zemple, *Community Is Messy: The Perils and Promise of Small Group Ministry* (Downers Grove, IL: InterVarsity, 2012).

32. Ross Parsley, *Messy Church: A Multigenerational Mission for God's Family* (Colorado Springs: David C. Cook, 2012).

33. Brett McCracken, *Uncomfortable: The Awkward and Essential Challenge of Christian Community* (Wheaton: Crossway, 2017).

34. Christopher C. Smith and John Pattison, *Slow Church: Cultivating Community in the Patient Way of Jesus* (Downers Grove, IL: InterVarsity, 2014).

35. For example, see Henry Cloud and John Townsend, *Making Small Groups Work: What Every Small Group Leader Needs to Know* (Grand Rapids: Zondervan, 2003); Stephen P. Greggo, *Trekking toward Wholeness: A Resource for Core Group Leaders* (Downers Grove, IL: IVP Academic, 2008); and Jan Paul Hook, Joshua N. Hook, and Don E. Davis, *Helping Groups Heal: Leading Small Groups in the Process of Transformation* (West Conshohocken, PA: Templeton Press, 2017).

Chapter 15 Integrity and Ethics

1. Jerry A. Johnson, "Testimony: The Pastor and His Ethics," in James W. Bryant and Mac Brunson, *The New Guidebook for Pastors* (Nashville: B&H, 2007), 179; see also 180–87.

2. See recommended readings at the end of this chapter.

3. William H. Willimon, *Pastor: The Theology and Practice of Ordained Ministry*, rev. ed. (Nashville: Abingdon, 2016), 311–12.

4. Willimon, *Pastor*, 319–39.

5. Willimon, *Pastor*, 312.

6. Willimon, *Pastor*, 330–34.

7. Willimon, *Pastor*, 325–27.

8. Willimon, *Pastor*, 338.

9. Adapted from Michael Todd Wilson and Brad Hoffmann, *Preventing Ministry Failure: A ShepherdCare Guide for Pastors, Ministers and Other Caregivers* (Downers Grove, IL: Inter-Varsity, 2007), 5–7. See also Rae Jean Proeschold-Bell and Jason Byassee, *Faithful and Fractured: Responding to the Clergy Health Crisis* (Grand Rapids: Baker Academic, 2018).

10. Bryant and Brunson, *New Guidebook for Pastors*, 180–87.

11. Bryant and Brunson, *New Guidebook for Pastors*, 180–85.

12. Bryant and Brunson, *New Guidebook for Pastors*, 181.

13. Bryant and Brunson, *New Guidebook for Pastors*, 181–82.

14. Bryant and Brunson, *New Guidebook for Pastors*, 182. See also Billy Graham, *Just As I Am* (San Francisco: Harper, 1997), 127–29; Marie Fortune, *Is Nothing Sacred? When Sex Invades the Pastoral Relationship* (San Francisco: Harper, 1989); and Stanley J. Grenz and Roy D. Bell, *Betrayal of Trust: Confronting and Preventing Clergy Misconduct*, 2nd ed. (Grand Rapids: Baker Books, 2001).

15. Bryant and Brunson, *New Guidebook for Pastors*, 183–84.

16. See Rollie Dimos, *Integrity at Stake: Safeguarding Your Church from Financial Fraud* (Grand Rapids: Zondervan, 2016).

17. Bryant and Brunson, *New Guidebook for Pastors*, 184–85.

18. Joe E. Trull and R. Robert Creech, *Ethics for Christian Ministry: Moral Formation for 21st Century Leaders* (Grand Rapids: Baker Academic, 2017), 235–38 (appendix D).

19. Adapted from Bryant and Brunson, *New Guidebook for Pastors*, 185–86.

20. Joe E. Trull and James E. Carter, *Ministerial Ethics: Moral Formation for Church Leaders* (Grand Rapids: Baker Academic, 2004), 39–40. See also and Trull and Creech, *Ethics for Christian Ministry*, 21–22; and Bryant and Brunson, *New Guidebook for Pastors*, 186–87.

21. Willimon, *Pastor*, 316–18.

22. Willimon, *Pastor*, 313. See also Rebekah Miles, *The Pastor as Moral Guide* (Minneapolis: Fortress, 1999); and Rebekah Miles, "Keeping Watch Over the Shepherds by Day and Night," *Circuit Rider* 23, no. 3 (May/June 1999): 15.

23. Trull and Creech, *Ethics for Christian Ministry*.

24. Trull and Creech, *Ethics for Christian Ministry*, vii.

25. Adapted from Randolph K. Sanders, "A Model for Ethical Decision-Making," in *Christian Counseling Ethics: A Handbook for Psychologists, Therapists and Pastors*, ed. Randolph K. Sanders, 2nd ed. (Downers Grove, IL: IVP Academic, 2013), 510–18.

26. Sanders, "Model for Ethical Decision-Making," 511.

27. Sondra Wheeler, *The Minister as Moral Theologian: Ethical Dimensions of Pastoral Leadership* (Grand Rapids: Baker Academic, 2017).

28. Wheeler, *Minister as Moral Theologian*, xv.

29. Wheeler, *Minister as Moral Theologian*, 1–25.

30. Wheeler, *Minister as Moral Theologian*, 58; see also 26–58.

31. Adapted from Wheeler, *Minister as Moral Theologian*, 59–84.

32. Adapted from Wheeler, *Minister as Moral Theologian*, 85–110.

33. Wheeler, *Minister as Moral Theologian*, 111–37.

34. Wheeler, *Minister as Moral Theologian*, 124.

35. Wheeler, *Minister as Moral Theologian*, 137.

36. Sondra Wheeler, *Sustaining Ministry: Foundations and Practices for Serving Faithfully* (Grand Rapids: Baker Academic, 2017).

37. Adapted from Wheeler, *Sustaining Ministry*, xvii–xviii.

38. Adapted from Wheeler, *Sustaining Ministry*, 36–52.

39. Adapted from Wheeler, *Sustaining Ministry*, 53–76.

40. Adapted from Wheeler, *Sustaining Ministry*, 91–104.

41. Adapted from Wheeler, *Sustaining Ministry*, 104–7.

42. Wheeler, *Sustaining Ministry*, 107–10.

43. Wheeler, *Sustaining Ministry*, 111–30.

44. Bill Blackburn, "Pastors Who Counsel," in Sanders, *Christian Counseling Ethics*, 368–81, especially 376–78.

45. Adapted from Blackburn, "Pastors Who Counsel," 378–81.

46. Henry Cloud and John Townsend, *Boundaries: When to Say Yes, How to Say No to Take Control of Your Life*, rev. ed. (Grand Rapids: Zondervan, 2017).

Chapter 16 Leaving and Retiring

1. See James W. Bryant and Mac Brunson, *The New Guidebook for Pastors* (Nashville: B&H, 2007), 200–216 (chap. 18 on the pastor changing churches) and 226–33 (chap. 20 on the pastor's retirement).

2. For some recent helpful books on pastoral succession, see recommended readings at the end of this chapter.

3. For some recent helpful books on CEO succession, see recommended readings at the end of this chapter.

4. William Vanderbloemen and Warren Bird, *Next: Pastoral Succession That Works* (Grand Rapids: Baker Books, 2014), 9.

5. Quoted in Vanderbloemen and Bird, *Next*, 10 (emphasis in original).

6. Adapted from Bryant and Brunson, *New Guidebook for Pastors*, 202–7.

7. Bryant and Brunson, *New Guidebook for Pastors*, 213–15.

8. Bryant and Brunson, *New Guidebook for Pastors*, 247–48. For example, pastors who need help can contact Lifeway LeaderCare at leadercare@lifeway.com; Focus on the Family at www.parsonage.org and pastors@family.org; and the Restoration Ministry at Sagemont Baptist Church in Houston, Texas, at www.sagemontchurch.org and stress-in-the-ministry.org.

9. Adapted from Gordon MacDonald, *Building Below the Waterline: Strengthening the Life of a Leader* (Peabody, MA: Hendrickson, 2011), 243–48.

10. Adapted from Vanderbloemen and Bird, *Next*, 40–47.

11. Bryant and Brunson, *New Guidebook for Pastors*, 216.

12. Vanderbloemen and Bird, *Next*, 22

13. Vanderbloemen and Bird, *Next*, 25.

14. Vanderbloemen and Bird, *Next*, 29.

15. Adapted from Vanderbloemen and Bird, *Next*, 33–36.

16. Vanderbloemen and Bird, *Next*, 178.

17. Vanderbloemen and Bird, *Next*, 182.

18. Adapted from Warren Bird, "Putting 'Success' in Succession," *Christianity Today*, November 2014, 50–53.

19. Bird, "Putting 'Success' in Succession," 53.

20. Adapted from Bird, "Putting 'Success' in Succession," 53.

21. Adapted from Vanderbloemen and Bird, *Next*, 49–50.

22. Adapted from Vanderbloemen and Bird, *Next*, 142–43.

23. Adapted from Vanderbloemen and Bird, *Next*, 50.

Epilogue

1. For examples of some helpful books on church revitalization, or church renewal and revival, see recommended readings at the end of this chapter.

2. Aubrey Malphurs and Gordon E. Penfold, *Re:Vision: The Key to Transforming Your Church* (Grand Rapids: Baker Books, 2014), 13.

3. For example, see D. Randy Berkner, *Quantum Ministry: How Pastors Can Make the Leap* (Kansas City, MO: Beacon Hill, 2007); Nelson Searcy with Jennifer Dykes Henson, *The Renegade Pastor: Abandoning Average in Your Life and Ministry* (Grand Rapids: Baker Books, 2013); James Emery White, *Meet Generation Z: Understanding and Reaching the New Post-Christian World* (Grand Rapids: Baker Books, 2017), 157–59; and Andreas J. Kostenberger, *Excellence: The Character of God and the Pursuit of Scholarly Virtue* (Wheaton: Crossway, 2011). Although Kostenberger emphasizes excellence, he does carefully describe it biblically as vocational excellence (with diligence, courage, passion, restraint, creativity, and eloquence), moral excellence (with integrity, fidelity, and wisdom), and relational excellence (with grace, humility, interdependence, and love) in academic or scholarship as well as in ministry contexts. See also L. Gregory Jones and Kevin R. Armstrong, *Resurrecting Excellence: Shaping Faithful Christian Ministry* (Grand Rapids: Eerdmans, 2006). Jones and Armstrong also carefully emphasize excellence based on the excellence of the Triune God, who calls us into ministry with him and for his kingdom.

4. See Zack Eswine, *The Imperfect Pastor: Discovering Joy in Our Limitations through a Daily Apprenticeship with Jesus* (Wheaton: Crossway, 2015); and Mandy Smith, *The Vulnerable Pastor: How Human Limitations Empower Our Ministry* (Downers Grove, IL: InterVarsity, 2015).

5. See Jared C. Wilson, *The Imperfect Disciple: Grace for People Who Can't Get Their Act Together* (Grand Rapids: Baker Books, 2017).

6. See J. R. Briggs, *Fail: Finding Hope and Grace in the Midst of Ministry Failure* (Downers Grove, IL: InterVarsity, 2014).

7. Simon Chan, *Spiritual Theology: A Systematic Study of the Christian Life* (Downers Grove, IL: InterVarsity, 1998), 75–76.

8. Vernon Grounds, "Faith to Face Failure, or What's So Great about Success?" *Christianity Today*, December 9, 1977, 12.

9. Grounds, "Faith to Face Failure," 13.

10. See Siang-Yang Tan, *Rest: Experiencing God's Peace in a Restless World* (Vancouver: Regent College Publishing, 2003), 179. See also Skye Jethani, *Immeasurable: Reflections on the Soul of Ministry in the Age of Church, Inc.* (Chicago: Moody, 2017).

11. Alan Fadling, "Developing Pastors and Churches of the Kingdom," in *Eternal Living: Reflections on Dallas Willard's Teaching on Faith and Formation*, ed. Gary W. Moon (Downers Grove, IL: InterVarsity, 2015), 200.

12. Fadling, "Developing Pastors and Churches of the Kingdom," 202. See also Gary W. Moon, *Becoming Dallas Willard: The Formation of a Philosopher, Teacher, and Christ Follower* (Downers Grove, IL: InterVarsity, 2018).

13. Chad Bird, *Your God Is Too Glorious: Finding God in the Most Unexpected Places* (Grand Rapids: Baker Books, 2018).

Scripture Index

Subject Index

Rev. Dr. Siang-Yang Tan was director of the PsyD (Doctor of Psychology) program in clinical psychology (1989–97) and is now professor of psychology in the Graduate School of Psychology at Fuller Theological Seminary in Pasadena, California. He is a licensed psychologist with a PhD in clinical psychology from McGill University and a fellow of the American Psychological Association (APA). He has published articles on lay counseling and lay counselor training, intrapersonal integration and spirituality, religious psychotherapy, cognitive behavior therapy, epilepsy, pain, and cross-cultural counseling with Asians and Hispanics as well as fifteen books, including *Rest: Experiencing God's Peace in a Restless World* (Vancouver: Regent College Publishing, 2003); *Managing Chronic Pain* (Downers Grove, IL: InterVarsity, 1996); *Full Service: Moving from Self-Serve Christianity to Total Servanthood* (Grand Rapids: Baker Books, 2006); with Dr. Eric Scalise, *Lay Counseling: Equipping Christians for a Helping Ministry*, rev. ed. (Grand Rapids: Zondervan, 2016); with Dr. Doug Gregg, *Disciplines of the Holy Spirit* (Grand Rapids: Zondervan, 1997); with Dr. Les Parrott III, *Exercises for Effective Counseling and Psychotherapy* (New York: McGraw-Hill, 1997); with Dr. Les Parrott III, *Exercises for Effective Counseling and Psychotherapy*, 2nd ed. (Pacific Grove, CA: Brooks/Cole, 2003); with Dr. John Ortberg, *Coping with Depression*, rev. ed. (Grand Rapids: Baker Books, 2004); and a major textbook, *Counseling and Psychotherapy: A Christian Perspective* (Grand Rapids: Baker Academic, 2011).

He was the 1993 recipient of the Award for Contributions to Racial and Ethnic Diversity from the National Council of Schools and Programs of Professional Psychology (NCSPP), the 1999 recipient of the Distinguished Member Award from the Christian Association for Psychological Studies (CAPS) International, the 2001 recipient of the Gary R. Collins Award for Excellence in Christian Counseling from the American Association of Christian Counselors (AACC), the 2002 recipient of the William Bier Award for Outstanding and Sustained Contributions from Division 36 (Psychology of Religion) of the APA, and the 2011 recipient of the Distinguished Silver Award for Outstanding Influence and Leadership in the Development and Advancement of

Christian Counseling Around the World and the James E. Clinton Award for Excellence in Pastoral Care and Ministry from AACC.

Dr. Tan is associate editor of the *Journal of Psychology and Christianity* and serves or has served on the editorial boards of the *Journal of Consulting and Clinical Psychology*, *Professional Psychology: Research and Practice*, *Journal of Psychology and Theology*, *Christian Psychology: A Transdisciplinary Journal*, and *Journal of Spiritual Formation & Soul Care*. He was president of Division 36 (Psychology of Religion) of the APA (1998–99).

Dr. Tan also serves as senior pastor of First Evangelical Church Glendale in Glendale, California. He lives in Pasadena with his wife, Angela, and they have two grown children, Carolyn and Andrew (who is married to Jenn). Dr. Tan is originally from Singapore.